CASPIAN SEA

Nineveh •

ASSYRIA

River Tigris

• Babylon

• Susa

BABYLONIA

• Ur

PERSIA

ARABIA

PERSIAN
GULF

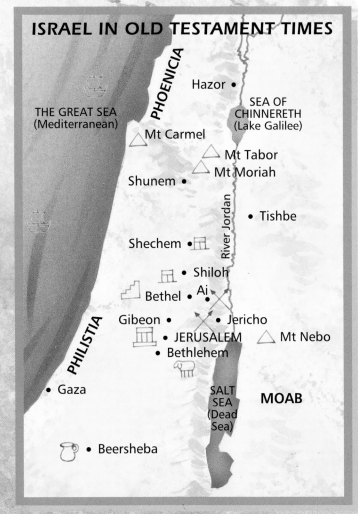

ISRAEL IN OLD TESTAMENT TIMES

PHOENICIA

Hazor •

THE GREAT SEA
(Mediterranean)

SEA OF
CHINNERETH
(Lake Galilee)

△ Mt Carmel

△ Mt Tabor
△ Mt Moriah

Shunem •

River Jordan

• Tishbe

Shechem •

Shiloh

Bethel • Ai

Gibeon • • Jericho

△ Mt Nebo

JERUSALEM

• Bethlehem

PHILISTIA

• Gaza

SALT
SEA
(Dead
Sea)

MOAB

• Beersheba

HOW TO USE THIS BIBLE

The Bible is full of stories.
It starts with the beginning of the world, and ends with a vision of the future.

Although the people in these stories lived a long time ago,
they were people who lived in families and had feelings just like us.

The Bible also tells us how God relates to the world
and the people he has made,
and how the birth, death and resurrection of Jesus Christ
changed that relationship for ever.

This Bible has been specially written for children at the start of the
21st Century.
It can be read in several different ways.

365 stories

Look at the Contents. You can choose whether to start with Jesus, or the
adventures of the apostle Paul. Read about Moses and the plagues in Egypt,
or about Samson fighting a lion with his bare hands. Or you could begin at
the beginning with the story of creation and how the earth was saved from a
terrible flood.

Information panels

As you read the stories, see where you can find them in your Bible. Look these
up if you want more of the details.

You'll also find helpful information about the places or the people or the time
in which they lived; there are pictures, too, to explain some of the facts behind
the stories.

Features

If you want to know more about the background to the Bible and life in Bible
times, look up the special features. Find out about what happened when
someone was born or died; about what they ate or where they slept; what
jobs they did and what they believed.

Maps

Look at the maps to see where everything happened. Work out just how long
some of those journeys were!

Indexes

If you want to read about someone in particular – Elijah or Stephen – and you
don't know where to find them; or you want to find out about chariots or
crocodiles, spears, ships or soldiers: look them up in one of the indexes at the
back. This will tell you which story to read or which page to find the
information in.

There are 365 stories altogether. You could even choose to begin at the
beginning and read one every day of the year!

THE 21ST CENTURY
Children's
BIBLE

by Stephanie Jeffs and Derek Williams
Illustrated by Tony Morris and Chris Saunderson

Marshall Pickering
An Imprint of HarperCollinsPublishers

WHAT IS THE BIBLE?

The Bible is one of the oldest, best-known and bestselling books in the world. It is in fact a collection of sixty-six different books, with two main sections. The Old Testament is the history of the Jewish people, including the Law given to Moses and the writings of the prophets. The New Testament is the story of Jesus and the first Christians.

For Christians it is a very special book because they believe it tells the story of how God has made himself known to the world, and especially through his son, Jesus Christ. The Bible contains God's teaching on how to live and how to understand God and the world he has made.

The Old Testament

The books of the Old Testament include history, drama, poetry, letters, laws and stories of people's lives. In Old Testament times, only a few people could read and write. Most people used a 'scribe' to write letters for them. From about 500BC scribes became very important as teachers of God's Law. Those who copied the Bible books took great care to make sure nothing was left out. Sometimes a second scribe checked over the work of the first. It took a long time to copy these scrolls so they were very valuable. The person reading the scroll used to unroll one end and roll up the other as he went along.

Who wrote it?

At least thirty-five different people, who believed in God and listened carefully to him, wrote the Bible books. The Old Testament was written in Hebrew, the language of the Jewish tribes of Israel, but nobody knows how and when all the writings started to be put together in one book. The Old Testament is the most important holy book for the Jews.

The New Testament was written in Greek, the common language of the first century AD. Christians believe that God guided or 'inspired' the human writers of the Bible to make his message clear. Other religious books were written, but over a long time people accepted that some of them had God's special authority. These were included in the Bible.

When the Old Testament writings were first gathered together and translated from Hebrew into Greek in about 250BC, the translation included some books which were not in the Hebrew Bible, and are now known as the 'Deuterocanonical books'. In the sixteenth century the Protestant churches in Europe decided to use only books from the Hebrew Bible in their Old Testament. The list of New Testament books was generally agreed by about AD350.

The Bible's message

The Bible's message is so important that it has now been translated into hundreds of different languages. The first Greek translation of the Old Testament was made 250 years before Jesus was born. By AD100

the New Testament books had been written in Greek, and were translated into Latin. But for hundreds of years after the birth of Jesus very few people could read or write.

The invention of the printing press in the fifteenth century meant that Bibles no longer had to be copied out by hand, and the first English translations that followed meant that people could read the Bible in their own language for the first time.

Since then the whole Bible has been translated into 330 languages. The New Testament is in 770 languages, and more than 900 other languages have a small part of the Bible.

ARCHAEOLOGY AND THE BIBLE

Artefacts and written records have been found in Bible lands which help to show that many of the accounts in the Bible were written in particular historical times. Ancient writings and pottery and other objects found in remains of old cities give us clues about how and when people lived.

The New Testament

The books of the New Testament were written in Greek by the followers of Jesus Christ. The Greek word for books is biblia, from which we get the name for the Bible. These were not written as scrolls, but sheets of parchment were placed on top of each other and bound together at one edge. This was called a codex and looked more like the sort of book we read today.

A scroll This was made of parchment (leather) or papyrus, sewn together into one long strip and rolled up from both ends.

Bible stories Ordinary people in medieval Europe could not read, so they listened to Bible stories in church and looked at the pictures in stained glass windows.

The Lindisfarne Gospels This manuscript from the tenth century was carefully copied and decorated by hand by monks.

THE DEAD SEA SCROLLS

In 1947 an Arab shepherd boy found some clay pots in caves in the desert near the Dead Sea. Inside were several very old scrolls. They were copies of parts of the Old Testament. Back in Roman times, when Jesus was alive, there had been a monastery in that area called Qumran and it is thought that the monks hid the scrolls in the caves to prevent them being destroyed. These are the oldest copies of Old Testament texts which still exist.

The Bible today For Christians, the Bible is not just a guide for living. Through reading the Bible, people can find faith in God.

CONTENTS

TIME-LINE

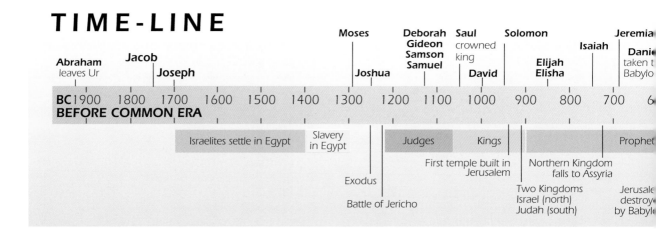

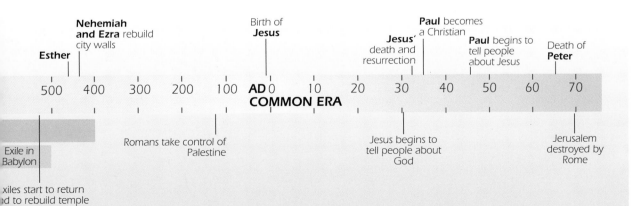

Esther

Nehemiah **and Ezra** rebuild city walls

Birth of **Jesus**

Jesus' death and resurrection

Paul becomes a Christian

Paul begins to tell people about Jesus

Death of **Peter**

500 400 300 200 100 **AD** 0 10 20 30 40 50 60 70
COMMON ERA

Romans take control of Palestine

Jesus begins to tell people about God

Jerusalem destroyed by Rome

Exile in Babylon

Exiles start to return and to rebuild temple

THE OLD TESTAMENT

The Old Testament contains thirty-nine books which were written down over many hundreds of years. These books are about the history and religion of God's people, the Jews. As a Jew, Jesus knew these holy writings, or 'scriptures' and they were an important part of his teaching. The Old Testament is also seen as 'God's word' for Christians today.

The thirty-nine books can be divided into different styles of writing, collected together for different purposes.

The history of God's people

History – battles and wars; good kings and bad kings – is a way of looking back at what has happened to people. God had promised Abraham a land many years before, and the book of Joshua starts with how God's people came to live in the land of Canaan, the Promised Land. These books tell of the leaders, judges and kings of Israel and of the many battles with their enemies.

Poetry and wisdom

Poetry expresses what people think and feel in a way that is different from writing down history. The poems and songs of worship, called psalms, are still used in worship by both Christians and Jews today. Many of these were written by King David, and they are about his relationship with God in very different situations and moods. There are also two books of wise sayings, some of which were written by King Solomon who was famous for his wisdom, a gift from God. The book of Job, which is about sadness and suffering, has been called the hardest book in the Bible.

The first five books

These five books form the basis for the Jewish religion. Called the Pentateuch, or the Law, these books start with why the world began, and God's promise to Abraham and his descendants, the Jewish people. The promise was a 'covenant' (an agreement, or 'testament') that if God's people obeyed and trusted him, and kept his laws, God would always love and protect them.

In these books are recorded the Ten Commandments and other laws from God which give guidance for the way God's people should worship him and behave. Here also is the story of how Moses led God's people out of slavery in Egypt, through the desert and towards the Promised Land.

Prophets

The last section of the Old Testament is a mixture of history, poetry and prophecy. Many times, God's people forgot his laws and disobeyed him, so God had to send a prophet to remind them of how they should live. Prophets were often very unpopular. Many of the prophets had to warn God's people of the terrible things that would happen to them if they did not obey his laws. And indeed, terrible things did happen. But the prophets also brought good news – of God's Saviour, or 'Messiah' who would come to show God's love to all people everywhere.

THE TEN COMMANDMENTS

1 I am God, who rescued you from slavery. Worship only me.
2 Do not make idols to worship.
3 Keep my name holy.
4 Make sure you keep my day of rest, the Sabbath.
5 Respect your parents.
6 Do not murder another human being.
7 Be faithful to your marriage partner.
8 Do not steal.
9 Do not tell lies.
10 Do not be jealous of what other people have.

The world of the Old Testament

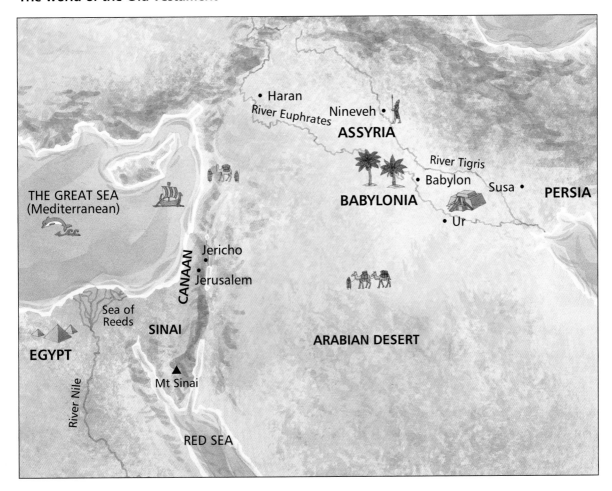

THE BEGINNING OF ALL THINGS

All over the world, different peoples and cultures have traditional stories about how the world was made. The Bible starts with the creation story which sets out Hebrew and Christian beliefs.

The very first words of the Bible are 'In the beginning', and the story begins with God himself. We read that God has always existed – no one made God. It was God who made the entire universe. He planned it carefully; nothing was left to chance, from the vast number of the stars to the tiniest creatures on the bed of the ocean. And, we are told, everything God made was good.

The creation story doesn't say exactly how God made the universe. The point of the story is not to tell us about things like how old rocks are or how stars are formed, but to help us begin to answer some of the big questions in life: Why is the world like it is? Why are people like they are?

We read that people

(represented by Adam and Eve) were created to be like God: able to create, to love, to care for the world, and to enjoy friendship with God. But that friendship was spoiled when they deliberately did what God had told them not to do. In the story, Adam and Eve are sent away from the Garden of Eden, away from God's presence.

After this, things went from bad to worse. People did all kinds of evil things until God decided to make a fresh start with Noah, whom he rescued from a great flood. Even after this, people still tried to live their lives without God. But God never stopped loving them.

---

1 Genesis chapter 1, verse 1 to chapter 2, verse 3.

Order of events

The story of creation is told as if someone on earth is watching it happen. So the sun and moon appear after 'light' as if the clouds have cleared and the sky can be seen.

A day of rest

The Bible divides God's work of creation into six days, and says that on the seventh day he rested. He set an example for people to stop their work, to rest, and to think about him.

1 The creation of the world

In the beginning God made the earth out of nothing. It was dark and empty and shapeless.

Then God spoke. 'Let there be light!' he said. As soon as he had said the words, light came into existence. God divided the light, so that he made day and night.

God made the air which surrounds the earth. He put water onto the earth and created seas and dry land.

Then God began to fill the world that he had made. He took the land and filled it with plants, flowers, seeds and fruit.

He filled the day time sky with the sun, and the night sky with the moon. He scattered the universe with stars and planets. He marked out time, with seasons, days and years.

God filled the sky with birds and the sea with fish and other living creatures. He brought life to the earth by making every kind of reptile, animal and insect.

God looked at everything that he had made and saw that it was good.

Then God made man and woman. He put them in charge of his creation, and he loved them.

When his creation was complete, God rested.

2 The garden of Eden

God's beautiful garden was filled with trees and a river ran through it. Some of the trees had fruit and seeds which were good to eat. Other trees were made in wonderful colours, shapes and textures, and were lovely to look at. In the middle of the garden were two special trees. One was called the tree of life and the other was called the tree of the knowledge of good and evil.

God gave Adam, the first man, and Eve, the first woman, the garden to live in. It was full of everything God had made. He wanted Adam and Eve to enjoy it all. God loved to be with Adam and Eve. He spent time walking and talking with them in the garden.

'You may choose to eat the fruit from any of these trees,' God told Adam. 'But there is one exception. You are not to eat from the tree of the knowledge of good and evil. If you do, you will die.'

3 The cunning snake

One of the creatures in the garden was a snake. He was God's enemy. He was cunning and crafty, and wanted to destroy God's beautiful garden, and everything in it.

He slithered up to Eve. 'Did God really forbid you to eat from any of the trees in the garden?' he hissed.

'God told us we can eat from every tree, except the tree in the middle of the garden,' said Eve. 'If we eat from the tree of the knowledge of good and evil, we will die.'

'That's not true!' said the snake. 'God does not want you to eat from that tree because if you do, you will become just like him.'

Eve looked at the tree, and the fruit which hung from its branches. She thought about what the snake had said, and she longed to be just like God.

'Come on,' she said to Adam. 'Let's eat.' She picked some fruit, and handed some to Adam.

As soon as they had eaten, Adam and Eve knew what they had done. They had spoiled everything. They had disobeyed God. Suddenly, they did not feel happy being in the garden. And when they heard God coming, they looked at each other, and ran to find somewhere to hide.

2 Genesis chapter 2, verses 4-25.

The tree of the knowledge of good and evil
If Adam and Eve ate from this tree, they would find out what it was like to do wrong. There was probably nothing different about its fruit. God simply made a rule which he expected Adam and Eve to obey.

Working life
Adam and Eve were given work to do. They looked after the garden God had given them to live in and enjoyed their work.

3 Genesis chapter 3, verses 1-7.

The snake
The snake stands for the devil or Satan. He is God's enemy, telling lies to Adam and Eve to make them break God's rules.

In medieval Europe most people could not read, so churches used stained-glass windows to teach Bible stories. Other pictures told them that Jesus came to defeat the powers of evil.

Somewhere to hide
Once Adam and Eve had tasted the fruit they knew they had done wrong. They didn't want to face God and be found out. But he knew at once, of course.

4 Genesis chapter 3, verses 8-24.

The first clothes
Before they had broken God's rules, Adam and Eve had been naked in the garden of Eden. Just like little children they were happy to have no clothes on. But when they felt guilty and ashamed of their behaviour they felt the need to make clothes.

Adam and Eve sewed together leaves from the fig tree to cover themselves.

5 Genesis chapter 4.

Farmers
Cain would have grown barley or wheat to make bread. He picked fruit from olive trees, vines and date palms. Abel would have kept flocks of sheep and herds of goats.

📖 See Feature pages 178-79.

Presents for God
Cain and Abel offered a sacrifice to God. In those days people often gave the best of what they had to God to show they loved him, or were sorry for being bad.

4 Adam and Eve leave the garden

That evening, God came to walk in the garden. He looked for Adam and Eve.

But Adam and Eve hid among the trees. They picked leaves and made some clothes. They were very unhappy with themselves.

'Where are you, Adam?' called God.

'I'm hiding!' replied Adam. 'I was afraid of you, because I was naked.'

'How did you know you were naked?' God asked. 'Have you eaten from the tree of the knowledge of good and evil?'

'It wasn't my fault!' replied Adam. 'Eve made me do it.'

'It wasn't my fault!' said Eve. 'The snake tricked me.'

God was very sad. 'Because you have disobeyed me you can no longer enjoy living in this garden. You will have to work hard. You will know what it is like to feel unhappy, and tired and in pain. You will see ugliness and sadness. Eventually you will die. This is what you have chosen. It is not what I wanted for you.'

Before they left, God made Adam and Eve some clothes out of animal skins. Then he sent them away from the garden of Eden.

5 Cain and Abel

Adam and Eve had two sons. The eldest was called Cain, and the youngest was called Abel.

Both grew up to be farmers. Cain planted seeds and harvested crops. Abel kept animals.

One day, both brothers decided to give God a present. Cain brought some of his crops, and Abel brought the first of his new-born lambs.

God looked at both presents. They were good. But then God looked at both brothers. He knew what they were like inside. He knew that Cain did not really care about God. God could not accept his present.

Cain was angry. And he was jealous.

'Don't be angry!' said God. 'Be careful! You are in danger of getting into worse trouble. Do what is right, and you will be accepted.'

But Cain did not listen. He went into the fields with Abel, and he killed his brother.

'Where is Abel?' asked God.

'I don't know!' lied Cain.

'I warned you,' said God, 'but you did not listen. Now you will be punished.'

Cain realized God knew everything. 'When people discover I have murdered my brother, they will kill me!' he cried.

'Because you have done such a terrible thing, your life will be very hard. Your crops will not grow well. But you will not be killed, because I will protect you,' promised God.

6 Noah builds a boat

As more people lived on the earth, fewer of them thought about God. They did what they wanted. They hurt one another. They continued to spoil the world God had made. God saw everything that happened, and it made him very sad.

Only one man, called Noah, remembered God.

'The world has been spoiled,' God told Noah. 'It must stop! I have seen all the terrible things men and women are doing. I am going to flood the earth with water until nothing is left. But I promise to save you and your family.'

God told Noah to build an ark. He told him how long it was to be, how many decks it should have, and where to put the door. God told Noah to coat the ark with pitch, and to fill it with supplies of food. Finally, God told Noah to collect two of every kind of living creature to take on board the ark.

'In seven days it will start to rain,' God warned Noah. 'But you and your family will be safe.'

7 The great flood

Noah and his family went on board the ark. They waited with the animals for seven days. Then it started to rain.

As the rains fell upon the earth, the rivers rose and burst their banks. Sea water gushed onto the land, and underground springs broke through the earth.

For forty days and forty nights the rain fell and the waters rose. Everything that had lived upon the earth was destroyed by the flood. But God kept Noah, his family and the animals safe inside the ark.

6 Genesis chapter 6.

The ark
The ark was meant to float on the flood waters, not to sail like a ship, so it was more like a box. The length of the ark was 300 cubits (about 137m/450ft long). This is about half the length of a modern ocean-going liner.

Pitch
This was a kind of thick oily tar used by people in Bible times to make things waterproof or to stick them together. Moses' mother also coated her baby's basket with pitch to keep the water out (see story 39).

7 Genesis chapters 7 and 8.

The flood
Many ancient peoples had stories like this about a great flood.

Nobody knows if the whole world was under water, or just the part of the world known to Noah's family.

8 Genesis chapter 9.

God's promise
After the flood God gave the rainbow a special meaning. It was a sign that he would keep his promise. This was the first promise or 'covenant' God made in the Bible. Later he made other promises to his people and expected them to love and obey him.

9 Genesis chapter 11, verses 1-9.

The tower of Babel
Babel may be the place which is later called Babylon in the Bible. The tall building was probably similar to the ziggurats (temple towers) that existed there in ancient times.

Mud bricks
These were probably made from mud and straw, which were pressed into wooden moulds and baked in the hot sun. Some people in the Middle East still make bricks in this way.

8 The rainbow

The rain stopped. Slowly the waters began to go down. The ark rested on rocks lying under the water.

Noah opened a window. He took hold of a raven and set it free in the air. The bird stretched its wings and flew, but there was nowhere for it to land. The earth was still covered with water.

Noah chose a dove, but the dove returned to the ark.

After seven days, Noah sent out the dove again. This time the bird returned with an olive leaf in its beak. Noah knew that the waters were going down.

He waited a little longer, and sent the dove out for a third time. When the bird did not return, Noah knew that it had found somewhere to rest.

'You may come out of the ark,' said God. 'Bring your family and all the animals out onto the earth. It is yours to enjoy!'

So Noah and his family left the ark. They thanked God for keeping them safe.

'I will never destroy all the earth with water again,' promised God. 'I have put a rainbow in the sky, as a sign of my promise.'

9 The tower of Babel

Many years after the flood, the earth was full of people once more. They all spoke the same language, and they moved about from place to place looking for somewhere to settle.

'Let's build a city!' said one group of people.

They didn't build with stones. Instead they baked bricks in the hot sun. They were very pleased with themselves.

As the people started to build, they began to think that a city was not important enough.

'We should build a tower!' some suggested.

'Yes,' others agreed, 'but not an ordinary tower. A tower that reaches up to heaven! Then everyone will know how important and clever we are. No one will dare do anything against us!'

But God saw the people as they built the tower. He knew how important they thought they were. He knew how little they thought about him.

'I shall make them speak different languages,' said God. 'I will scatter them all over the earth, so they will not be able to plot together. Maybe then they will spend more time thinking about me.'

THE PATRIARCHS

A 'patriarch' is the head of a tribe or family. The patriarchs of the Old Testament were Abraham, Isaac and Jacob. These men were chosen by God to be the fathers of the families that began the nation of Israel.

For many years after the Tower of Babel, God watched the people of the world. He wanted to find another fine and honest man like Noah. God needed someone who loved and trusted him so much that he would obey his commands. This person was to be chosen by God to start a new and special nation. Finally he found Abraham.

Abraham was born into the Semite race who lived in Mesopotamia, now part of the country of Iraq. When Abraham was seventy-five years old, God asked him to leave his home in Haran and take his family to the land of Canaan.

Abraham lived in a country where there were all kinds of different religions and the people worshipped many gods. For Abraham to hear the call of the 'true God' and to obey him shows that he was a very special person.

Abraham had great faith in God and obeyed his commands. He left his home and everything he knew, took his family and set off for the 'Promised Land'.

God tested Abraham's obedience many times, and because Abraham never failed him, God gave him what he had always promised – a son and heir.

When Abraham's son, Isaac, grew up, he also obeyed God's commands. Isaac trusted God to find him a wife from his own race.

Although their son, Jacob, plotted and schemed for his own success, God finally won his trust and obedience, too.

When God was sure of Jacob's love, he changed his name to Israel. Jacob's twelve sons became the fathers of twelve tribes. These tribes grew into the nation of Israel that exists today.

10 The journey begins

Noah's son, Shem, had many descendants. One of them was called Terah. He had three sons, one of whom was called Abram.

Abram was married to Sarai, but they did not have any children. They lived in the prosperous city of Ur of the Chaldeans.

One day, Terah decided to move, and his whole family set off to go to Canaan. But they did not reach there. Instead, they settled in Haran.

10 Genesis chapter 11, verses 27, 31.

The city of Ur
This was a large city near the River Euphrates in South Babylonia. The people there were rich and clever. They could read and write and they were skilled craftsmen and merchants.

On the move
Lots of people were moving from place to place at this time. Abram's long journey was not unusual.

11 Genesis chapter 12, verses 1-9.

The land of Canaan
At this time (about 2000BC) this was a fertile land with many towns and small cities.

Altars
An altar was a stone slab or a pile of stones with a flat top. People sacrificed animals and other foods to God on it (see story 5).

See Feature pages 44-45.

12 Genesis chapter 13.

Nomads
Abram and his family went from place to place to find grazing land for their sheep and goats.

Tents
Tents, light enough to be carried, were made from animal skins stretched over a wooden frame. They usually had two rooms, one for men and guests, and one for women and children.

See Feature pages 140-41.

13 Genesis chapter 15.

God's promise
God made a promise or 'covenant' with Abram just as he had done before with Noah (see story 8).

Inheritance
When a man died, his wealth passed to his eldest son. If he had no son, he would adopt someone to inherit his wealth. Abram had adopted Eliezer.

11 The Promised Land

One day, while Abram was living in Haran, God spoke to him.

'You must leave here,' said God. 'I will show you where you must go. I am going to make your family into a great nation.'

Abram did as God had told him. He packed up his possessions, prepared his servants, and said goodbye to the rest of his family. Only his wife, Sarai, and his nephew Lot, went with him.

When they arrived in Canaan, God spoke to Abram again. 'This is the land I have promised to give to you and your children,' he said.

Abram built an altar there and thanked God. He believed God's promise, even though there were other people already living in Canaan.

12 Lot chooses where to live

Abram and Lot stayed together. During a famine they went to Egypt to find food. They returned to Canaan together.

Both men had become wealthy. They had many servants and lots of animals. But the place where they had chosen to live was not big enough to support two such large families and the servants started to quarrel.

'Let's not quarrel,' said Abram to Lot. 'We have a whole land to choose from. You decide where you want to live, and I will take my family somewhere else.'

Lot looked about. He saw the plain before him was green and fertile. There was plenty of water. It would be a good place to live, and Lot wanted all of it.

'I shall live here,' Lot said. He left Abram, and pitched his tents close to the city of Sodom.

'I have not forgotten my promise,' said God to Abram when Lot had gone. 'This land is yours. You will have so many descendants that no one will be able to count them. Go and explore the land I will give you!'

13 God's promise to Abram

Abram felt confused. God had promised to make his descendants into a great nation, but still he and Sarai had no children of their own.

One day God spoke to Abram. 'Don't be afraid!' said God. 'I will protect you. I will reward you.'

Abram plucked up courage. 'Oh, Lord,' he said, 'how can you reward me, and make my descendants great, when Sarai and I have no children? My servant, Eliezer, will inherit everything I have.'

'No, he won't,' said God. 'Look up into the night sky and see if you can count the stars. There are too many of them! I promise that you will have so many descendants they will be like the stars in the night sky.'

Abram looked, and he believed what God had told him.

14 Hagar and Ishmael

After ten years of living in Canaan, Sarai still had not become pregnant. She decided to take matters into her own hands.

'Take my servant Hagar, and treat her as your wife,' said Sarai to Abram. 'Perhaps she will have some children.'

Abram listened to his wife, and before long Hagar became pregnant.

Once Hagar knew that she was expecting Abram's child, she did not want Sarai to treat her like a servant any more. She looked down on Sarai because she could not have children.

'It's all your fault!' Sarai complained to her husband. 'Hagar despises me. What shall I do?'

'Do whatever you like!' replied Abram.

So Sarai took her revenge. She made sure that Hagar suffered. She ill-treated her.

Hagar had had enough. She was so unhappy she decided to run away. But when she reached the desert an angel found her.

'Go back to Sarai!' commanded the angel. 'Be her servant again. God has seen how miserable you are. You will have a son called Ishmael. He will have many descendants.'

Hagar was amazed. 'Now I know that God sees everything!' she said, and went back home. Some time later, Ishmael was born.

15 The special visitors

When Ishmael was thirteen years old, God spoke again to Abram. 'I have not forgotten my promise,' he said. 'It will come about very soon. I am giving you both new names. You will now be called Abraham and Sarah. By this time next year, Sarah will have a son called Isaac.'

Not long after, Abraham was sitting outside his tent. It was hot. He noticed three strangers and went out to meet them.

'Come and rest!' Abraham said to them. 'Let me bring you water to wash your feet, and some food to eat.'

The men accepted Abraham's invitation.

'Where is Sarah?' they asked.

Immediately Abraham knew that the men were messengers from God.

'By this time next year, she will have a son,' they said.

Sarah was listening at the entrance to the tent. She laughed to herself. 'I'm far too old to have a baby!' she thought.

14 Genesis chapter 16.

Second wives
Men were allowed more than one wife. A servant was already treated as part of the family, so her child would be part of the family too.

📖 *See Feature pages 22-23.*

Angels
'Angel' means 'messenger'. God used angels to give his messages to people. Sometimes angels looked like the people they visited. At other times they looked like creatures from heaven, pure and powerful like God, and shining brightly.

15 Genesis chapter 17, verse 1 to chapter 18, verse 15.

Visitors
The kind way Abraham treated his visitors was typical of people of that time. He provided water for them to wash their feet, told his servants to bake bread for them to eat, and killed his best calf so that it could be cooked for them. Then he stood nearby, in case they needed anything else.

📖 *See Feature pages 54-55.*

Hebrew names
A Jewish name usually described something about a person. 'Abraham' means 'father of many nations' and 'Sarah' means 'princess'. 'Isaac' (their son) means 'laughter' because Sarah laughed when she was told she would have a child.

FAMILIES

In Bible times a family included all parents, children, grandparents, aunts, uncles, cousins, nephews, nieces and even servants. Belonging to a family was so important that it was very unusual for a man or woman not to marry, and most people usually stayed in the same village or town all their lives. Divorce was extremely rare. Everyone in the family had work to do, even children.

Family life

For all Jewish families God was at the centre of family life. Children were 'a gift from God' and having many children was thought to be good. In Old Testament times some men had more than one wife.

Fathers and mothers had to teach their children about God, as well as pass on to them their trade or how to grow food or run the household. The father of the family was the most important person, and had complete authority.

Women's work

As well as looking after the children, women had to run the household and help grow food. Every day a woman had to fetch water from the village well, grind the grain and make bread, milk the goat, fetch firewood and cook the food. Women would spin and weave cloth to make clothes for the family and go to the nearest stream or river to wash the family's clothes.

Women could not usually inherit property. They could not earn a living on their own and had to obey their husbands. The religious teachers in Jesus' time were shocked when Jesus talked to women as equals.

New baby

After her baby was born, the mother rubbed salt into its arms and legs and then wrapped it tightly in strips of cloth called swaddling bands. This was thought to make the baby's limbs grow straight. The parents often chose a name which described their feelings or the child's looks.

After eight days, a Jewish baby boy was circumcised. This was a small operation in which the foreskin was removed from his penis. Circumcision was the sign of belonging to God's people.

A wedding

Wedding celebrations sometimes lasted a week and took place in the bridegroom's house. On the eve of the wedding the bridegroom and his friends went to the bride's house to collect her. Garlands of flowers were placed on the heads of both bride and groom. Then the friends and relatives lined the street as the wedding procession went by. There was feasting, music, singing and dancing.

Men's work Most men worked as farmers or craftsmen. This boy will be a potter when he grows up.

Widows They were often very poor and had to rely on other people to look after them.

EDUCATION

The father had to teach his son God's Law. In the time of Jesus, boys went to the synagogue school, where they learned by heart the Scriptures (holy writings) of the Jewish religion, and the laws which they had to keep. Girls were taught God's Law by their mothers as well as how to do all the different jobs required at home.

Children's work Children had to work to help the family – milking the goat to make cheese; or leading a donkey with panniers on its back, full of wool, ready to be spun.

Death When someone died the whole family went into mourning. Sometimes rich families hired professional mourners to weep and wail with them. After someone died, their body was washed and put in special graveclothes and buried straight away. Rich people were buried in tombs cut out of rock; poor people were buried in caves.

GOD'S LAWS

Every child learned this:
'Love God with all your heart, with all your soul and with all your strength.'
   Fathers were told:
'Teach God's commands to your children. Repeat them when you are at home and when you are away from home, when you are resting and when you are working. Write them on the doors of your house and on your gates.'

16 Genesis chapter 18, verses 16-33.

God cares

It seems at first that Abraham is making God change his mind. But in fact God is showing Abraham that he cares very much for people who do as he asks.

17 Genesis chapter 19, verses 1-29.

Gateway meeting

City leaders usually met each other at the gateway to a city because there was no 'council office'. So Lot was probably a respected leader in Sodom.

Burning rain

The land around the Dead Sea, where Sodom and Gomorrah were, contains chemicals and bitumen, which is a kind of tar. It is thought that an earthquake sent chemicals shooting into the air, which then rained down on the city and were set alight by the fires people used for cooking on.

A pillar of salt

The Dead Sea got its name because it is so full of salt that nothing can live in it. The salt would have mixed with the other chemicals released by the earthquake. It poured down from the sky and buried Lot's wife.

You can still see large craggy mounds of salt around the Dead Sea today.

16 Abraham pleads for Sodom

The three visitors stood up to leave. Two were really angels, and the third was God. Abraham went with them a little way. They looked out across the plain to the cities of Sodom and Gomorrah.

'People say that nobody living there remembers God,' they said. 'We will visit them to see if it's true. Then we will destroy them.'

Abraham looked down towards Sodom and thought about the people who lived there.

'What if you find fifty good men?' Abraham asked God. 'Surely you won't destroy the city.'

'No!' replied God. 'If I find fifty good men, it will be saved.'

'What if you find forty-five good men?' asked Abraham.

'I won't destroy the city,' replied God.

'Forty?' Abraham pleaded.

'I won't destroy the city,' said God.

Abraham took a deep breath. 'Don't be angry with me,' he cried. 'But what if you find thirty good men?'

'I will spare the city,' promised God.

Once more Abraham spoke. 'Twenty?'

God promised to spare the people of Sodom.

'What if you find just ten good men in the whole of the city?' asked Abraham.

'For the sake of ten good men, I will not destroy it!' said God finally.

17 Angels rescue Lot

Lot, Abraham's nephew, was sitting in the gateway to the city of Sodom, when the two angels arrived. He stood up to greet them.

'Come and stay in my house,' he insisted.

That night, every man in Sodom made his way to Lot's house.

'We know you have two men staying with you!' they screamed. 'Hand them over!'

Lot ventured outside, and tried to calm the crowd. But they were too angry to listen. 'You're not one of us,' they shouted to Lot. 'If you don't hand them over we'll hurt you too!'

The two angels quickly pulled Lot inside. The angry crowd surged forwards ready to force down the door. As they moved, everyone who stood outside the house became blind. They stumbled about, unable to find the way in.

'Get out of here,' said the angels to Lot, 'and take your wife and children with you! This city will be destroyed!'

'But...' began Lot. The angels grabbed them by the hand and led them out of Sodom.

'Now run for your lives!' ordered the angels. 'And don't look back!'

Lot and his family ran. As morning came, God sent down burning rain, until Sodom and Gomorrah were destroyed.

But Lot's wife forgot the angels' warning. She looked back to see what had happened, and she was turned into a pillar of salt.

18 God protects Ishmael

'Who would believe that Abraham and I would have a son in our old age?' said Sarah, as she nursed Isaac. But Ishmael, Hagar's son, made fun of Isaac. Sarah did not like it.

'Get rid of them,' she said to Abraham. 'Tell Hagar to go away – and to take the boy with her.'

Abraham was very upset. Ishmael was his son.

'Don't worry,' God said. 'I will look after Ishmael.' So Abraham gave Hagar food and water and they set off.

After a while they ran out of water, and Hagar knew that they would die. She laid Ishmael under a bush, and walked away.

'I cannot watch my boy die!' she sobbed.

But God heard Ishmael cry. An angel spoke to Hagar. 'Don't be frightened,' he said. 'God knows. Hold Ishmael by the hand and carry on. I have promised to make him great.'

Suddenly Hagar saw a well. She went and got Ishmael a drink. God looked after Ishmael as he grew up.

19 God tests Abraham

One day, God spoke to Abraham.

'I want you to take your precious son, Isaac, to a mountain in Moriah, and sacrifice him to me there.'

Stunned with grief, Abraham obeyed God. He cut some wood for a fire and prepared his servants and his son for the journey.

After three days, Abraham left his servants and walked with Isaac towards the mountain. 'Father,' asked Isaac. 'I know we're going to make a sacrifice to God, but where's the lamb?'

'God will provide a lamb,' said Abraham sadly.

Abraham made an altar out of stones and laid the wood on it. He tied up his son, laid him on the altar and picked up his knife.

'Stop!' a voice called from heaven. 'Don't hurt him! You have shown how much you love God. You will be blessed, and your descendants will be as great as the stars in the sky!'

Abraham suddenly saw a ram caught in a bush. God had provided a sacrifice. He set Isaac free.

20 Rebekah and Isaac

'I want you to find a wife for Isaac,' said Abraham to his servant one day. 'He must marry a woman from our own people.'

So the servant took some camels and expensive gifts and set out. When he reached the well at Nahor he prayed, 'You are the God of my master Abraham and you always keep your promises. May the first girl who offers to give me and my camels some water be the wife you have chosen for Isaac.'

Before he had finished praying, Rebekah came to the well and offered him water.

'She will be a good wife for Isaac,' he thought. Rebekah's family agreed to the marriage, and when Isaac met Rebekah, he fell in love with her.

18 Genesis chapter 21, verses 1-21.

19 Genesis chapter 22, verses 1-19.

Mountains of Moriah
These mountains were about 80km/50 miles from Abraham's home. The journey there took him three days. The hill where he sacrificed the ram is thought to be where Jerusalem is today.

Sacrifice
To 'make a sacrifice' means to give up something that is precious to you (see story 5). Some people at the time sacrificed children to false gods, but God's people were never allowed to do that. God was testing Abraham's faith, to see if Abraham loved him more than he loved Isaac.

20 Genesis chapter 24.

Arranged marriages
In ancient Israel marriages were usually arranged by people's parents, although sometimes the couple could ask to marry. When they were 'betrothed' the groom often gave his future wife rings and bracelets. Nose rings were very popular at that time.

See Feature pages 22-23.

A long walk
Nahor was another name for Haran (see story 10). It was about 640km/400 miles north of Hebron, where Abraham now lived.

21 Genesis chapter 25, verses 19-34.

The inheritance
The inheritance or 'birthright' was given to the eldest son of a Jewish family when his father died (see story 13). He received the right to take over as head of the family, and twice as much of his father's possessions as anyone else.

Twin sons
When the twins were born, Jacob was gripping Esau's heel. 'Jacob' means 'he grasps' (or 'deceives').

22 Genesis chapter 26.

The Philistines
The Philistines were a fierce tribe of warriors. Later they became a powerful and dreaded enemy of the Israelites. The land of Palestine (also called Canaan) took its name from them.

See Feature pages 44-45.

23 Genesis chapter 27.

The blessing
This was both a prayer and a legal oath given by a father. It confirmed that his eldest son would be head of the family when the father died. The father laid his hands on his son and prayed over him. Once the blessing had been given, it could not be changed or given to someone else.

21 Jacob and Esau

For a long time Rebekah did not have any children. But Isaac knew about God's promise to Abraham and he prayed for his wife. After a while Rebekah gave birth to twins.

Esau was the eldest and Isaac loved him most of all. He became a good hunter, and enjoyed being outside. Jacob preferred to stay at home. Rebekah loved him the best.

One day, Esau came home from hunting. He was hungry and desperately wanted something to eat. Jacob was cooking a stew.

'Give me some of that!' demanded Esau.

Jacob seized his chance and said, 'Give me your inheritance.'

'Agreed!' said Esau, who wasn't really thinking.

22 God looks after Isaac

When a famine came, Isaac moved to the more fertile land where the Philistines lived. 'I will protect you,' God reassured him.

Abimelech, the Philistine king, ordered his people to leave Isaac and his family alone. Isaac planted some crops, which grew well, and provided a good harvest.

After a while, Abimelech changed his mind. 'You are growing too rich and powerful,' he said. 'You will have to leave!'

So Isaac moved on.

'I am with you,' God told Isaac, 'just as I was with your father.'

Abimelech came to find Isaac.

'Why have you come?' asked Isaac.

'I know God is with you,' said the king. 'We do not want to fight you. Let us agree not to hurt each other.'

So Isaac and the king of the Philistines made a solemn promise to one another, and left each other in peace.

23 Jacob steals the blessing

The years passed. Isaac was an old man. He was almost blind, and he had not long to live. One day he called for his eldest son, Esau.

'Go and hunt some wild game and make me a meal,' he said. 'Then I will bless you.'

Esau took his bow and arrow and set off. He had forgotten the rash promise he had made to his brother years before.

Rebekah overheard her husband's conversation. She wanted

Jacob to receive Isaac's special blessing.

'Go and kill two goats and give them to me,' she ordered Jacob. 'I will cook for your father, and he will bless you.'

Jacob was unsure. 'But Esau has hairy skin,' he protested. 'Father can't see me but when he touches me he'll know I'm not Esau.'

Rebekah dressed Jacob in Esau's clothes and tied goatskin on his arms and neck, and sent him to his father.

Isaac touched his son and smelled his clothes. Then he blessed him.

When Esau returned and found out he had been tricked, he was furious and wanted to kill Jacob. But Rebekah urged Jacob to run away, and escape to her brother, Laban.

24 Jacob's dream

Jacob set out towards Haran, where his uncle Laban lived.

At night Jacob lay down to sleep. He had a vivid dream.

He saw a long flight of stairs, stretching from the earth to heaven. Angels moved up and down the staircase, and at the very top, Jacob saw God.

'I am the God of your father and grandfather,' said God. 'I promise to give you and your descendants the land you are lying on. I will watch over you and will never leave you.'

When Jacob woke, he was afraid. He knew that he had seen God. He took the stone he had used as a pillow and put it up like a pillar to mark the special place.

'If you look after me as you have promised, I will obey you and follow you,' said Jacob.

Then he continued on his journey.

25 Jacob meets Rachel

Jacob went eastwards. He saw some shepherds and their sheep waiting by a large well. Jacob went up to them.

'Where are you from?' he asked the shepherds.

'Haran,' they replied.

Jacob was delighted. That was where his uncle lived.

'Do you know Laban?' he asked hopefully.

'Yes,' they replied.

Jacob looked up. He saw a shepherdess leading her flock of sheep towards the well.

'That's Laban's daughter, Rachel,' said the shepherds. Jacob went to meet Rachel.

When Rachel heard that Jacob was Rebekah's son, she ran to fetch her father, Laban. He hurried to meet his nephew and greeted him like a father, and took him home.

'You are part of my family,' said Laban.

'At last I am safe,' thought Jacob.

24 Genesis chapter 28, verses 10-22.

God's promise
Although Jacob had done wrong and tricked his father, the blessing he had been given meant Jacob would be the father of the twelve tribes of Israel.

The stone pillar
The stone pillar that Jacob set up was at a place called Bethel, which means 'house of God'. Jacob wanted to mark the spot where God had spoken to him.

25 Genesis chapter 29, verses 1-14.

Water
There were no taps even in cities. People collected water from wells or rivers and stored it in large clay pots.

Women's work
It was the job of the women and girls to fetch water for the household and their animals. Rachel was doing what Jacob's mother, Rebekah, had done many years before.

📖 See Feature pages 22-23.

26 Genesis chapter 29, verses 15-30.

Marriage custom
It was the custom of the time for the bride to be veiled throughout the wedding service. So Laban was able to trick Jacob into marrying the wrong woman. It was only after Jacob had married Leah that he saw who she was.

See Feature pages 22-23.

27 Genesis chapter 30, verse 25 to chapter 31, verse 55.

Jacob's wives and children
Jacob had four wives: Leah and her servant, Zilpah, and Rachel and her servant, Bilhah. He had twelve sons, Reuben, Simeon, Levi, Judah, Dan, Naphtali, Gad, Asher, Issachar, Zebulun, Joseph, Benjamin, and a daughter, Dinah.

Sheep and goats
Jacob learned to breed strong animals with other strong animals, and so his herds were of a much better quality. He chose the speckled ones so that there could be no arguments about which sheep were his.

26 Laban cheats Jacob

'You have stayed with us for a month now,' said Laban to Jacob, 'and I have not paid you for the work that you have done for me. Name your price.'

Jacob thought carefully. He had only been with Laban a short time, but he had fallen in love with Laban's youngest daughter, Rachel.

'I will work for you for seven years, if you let me marry Rachel,' said Jacob.

Laban agreed and Jacob worked hard.

At the end of the seven years, Laban organized a big feast to celebrate his daughter's marriage. But Laban intended to trick Jacob. Instead of marrying Rachel, Jacob married Leah, Laban's eldest daughter. When he found out, it was too late.

'Why did you trick me?' asked Jacob angrily. He didn't love Leah at all.

'Because it is our custom that the eldest daughter should marry first,' replied Laban. 'But I will let you marry Rachel now, if you agree to work for me for another seven years.'

Jacob agreed. He loved Rachel very much.

27 Jacob runs away

After twenty years, God told Jacob to go back home. Jacob had worked hard, but Laban had often treated him unfairly. Now he wanted to take his wives and children back to his father, Isaac.

'Don't go!' begged Laban. 'God has blessed me because you are here.'

'Very well,' sighed Jacob. 'But let me have any spotted or speckled sheep or goat from your herd, so I can build up my own.'

Laban agreed. He wanted Jacob to stay. But the sheep and goats Jacob chose grew to be strongest. Soon Jacob owned good, healthy livestock, while Laban's animals were weak and inferior.

'Can't you see what Jacob is doing?' Laban's sons asked their father. 'He is taking your finest animals.'

Laban saw what had happened. He began to feel differently towards Jacob. Jacob noticed the change. He did not trust his uncle.

'Go home!' God told Jacob. 'I will be with you.'

Secretly, Jacob prepared his wives and children for the long journey. He did not tell Laban they were going.

When Laban discovered Jacob had gone, he chased after him.

'Don't say anything against Jacob,' God warned Laban in a dream.

When Laban caught up with Jacob, he challenged him. 'Why did you run away?' he asked. 'Why didn't you tell me you were going?' He searched through Jacob's possessions, making sure nothing had been stolen.

Now Jacob was angry. 'I have worked hard for you for twenty years,' he said, 'and God has seen how you have cheated me!'

Laban looked at Jacob, his daughters and his grandchildren, and his healthy sheep and goats. 'Everything that belongs to you was mine,' he said. 'Let us promise not to hurt each other.'

So Jacob and Laban set another pillar in the ground, and made their promise. 'May God see what we have promised,' they said.

28 Jacob wrestles with God

It was night and Jacob was alone. His wives and children had gone on ahead of him. Suddenly, out of the darkness a stranger appeared. He grabbed Jacob and began to wrestle with him. Jacob faced the strange man, and gripped him tightly. Hour after hour the two men fought. Hour after hour they were locked together in conflict. Neither would let go. Neither would give up.

The sun began to break through the night sky, and the stranger touched Jacob's hip. Immediately his hip bone jumped out of its socket. But Jacob did not loosen his grasp.

'Let me go,' said the stranger.

'Not until you bless me,' said Jacob. He knew that this stranger was not an ordinary man.

'What's your name?' asked the stranger.

Jacob told him.

'I will give you a new name,' said the stranger. 'You will be called Israel because you have wrestled with God and other people, and you have won.'

'Please tell me your name,' asked Jacob.

The stranger refused, but he blessed Jacob.

Jacob limped away. He knew he had wrestled with God.

29 The brothers make friends again

Jacob was frightened. Many years had passed and now his twin brother Esau was coming to meet him, bringing 400 men with him. Jacob was certain Esau wanted to kill him.

In panic, Jacob prayed to God. 'You told me to go back home,' said Jacob. 'You promised to protect me!'

Quickly Jacob divided his family and herds into small groups. He hoped if Esau attacked one, the rest would escape. He also chose some animals as a present for Esau.

When he saw Esau approach, Jacob bowed down to the ground. But his brother had not come to fight. When Esau saw Jacob he threw his arms around him, and hugged him.

Both men started to cry. Esau had forgiven Jacob. He was no longer angry. Neither was jealous of the other. They were friends and brothers once more.

Pillar in the ground
The pillar which Jacob set up was like a memorial. It was a sign that he and Laban had made an agreement. If it was ever doubted, people could point to the pillar to prove it. People also set up pillars as boundary stones.

28 Genesis chapter 32, verses 22-32.

Israel
When Jacob refused to let go, God knew that Jacob was at last willing to obey him. So he gave him the new name 'Israel', which means 'one who struggles with God'. The nation was later called by his name.

29 Genesis chapter 33.

A big present
Jacob chose 220 goats, 220 sheep, 50 cattle, 40 donkeys and 30 camels to give to Esau. It was the custom to give presents as a sign of peace. The size of the present showed that Jacob was wealthy and powerful.

Bowing low
Jacob bowed down to the ground seven times in front of Esau. It showed that he was sorry and wanted to be forgiven. It also showed that he respected his brother and did not want to cheat him again.

30 Genesis chapter 29, verse 31 to chapter 30, verse 22 and chapter 35, verses 16-26.

Childlessness
People thought that women who could not have children were cursed by God. Each couple wanted as many sons as possible to keep the family name alive and help with the work.

Benjamin's name
'Ben' in Hebrew means 'son of'. So Ben-Oni meant 'son of trouble', but Ben-jamin meant 'son of the right hand' – that is, lucky.

See Feature pages 22-23.

31 Genesis chapter 37, verses 1-4.

Joseph's coat
The special coat given by Jacob to Joseph was probably an ankle-length tunic with long sleeves down to the wrists. This was the kind of coat worn by an important person or someone on special occasions. An ordinary worker's tunic had no sleeves and only came down to the knees.

32 Genesis chapter 37, verses 5-11.

The dreamer
Joseph's dreams were looking into the future (see stories 36, 38). Later, the things his family feared would happen came true.

30 Rachel's sons

Jacob had many children by his other wives. But he loved Rachel the most, and for years she did not have a baby.

At last she gave birth to a son, and she called him Joseph.

'Please give me another son,' she asked God.

Some time later Rachel became pregnant again. But this time she had difficulty giving birth.

'You have another son,' the midwife told Rachel.

'Call him Ben-Oni,' whispered Rachel weakly. She knew she was going to die.

'I will call him Benjamin,' said Jacob, as he looked at his new-born son.

31 Jacob's special son

Jacob had twelve sons but he loved Joseph more than his other children, and Joseph knew it.

By the time he was seventeen, Joseph helped his brothers to look after his father's flocks. But Joseph watched them and listened to them, and then told his father the bad things they said and did.

Jacob gave Joseph a very special long-sleeved coat. When Joseph's brothers saw it, they knew that he was loved much more than they were. They hated him.

32 Joseph's dreams

One night, Joseph had a dream.

'Listen everyone,' he said grandly. 'I dreamed that we were all binding sheaves of corn when suddenly my sheaf stood up straight, and your sheaves bowed down before mine!'

'What are you trying to say?' asked his brothers angrily. 'Do you really think we are going to bow down before you?'

Then Joseph had another dream. 'I dreamed that the sun, the moon and eleven stars all bowed down before me!' he boasted.

'Are you suggesting that your mother and I will bow down before you?' asked his father.

His brothers said nothing. But they hated him even more.

His father began to wonder what would become of Joseph.

33 Joseph is sold

One day Joseph set off, looking for his brothers who were taking care of the flocks.

Long before Joseph had reached them, they saw him. They recognized his coat.

'Here comes the dreamer boy!' they said. 'Let's kill him while we have the chance.'

But Reuben did not agree. 'Put him in a pit,' he said. 'Let's not be guilty of murder.'

The brothers agreed.

As soon as Joseph reached them, the brothers tore off his coat, and threw him in the pit. Then they sat and ate a meal.

After a while they saw a group of traders. 'Even better!' said Judah. 'Let's not harm our brother at all. Let's sell him!'

So they sold Joseph, dipped his special coat in animal blood, and told their father that he was dead.

Joseph was taken as a slave to Egypt where he was sold to Potiphar, the captain of Pharaoh's guard.

34 Joseph in prison

At first Joseph did well in Potiphar's household. Soon Potiphar trusted him with everything he owned. But one day Potiphar's wife told lies about him, and Joseph was flung into prison.

For many years, nobody remembered Joseph. But God had not forgotten him.

Pharaoh's cupbearer and baker were also in prison. Both men had strange dreams, and when they told Joseph about them, God helped him to understand the meaning of their dreams. The cupbearer was released, just as Joseph predicted.

35 Pharaoh's strange dreams

Some time later, Pharaoh also had strange and disturbing dreams. No one knew what they meant. Suddenly the cupbearer remembered Joseph. 'He can explain dreams,' he said.

Pharaoh sent for him. 'In my dreams, seven thin cows eat up seven fat, healthy cows,' said Pharaoh, 'and seven thin, poor ears of corn swallow up seven healthy ears of corn. What does this mean?'

'God is warning you what will happen,' said Joseph. 'There will be seven years of plentiful harvest, followed by seven years of famine. Store up the grain wisely, and all will be well.'

Pharaoh was impressed. He put Joseph in charge of everything. He could see that God was helping him.

33 Genesis chapter 37, verses 12-36.

Pit
The pit into which Joseph was thrown was a large, empty hole in the ground used for storing water. These were sometimes 30m/100ft deep.

Slave trade
Children (and adults who could not pay their bills) were sometimes sold as slaves. They would have to work hard for someone and had no rights of their own. The traders were spice merchants going to Egypt.

34 Genesis chapters 39 and 40.

Prisoners
'Pharaoh' was the Egyptian word for king. The cupbearer to the Pharaoh was the man in charge of his wine. The 'baker' probably means cook. They may have been thrown into prison because the Pharaoh thought they were poisoning him.

35 Genesis chapter 41.

Dreams
The people of ancient Egypt thought dreams were very important. Wise men wrote books to help people understand what they had dreamed. God gave Joseph the ability to explain Pharaoh's dreams.

36 Genesis chapter 42.

Famine
The River Nile is a long river that flows through Egypt. It was the only source of water for the Egyptians' food crops. If the water level fell too low, it would not flood the fields and ditches which watered them. In Canaan, where Jacob lived, the famine would have been caused by too little rainfall.

37 Genesis chapters 43 and 44.

Egyptian style
It was not surprising that Joseph's brothers did not recognize him. Joseph was now a powerful man dressed in the fine clothes and headdress of an important official of Egypt. It was also over thirteen years since his brothers had sold him into slavery.

Judah's kindness
Judah knew how much his father, Jacob, missed Joseph. Now he wants to save Jacob from the sadness of losing Benjamin, Rachel's other son. Joseph could see that his brothers had changed.

38 Genesis chapters 45 to 50.

The Israelites
There were about seventy people in Jacob's whole family when he went to live in Egypt. The descendants of Jacob became known as the 'Children of Israel' or 'Israelites'.

📖 See Feature pages 44-45.

36 Joseph and his brothers

Everything happened just as Joseph had said. During seven good harvests, Joseph stored the extra grain, ready for the famine. Back in Canaan, Jacob heard that there was grain in Egypt, so he sent his sons to buy some.

When the brothers arrived, they bowed down before the Egyptian governor. They did not recognize their brother.

'Are you spies?' Joseph asked. He knew who they were.

'No, sir,' they replied. 'We are brothers from Canaan. Our youngest brother is at home with our father. Can we buy food?'

Joseph made them wait three days. He sold them grain.

'Return home,' he said, 'but as proof that you are not spies, leave one brother here and return with your youngest brother.'

On the way home, the brothers opened the grain sacks, and found that the money they had paid for the grain had been returned. They were frightened. They told their father what had happened.

But Jacob refused to let Benjamin, his youngest son, go to Egypt.

37 The silver cup

When the famine continued, Jacob had no choice. Reluctantly he let his sons leave Canaan and return to Egypt with Benjamin.

When Joseph saw his brothers, he invited them to his house to attend a feast. But still they did not recognize him.

Joseph arranged for his brothers to be given grain. He also asked his servant to put his own silver cup in Benjamin's sack.

As the brothers left the city, Joseph ordered his men to catch up with them and accuse them of theft.

The brothers denied Joseph's accusations, but when the cup was found in Benjamin's sack, they tore their clothes in disbelief and grief.

'Do not harm Benjamin!' Judah pleaded as he stood before Joseph. 'Let me take the blame instead!'

38 Jacob moves to Egypt

Joseph could keep up the pretence no longer. He ordered his servants to leave him alone with his brothers.

'I am your brother, Joseph,' he told them. 'You sold me to some traders, and you wished me harm, but that was in the past. God had a greater plan, and now I am able to help my whole family.'

When Pharaoh heard that Joseph's brothers had come to Egypt, he invited their whole family to leave Canaan and live in Egypt.

The brothers returned home, and told their father the whole story. 'Joseph is alive!' they said.

So Jacob left with his children and grandchildren to go to Egypt.

'Don't be afraid to leave Canaan,' God told Jacob. 'I will go with you. I will make your family into a great nation.'

THE PROMISED LAND

This part of the Bible tells the dramatic story of how God's people,
the Israelites, escaped from Egypt where they were slaves,
and after forty years of wandering through the desert came to Canaan,
the land God had promised Abraham many years before.

The story starts in the book of Exodus, which describes how the Israelites were cruelly treated by the Egyptians and used as slave labour to build some of the cities of ancient Egypt. Jacob's family had come to Egypt 400 years earlier. Now they longed to go back to Canaan.

Moses, God's chosen leader, pleaded with the Pharaoh to let the people leave. But it was only after a number of plagues sent by God that the Israelites crossed over the Red Sea in what is known as the 'exodus' or 'going out'. The story of how the Israelites were freed from slavery is still celebrated by Jewish people today in the Passover festival.

The journey to Canaan, the Promised Land, was difficult. Food and drink were scarce, although God provided both for the people as they needed them. The people grumbled, complained and turned against God.

At Mount Sinai, Moses received the Ten Commandments and other laws from God. Time and again he reminded the people of God's promise to look after his people. When they reached the borders of Canaan, Moses sent spies in to report on the land. While two of them reported that the land was good and fertile, the others were frightened and refused to take the land. So the Israelites spent the next forty years wandering in the desert, and only entered the Promised Land when the generation that had left Egypt had died.

39 The baby in the basket

Years passed. Jacob and his sons died in Egypt. But their children stayed, and had children of their own until there were many Israelites living there. However, as other Pharaohs came to power, they forgot about Joseph. They did not treat his descendants kindly. Instead, they made them slaves, and forced them to build new cities for the Egyptians. But there were so many slaves the Egyptians came to hate and fear them. So Pharaoh ordered that all Israelite baby boys be killed at birth.

When an Israelite woman called Jochebed gave birth to a baby boy, she hid him until he was three months old. Then she put the baby in a basket, coated with tar and pitch, and told her daughter, Miriam, to hide it in the reeds along the bank of the River Nile.

When the Pharaoh's daughter came to bathe in the river, she heard the sound of a baby crying and felt sorry for him.

'Shall I find someone to nurse him for you?' asked Miriam, the baby's sister.

'Yes,' said the princess. Miriam went to fetch her mother.

'I will pay you to look after this baby for me until he is older,' said the princess. The real mother took her baby in her arms.

The princess named him Moses.

39 Exodus chapter 1, verse 1 to chapter 2, verse 10.

New cities
Egypt was very wealthy at this time. Many slaves including the Israelites were forced to build big store rooms and palaces at Pithom and Rameses. These were near where the Nile enters the Mediterranean Sea.

Pharaoh's daughter
The Egyptian king had many wives and children. The less important ones lived in a harem. The Egyptian princess who found Moses would have taken him back to the palace to be brought up and educated as an Egyptian boy.

40 Exodus chapter 2, verses 11-25.

Midian
The Midianites were descendants of Abraham. They lived in the desert, so Moses had to change his way of life. He became a shepherd. This prepared him for the hard years ahead when he would lead the Israelites in the desert.

41 Exodus chapter 3.

Burning bush
Moses saw the burning bush on Mount Sinai (also known as Horeb). This is the place where he later meets God again to receive the Law. In the Bible fire is often a sign of God's presence (see stories 47, 88).

See Feature pages 82-83.

Holy ground
It has always been the custom in the East to take off shoes as a sign of reverence and respect for anything holy.

42 Exodus chapter 4, verses 1-17.

Leprosy
In ancient times 'leprosy' described many different skin problems, especially those which made the skin go pale or patchy. True leprosy, which makes the hands and feet go numb, probably did not exist at the time of Moses.

Moses' stick
This stick or 'staff' may have been a shepherd's crook. Moses probably used it as a walking stick too.

40 Moses runs away

One day, when Moses was grown up, he saw an Egyptian beating an Israelite. Moses hated the way the Egyptians treated his people.

Looking round to make sure no one could see him, Moses seized the Egyptian and killed him. He quickly hid the body in the sand.

The next day, Moses saw two Israelites fighting. 'Don't fight each other,' he said to them.

'Why?' asked one of the men defiantly. 'Are you going to kill me as you killed that Egyptian?'

Moses was frightened. He knew he must have been seen.

When Pharaoh heard what Moses had done, he tried to kill him. But Moses had already run away, to Midian.

41 Moses and the burning bush

Moses stayed in Midian for many years. He married, and had a son.

One day, while Moses was looking after his father-in-law's sheep, he saw something strange. A bush was on fire but the flames did not burn it up.

Suddenly, Moses heard a voice, speaking from the bush.

'Moses! Moses!' called the voice.

'Yes, here I am,' he replied.

'Take off your shoes!' ordered the voice. 'You are on holy ground.' At once, Moses knew that God was speaking to him. He was so afraid, he hid his face.

'I have seen how my people, the Israelites, have suffered as slaves in Egypt,' said God. 'I want them to be free to live in the land I have promised them. I am sending you to rescue them.'

Moses was amazed. 'But I can't go to Pharaoh,' said Moses. 'He wouldn't listen to me!'

'I will be with you,' replied God.

42 Moses is afraid

Moses was afraid. He did not want to be the Israelites' leader.

'They'll never believe me,' argued Moses. 'What shall I say?'

'Take your stick and throw it on the ground,' ordered God.

Moses threw it. It hit the ground and turned into a snake. Moses ran.

'Pick it up by the tail!' said God.

As Moses picked it up, it changed into a stick once more.

'Put your hand inside your cloak,' said God.

Moses did as God asked. Then he took his hand out from under his cloak. It was covered with leprosy. Quickly, he put it back and when he removed it, his hand was healthy again.

'Show them these things,' said God, 'and they will know that you have been sent by me. If they still doubt, take some water from the River Nile. As you pour it onto the ground, it will turn to blood.'

But Moses said, 'I do not speak well. I have always found it difficult to speak to people. I don't want to go. Send someone else.'

God was angry with Moses. 'I made you, and I know all about you,' he said. 'Your brother Aaron can go with you. He will speak for you. But take your stick, so you can prove that I have sent you.'

So Moses made plans to return to Egypt.

43 A visit to the king

Moses and his brother Aaron went to see Pharaoh.

'We have come with a message from God. Let his people the Israelites leave Egypt,' they said.

'I don't know your God,' said Pharaoh, 'and I don't want to let the Israelites leave. They are slaves, and they are needed. I won't let them go!'

Moses and Aaron left. Pharaoh believed that they had stirred up trouble among the Israelite slaves.

'Make the Israelites work even harder,' Pharaoh told his slave-drivers. 'Make them gather their own straw to make bricks. But punish them severely if they make fewer bricks than before!'

'This is unfair,' said the Israelites to Pharaoh. 'How can we make the same number of bricks?'

'You are lazy,' said Pharaoh. 'Now you will have to make bricks without any straw. Get back to work!'

Some Israelites found Moses and Aaron. 'It's all your fault!' they complained. 'You have made Pharaoh hate us even more!'

Moses spoke to God. 'Why have you allowed me to cause such trouble?' he asked.

'They are my people,' promised God. 'I will rescue them.'

44 Frogs, gnats and boils!

Moses and Aaron went to see Pharaoh again.

'Let God's people go!' they said.

Pharaoh refused.

God spoke to Moses. 'Tell Aaron to stretch out his stick,' he said.

Aaron did as Moses told him, and as he stretched out his stick, all the water in Egypt turned to blood.

A week later, Moses returned to Pharaoh. 'If you don't let God's people leave, he will send a plague of frogs.'

Aaron stretched out his stick, and Egypt was covered in frogs.

'The Israelites can leave,' said Pharaoh. 'Only pray to your God to take the frogs away.'

Moses prayed and the frogs died. But Pharaoh changed his mind. He refused to let the Israelites go.

Seven more times Moses and Aaron asked Pharaoh to let the Israelites go. They stretched out their arms and plagues of gnats, flies and locusts filled the air. Every Egyptian animal died, and the people were covered in boils. Violent hailstorms battered the land, and finally the whole of Egypt was plunged into darkness.

Each time Pharaoh refused to let the Israelites go, his heart grew harder and harder. He could not change his mind.

43 Exodus chapter 5.

Slave labour
In Old Testament times it was common for nations to make others work for them as slaves. The Israelites had to work long hours in the heat making bricks to build Egyptian cities. The Israelites sometimes had slaves, but they were told by God to treat them kindly.

44 Exodus chapters 7 to 10.

Plagues
A plague is something nasty that spreads over a wide area and causes destruction, ill-health or death. These plagues happened over many months.

The 'blood' may have been thick red earth carried down by the flooding River Nile, along with weed and germs. It took oxygen from the water so the fish died. The frogs moved inland and may have caught a disease which later spread to cattle.

The insects multiplied in the heat and damp, and on the rotting flesh. Insects often carry disease. The darkness was probably a huge dust storm after the land had dried out.

45 Exodus chapter 11.

The firstborn
The word 'firstborn' here means the firstborn male. This was significant in the East as he usually became the next head of the family after the father died. The head of the family was very powerful. Perhaps the death of the firstborn Egyptians was a punishment for killing the Israelite baby boys at the time of Moses' birth.

📖 See Feature pages 22-23.

46 Exodus chapter 12, verses 1-30.

The Passover
The night in Egypt when death 'passed over' the homes of the Israelites was the most important event in Jewish history. It has been celebrated by the Jews every year ever since.

Unleavened bread
At the Passover feast the Jews eat the same meal that they ate in Egypt, lamb with herbs, and bread with no yeast added (see also stories 276-278).

📖 See Feature pages 54-55.

47 Exodus chapter 12, verses 31-42.

Pillars of cloud and fire
God is often represented by a cloud or fire in the Old Testament (see stories 41, 56, 88). The cloud reminded people that God was still with them though he could not be seen. Fire (used to purify metals) was a sign that he was perfect.

45 Disaster in Egypt

'I will give Pharaoh one more warning,' said God to Moses. 'If he still refuses to listen, every Egyptian, including Pharaoh, will beg my people to leave.'

Then God told Moses what he was going to do. 'After midnight tonight, every firstborn living thing which belongs to Egypt will die. Their children will die, and their animals will die. But I will keep my people safe.'

Moses warned Pharaoh, but Pharaoh took no notice. He refused to listen. He did not want the Israelites to leave Egypt.

46 The Passover

That night, after midnight, every firstborn Egyptian died.

But God had made sure that the Israelites were safe. He told Moses, 'Each Israelite family must prepare a special meal of roast lamb and eat it with unleavened bread and herbs. They must coat their door frames with blood from the lamb, so that death will pass over them. They are to eat ready for a journey, with their cloaks wrapped round them, their sandals on their feet, and a stick in their hands.'

Moses told the Israelites what to do. 'This is a solemn night,' he said. 'It is one we must never forget. We must tell our children and grandchildren everything that happens tonight.'

The Israelites did as they were told. Throughout the night, they heard the cries of the Egyptians.

47 Escape from Egypt

During the night Pharaoh summoned Moses and Aaron. He had heard the cries and screams of his people. He knew how they felt. His own son had died.

'Leave us!' he cried. 'And take your cattle and sheep with you!'

The Egyptians gave the Israelites everything they asked for. They gave them gold and silver. They just wanted them to go.

'God is leading us to Canaan,' Moses told the people. 'It is the land he promised to give to Abraham and his descendants.'

And the people saw that God was leading them. By day he appeared as a pillar of cloud, and by night as a pillar of fire. God did not leave them. They stopped and made camp by the Red Sea.

48 Exodus chapter 13, verse 17 to chapter 14, verse 31.

The Egyptian army
The Egyptians chased the Israelites (who were on foot) in fast, horse-drawn chariots.

48 Crossing the Red Sea

Pharaoh heard that the Israelites had stopped by the Red Sea. He began to regret that he had ever let them leave Egypt.

'What have we done?' he said to his officials. 'We have let our slaves just walk away from us. Prepare the army! The Israelites are trapped by the Red Sea. We will soon bring them back.'

When the Israelites saw the Egyptian army thundering towards them, they turned on Moses. 'Why have you brought us here? It's all your fault! We would have been happier dying in Egypt!'

'Don't be afraid,' said Moses. Suddenly the pillar of cloud moved behind the people, and stood between them and the Egyptians.

Then, listening to what God told him, Moses stretched out his hand over the waters of the Red Sea. A strong wind blew from the east. The sea waters rose and fell, until they divided in two, and a path appeared through the middle, on the sea-bed.

Moses led the Israelites safely to the other side.

The Egyptians followed. But as Moses stretched out his hand, from the safety of the far bank, the water moved freely once more. Pharaoh and his army were covered by the waters of the Red Sea. No one survived.

The Red Sea
The Israelites probably crossed a marshy area just north of the Red Sea. The wind blew the marsh dry, but when the wind stopped it got muddy again.

49 Exodus chapter 15, verses 1-21.

Music and dancing
The Israelites always danced and sang at a time of great rejoicing (see also story 126). The tambourine was probably an animal skin stretched over a wooden frame which had bronze pieces in it to rattle.

49 God is great

When Moses and the Israelites saw what had happened to the Egyptians, they were amazed. They wanted to tell God how great and wonderful he was. So Moses led the Israelites in a song of praise.

'Our God is great and mighty!
He threw horses and riders into the sea.
Our God is strong and mighty!
He came to rescue us all.
He came for us as he promised,
And loves us and leads us on.'

Then Miriam, Moses' sister, took her tambourine, and began to play and to dance. She wanted to thank God for all that he had done. The other Israelite women saw what she did, and they followed her, dancing and playing tambourines.

'Sing to the Lord God,' sang Miriam. 'He is the greatest!'

As well as using music to celebrate victory in battle, the Israelites used it at funerals, when a king was anointed, in battles and in their worship of God.

50 Exodus chapter 15, verse 22 to chapter 16, verse 36.

Quail
These brown birds belong to the partridge family and are considered a great treat to eat. Large flocks of them migrate across the Sinai Desert twice a year. As they fly low they are easily caught.

Water sweetener
The bark and leaves of some desert plants can be used to sweeten the water.

Manna
This was a miraculous food provided by God. Nothing like it has ever been seen since.

51 Exodus chapter 17, verses 1-15.

Water from the rock
Many of the rocks in the area absorb and hold water inside them.

Amalekites
These were nomads who were descended from Esau. They were enemies of Israel for another 500 years until they were destroyed.

Arms lifted
People prayed with their arms raised. So all the time Moses' arms were lifted he was praying for God's help to win the battle.

50 Sweet water in the desert

A few days later the mood in the Israelite camp changed.

Moses had led them into the desert. But they went for three days without finding water. When at last they found some, it was undrinkable.

The people complained, and Moses spoke to God.

'Throw that piece of wood into the water,' said God. 'Then it will taste sweet.'

Moses obeyed God, and the people drank.

They continued to travel through the desert. It was hot and tiring. There was no food and little water.

'We wish we had died in Egypt!' the people said to Moses. 'At least we had plenty of food.'

'Tell everyone that I have heard how much they grumble,' said God to Moses. 'I will make bread rain from the sky, and I will provide quail for my people to eat. There will be enough for everyone.'

That evening, the Israelite camp was full of quail, and the ground was covered in a thin layer of white flakes. It looked like frost. It was the bread God had promised, and it tasted like wafers made of honey.

The people called the bread 'manna'.

51 Battling with the enemy

The people moved on. Once more there was no water to drink.

'We want water!' they grumbled, ready to kill Moses.

'What am I to do?' cried Moses to God.

God told Moses to take his stick, and to strike a rock. As he did so, water streamed out from the rock, and the people drank.

But then the Amalekites came and attacked the Israelites.

Moses chose Joshua to lead the Israelite army. The two armies fought in the valley, while Moses took Aaron and Hur and climbed to the top of a hill. Moses held his stick high in his hands, and watched the battle. As soon as he lowered his arms, the Amalekites became stronger. But when he held the stick high, the Israelites took control of the battle.

Moses' arms grew tired, but he dared not lower them. Hur and Aaron found a stone for him to sit on. Then they stood on each side of him, holding up his arms until sunset when the Israelites had the victory.

52 God speaks on the mountain

The Israelites camped at the foot of Mount Sinai.

Then God called to Moses from the mountain. 'Tell the people that I promise that if they obey me, I will make them into a special nation. They will be precious to me.'

Moses told the people what God said and they promised to obey.

God told Moses that he would come down and speak to him on the mountain. Three days later, thick cloud covered the mountain. Thunder and lightning struck. At the sound of a trumpet blast the people trembled, and Moses led them to the foot of the mountain. There was fire and smoke, the ground shook, and the trumpet sounded over and over again.

The people stood still. They would die if they moved nearer, so great was God's presence.

God came down, and Moses went to meet him. God gave Moses the laws for his people to obey. He engraved them on two stone tablets, in his own hand.

53 A special place for God

While Moses was on the mountain, God told him how he wanted the people to worship him. They were to build a tabernacle, a special tent, made of precious materials, with special furniture. The gold, silver, fine cloth and jewels the Egyptians had given the Israelites would be needed for God's use.

'I have chosen Bezalel and Oholiab to do the work,' God said to Moses. 'I have filled Bezalel with my Spirit. He will be able to work with many different materials. I will help everyone who is a craftsman to use their gifts to work for me.'

54 Aaron makes a golden calf

Moses stayed on the mountain for forty days.

As the people waited, they grew tired and restless.

'Where has Moses gone?' they asked Aaron. 'Anything could have happened to him.' Then they had an idea. 'Give us a god we can see,' they demanded. 'Make one for us!'

Aaron did not hesitate. He told the people to give him all their gold jewellery. Then he melted it down, and made it into the shape of one of the Egyptian gods. It was a golden calf.

The people were delighted. They thanked the golden calf for leading them out of Egypt.

Aaron saw how pleased they were. He proclaimed the following day to be a festival. But God saw what they were doing.

'Go back to the people,' he told Moses angrily. 'Tell them I have seen their disobedience.'

52 Exodus chapter 19, verse 1 to chapter 20, verse 21.

Mount Sinai
This is the mountain of God, where he revealed himself to Moses in the burning bush (story 41) and then gave Moses the Ten Commandments. Mount Sinai (also called Horeb) is 2,300m/7,500ft high and is part of a range of mountains.

The Ten Commandments
These were written on slabs, called 'tablets'.
1 I am the Lord your God. You shall not have any other gods but me.
2 Do not bow down to or worship idols.
3 You shall not take a false oath in my name.
4 Remember the Sabbath day and keep it holy.
5 Honour your father and your mother.
6 Do not murder.
7 Do not take another person's wife or husband.
8 Do not steal.
9 Do not tell lies.
10 Do not be jealous.

53 Exodus chapter 31, verses 1-11.

God's Spirit
God's Spirit is given to people to help them do things for God. Here, Bezalel and Oholiab receive God's power to make the tent beautiful (see also story 59).

54 Exodus chapter 32, verses 1-14.

Idol worship
Pagan gods were often represented as strong and fearless bulls. The Egyptians sometimes offered their worship to live bulls.

See Feature pages 82-83.

55 Exodus chapter 32, verses 15-35.

Broken tablets
Moses smashed the stone tablets which held the rules God had given him. But God was not angry with Moses, but with the people because they had broken those rules.

Aaron's excuse
Aaron was worried about what the people thought of him. He should have been more afraid of disobeying God.

56 Exodus chapter 33, verses 1-3, 7-16.

A pillar of cloud
This showed the Israelites that God was with Moses (see stories 41, 47, 88).

God's threat
The people knew they needed God's help to get into Canaan, so they said sorry, and asked God to lead them again.

God's friend
Moses is the only person in the Bible who is called 'God's friend'. He spent much of his time listening to God and talking to him.

57 Exodus chapter 33, verse 17 to chapter 34, verse 8.

God's face
This does not mean God has a face like ours. It means Moses could not see God completely.

55 The people disobey God's Law

Moses hurried down the mountain. He carried the two stone tablets. As he neared the bottom he heard singing. He saw the people dancing before the golden calf.

Moses was angry. He threw the tablets onto the ground. They shattered into pieces. He took the calf and destroyed it.

'How could you be so disobedient?' he asked Aaron angrily.

'The people told me to do it,' muttered Aaron.

'God will punish us for breaking his rules!' said Moses. 'I will go and talk to him.'

But God punished the people with a plague.

56 Moses speaks for the people

God was very angry with the Israelites.

'I made a promise to Abraham, Isaac and to Jacob which I cannot break,' said God. 'I promised that their descendants would live in a land which I would give them. Leave this place, take the people, and go to the Promised Land. But because they have disobeyed me, I will not go with you.'

When the people heard what God had said, they were very upset. They wanted God to stay with them.

Moses used to pitch a special tent away from the main camp. Joshua, his assistant, would stand outside the tent. When Moses needed to ask God something, he would go inside the tent and a pillar of cloud would cover the tent entrance. Once inside, God would speak to Moses as to a friend.

The people would stand at the entrances to their own tents, and watch. They would worship God, until Moses returned to the camp.

Now Moses asked God, 'You say that we are your people. But what makes us different from any other group of people unless you go with us? Don't send us on without you.'

57 Moses sees God

God was pleased with Moses. 'I will do what you ask,' he said. 'I love you and I know you.'

'Now show me your glory!' asked Moses bravely.

'No one can see my face and live,' said God. 'But there is a space where you can stand on the mountain and I will pass by you. I will cover you with my hand to protect you. Then I will remove my hand so that you can see my back. But you cannot see my face.'

God told Moses to come to the mountain the following morning with two new stone tablets. 'You must come alone,' said God to Moses. 'Nothing else must be on the mountain – no other people or grazing animals – only you.'

Moses stood by the rock on Mount Sinai. God came and passed in front of him. God spoke. 'I am the Lord. I am faithful and compassionate. I long to forgive because I am love.'

Moses fell on the ground. He worshipped God.

58 New stone tablets

As Moses stayed in the space by the rock, God told him again how he wanted the people to live.

'I will make a covenant with you, a special promise,' said God. 'I will lead you to the land I promised to give Abraham and his descendants. But if you disobey my laws, I will punish you.'

Moses wrote on the tablets of stone the commandments God had given him.

When Moses came down from the mountain, and returned to the camp, the people were frightened to go near him. His face shone, because he had been in God's presence.

59 Making the tent of meeting

The people gathered around Moses.

'God has told us to make a special tent, where we can worship him,' he told them. 'We also need to make things to put in it – an ark, a table, an altar and a lampstand, and special clothes for the priests to wear. If you are willing, give God anything that can be used.'

The people brought their gold, silver, bronze and precious jewels. The women spun linen and made cloth out of goat's hair. They brought spices and olive oil. They worked for six days of the week, and rested on the seventh, as God had commanded.

'God has given Bezalel and Oholiab the ability to be master craftsmen,' said Moses, 'and he has made them good teachers. All who want to and are able, can help to make God's special tent.'

58 Exodus chapter 34, verses 10-30.

The covenant
God makes a promise with the people of Israel as he had made in the past with Noah (story 8) and Abraham (story 13). God tells them that he will keep this promise if the Israelites obey his laws.

Moses' face 'shone'
This means that his face was lit up with a great joy and happiness reflecting the goodness and holiness of God, because Moses had just been in God's presence.

59 Exodus chapter 35.

The tent of meeting
This is sometimes called the 'tent of the Lord's presence' or the tabernacle. It was the first 'house of God' made by the Israelites. God wanted the people to have a permanent reminder that he was with them.

📖 See Feature pages 82-83.

The ark of the covenant
This was a large wooden box covered in gold. On top were two golden cherubs or angels guarding the sacred tablets of Law kept inside.

Gold
The gold, silver and jewels that the Israelites owned had been given to them by the Egyptians to encourage them to leave their land (see story 47).

60 Exodus chapter 39, verse 32 to chapter 40, verse 38.

The High Priest
On the front of each High Priest's robe were sewn twelve precious stones. These represented the twelve tribes of Israel and reminded the priest that he served all the people.

61 Leviticus chapter 10, verses 1-5.

Aaron and the priests
The priests were in charge of making the sacrifices. Only Aaron, the High Priest, could go into the 'Holy of Holies'.

See Feature pages 82-83.

Incense
A censer was a small container that held the incense which was burned near the altar.

Incense is made from tree resin and smells very sweet when burned. The puffs of smoke that waft out of the censer represent prayers rising to God.

60 The cloud of God's presence

When the people had finished making everything for the tent of meeting, Moses inspected their work. They had made each part just as God had asked. Moses was pleased with them.

God told Moses how to put everything together. The special tent had four layers of coverings of different fabrics. Inside was the most special place, the 'Holy of Holies', where the ark containing the stone tablets of the Law was put. A curtain separated it from the table, the golden lampstand and the incense altar. Another curtain hung at the entrance. The tent of meeting was to be a sign of God's presence with his people.

Then Aaron and his sons came to the entrance. They washed themselves, and dressed in the special clothes God had designed for them. They were to be his priests.

Moses made sure that everything was just how God had planned it. Finally, he set a courtyard around the tent of meeting, made with more curtains.

Then a cloud covered the tent, and God's presence filled it. His presence was so great that Moses could not enter.

Each time the cloud lifted, it was time for the Israelites to move on. And God's presence remained with them.

61 God is holy

Aaron and his sons were priests. They were allowed special access to the tent of meeting and had important jobs to do. They made offerings to God on behalf of the people. They were to make sure that they were holy and obedient.

One day Aaron's eldest sons, Nadab and Abihu, were in the tent of meeting. They took some fire in their censers, added incense, and offered it to God. But they were careless and did not take the fire from the place God had commanded. Immediately, God's presence came down in a shaft of fire, and killed them.

'Remember: God is holy,' said Moses to Aaron.

62 Miriam and Aaron grumble

Whenever the cloud lifted, the Israelite camp moved on towards the land God had promised them. But they began to complain. They complained about their hardships and they complained about the food. They began to wish they were back in Egypt. They blamed Moses for everything.

Even Miriam and Aaron complained. They gossiped about Moses' wife, and spoke against their brother.

'Why is Moses so special?' they asked. 'God has also spoken through us!'

God heard what they said. He called the three of them to the tent of meeting and told Miriam and Aaron to step forward. They stood before God as he came down in a pillar of cloud.

'Listen carefully to what I have to say,' he said to them angrily. 'I have spoken to Moses face to face. He has seen me, and he is faithful to me. How dare you speak against him?'

The cloud lifted. Aaron turned towards Miriam and saw that her skin was covered in leprosy.

'We have been stupid!' cried Aaron to Moses. 'Forgive us! Don't let Miriam suffer like this!'

Moses cried out to God. 'Please heal her!' he begged.

'She must stay outside the camp for seven days,' said God, 'and then she can return.'

The people waited. They did not continue their journey until Miriam had returned.

63 The spies' story

As the Israelites approached Canaan, the Promised Land, God told Moses to send one man from each tribe to explore it.

They spied out the land for forty days. They noticed how the cities were fortified. They watched the people, and took note of the terrain. They brought back fruit, and cut off a branch bearing a single cluster of grapes. It was so heavy, two men carried it on a pole.

Moses gathered the people, and they listened to the spies' report.

'It is a fertile land,' said the spies, 'full of good things. Look at this fruit!'

But ten of the spies continued with bad news. 'The people who live there are strong and powerful,' they said. 'They are like giants, and they live in protected cities. They are much stronger than we are.'

When the Israelites heard what the ten spies said, they were miserable. They cried, and they grumbled.

'Let's choose another leader,' they said, 'and go back to Egypt.'

Moses and Aaron got down on their knees before the whole of the Israelite people. Two of the spies, Joshua and Caleb, joined them. 'The land is good,' they cried, 'and God has promised to give it to us. Don't make him angry by doubting his words.'

The Israelites did not listen. They planned to stone them.

Suddenly, God's presence appeared at the tent of meeting. 'How long will you refuse to believe me?' asked God.

'Forgive them,' pleaded Moses, 'and show how much you love them.'

'I will forgive them,' said God. 'But no one who has been disobedient and doubted me will enter the Promised Land, apart from Caleb and Joshua. They will wander in the desert for forty years until their children are ready to enter Canaan.'

62 Numbers chapter 12.

Miriam's punishment
Miriam was sent to live on her own for a week as God wanted everyone to see that she had been punished for speaking up against Moses. It was also usual for anyone with a disease to be kept separate until they were no longer infectious.

63 Numbers chapters 13 and 14.

The spies' mission
The spies probably walked about 800km/500 miles, with donkeys only to carry their supplies.

Stoning
It was common for people to be punished by being stoned (often until they died). The land was rocky and stones were easily available.

Joshua and Caleb
Unlike the other spies, they believed God would help the Israelites. They were the only people of their age who were allowed to settle in Canaan. All the others died before the Israelites got there.

Grapes and vines
Vines grew easily in Canaan, providing fresh grapes, raisins and wine. The big cluster showed how rich the land of Canaan was.

📖 See Feature pages 44-45.

THE LAND OF CANAAN

The land of Canaan was the 'Promised Land' for God's people. Today, Israel is in part of the old land of Canaan.

Abraham had settled in Canaan, but his grandson, Jacob, went with all his family to Egypt in a time of famine and stayed there (see stories 31 to 38). It was 400 years later that Moses led the Israelites out of Egypt to journey through the desert back to Canaan.

The city of Jericho One of the oldest cities of the ancient world, Jericho, was called 'city of palms' because of its springs. Archaeologists have found remains of a city dating from 8000BC.

Goodbye Egypt

The Israelites had been slaves in Egypt and by a series of miracles God had freed them. But they soon forgot the bad times, and started to grumble and complain on their desert journey. They disobeyed God and when they got to the borders of Canaan they refused to go in, imagining that the land was full of giants and hazards. For this reason their time in the desert was forty years, and Moses died before they could cross the River Jordan and enter the land.

The new land

Canaan had a number of walled cities built on the tops of hills so that the Canaanites could see their enemies coming and close the city gates. The small stone houses inside were then protected by the high, thick walls. The cities were difficult to attack, and it looked like an impossible task. But with his strong faith in God, Joshua used sieges, night raids and spies to capture some of them. Joshua had faith that God could win the battle (see story 75 to find out what happened at Jericho).

Enemies

There were a number of tribes living in Canaan, but the two main enemies were the Canaanites and the Philistines. Although they had strong cities and much better weapons, the Canaanites were terrified when they saw the vast numbers of Israelites entering their land, and so they lost the battles, city by city.

The Philistines or the 'sea people' were good at making weapons and had discovered how to make iron. This meant that their weapons were stronger and more effective than the bronze ones used by the Israelites. They wore feathered helmets and body armour, and carried spears and long straight swords.

The religion of the Canaanites

The Canaanites did not believe in God but would worship a number of false gods and idols made out of wood, metal or stone. They also practised witchcraft, which was against God's laws.

The main gods were Baal, the storm god, and Asherah, a fertility god. The Canaanites carved statues of the goddess Asherah like a wooden pole, which they placed on hilltops. Sometimes they sacrificed their children to the gods because they thought that this would make the gods give them what they needed. The Canaanites did not live in ways that were pleasing to the true God.

THE TWELVE TRIBES

After many years the Israelites had conquered most of Canaan and eventually Joshua divided up the whole land between the twelve tribes of Israel, the descendants of Jacob's twelve sons.

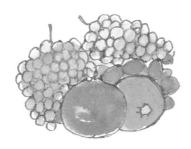

A fertile land The people sometimes talked about Canaan as a land 'flowing with milk and honey'. Compared to the desert lands around, it was very fertile and all kinds of fruit and vegetables could be grown, and sheep, goats and cattle could be grazed.

JOSHUA

Joshua is one of the great leaders of the Old Testament. As well as being a very good and brave soldier, he had great faith in God. As he was about to cross the Jordan river and enter Canaan, God told him, 'Be brave and strong, because I will always be with you.' The name Joshua means 'God saves' and is the Old Testament form of the name Jesus.

The River Jordan To enter the land of Canaan, Joshua had to cross the River Jordan. It is the main river in Israel and waters the land to make it fertile. More than a thousand years later, Jesus was baptized in the River Jordan.

Early writing The writings on rocks and stones in the Sinai desert, dating back to 1500BC, show that the Canaanites had an early form of alphabet. Here are some Canaanite letters alongside the Greek and Roman form.

Canaanite

Greek

Roman

64 Numbers chapter 14, verses 39-45.

The Canaanites
The people who lived in Canaan at this time had better weapons than the Israelites. If God did not guide Israel against the Canaanites they had little chance of victory.

Forty years
'Forty' here describes the long time the Israelites have to wander in the desert because of their disobedience.

65 Numbers chapter 20, verses 1-13.

Moses disobeys
Moses had become angry with the continual moaning of the Israelites. He lost his temper and so disobeyed God. God showed that even Moses had to be punished for not obeying him.

66 Numbers chapter 21, verses 4-9.

Snakes
These could have been sand snakes. Their venom causes terrible inflammation.

The bronze snake
Bronze is copper mixed with tin and other metals. The snake itself could not heal people. But looking at it reminded them of their sin and made them sorry, so God was willing to forgive and heal them.

64 Forty years in the desert

The Israelites were sorry.

'We will do what God wanted,' they said. 'We will go and take the land of Canaan.'

'It's too late!' cried Moses. 'You cannot enter the land now. You will be defeated because God is not with you.'

But the Israelites did not listen. They confronted the Canaanites, but were beaten by them.

Moses did not move from the camp. He stayed with the ark of God's covenant.

Then the Israelites moved back from the borders of Canaan, and made their way towards the desert, where they stayed for forty years.

65 Water from the rock

Life in the desert was hard. There was no grain or fruit or water.

The people gathered around Moses and Aaron. 'Why did you bring us here?' they moaned. 'This is a terrible place. We are thirsty, and there is nothing to drink.'

Aaron and Moses left the people, and went to the tent of meeting.

'Take your stick,' said God to Moses, 'and gather the people so that they can see what I am going to do. Speak to the rock, and it will pour out water. Then everyone will have plenty to drink.'

Moses took the stick and gathered the people as God had said. But he was angry with them. He was fed up with their moaning. Instead of obeying God, he held his stick in the air, and then hit the rock twice.

Immediately, water poured out from the rock.

But God was not pleased. 'You disobeyed me,' he said to Moses and Aaron. 'You did not do what I said. Now you will not be able to lead my people into the Promised Land.'

66 The bronze snake

As the Israelites went through the desert, they continued to be dissatisfied and impatient. They grumbled to one another. They complained about God and about Moses.

'Why have you brought us to the desert?' they moaned. 'We hate it. There is no bread or water. And the food is disgusting!'

God heard the Israelites' endless complaining. They had forgotten that God had rescued them. So God sent poisonous snakes to slither through the camp. Many people died.

The Israelites realized what they had done.

'We have sinned,' they cried to Moses. 'We shouldn't have complained. Ask God to take the snakes away.'

Moses prayed.

'Make a metal snake and put it on a pole,' said God. 'Anyone who has been bitten and who then looks at the snake can live.'

Moses made a snake out of bronze, and put it on a pole.

Those who looked at the snake lived.

67 Balaam's donkey

The years passed. Aaron and Miriam were dead. A new generation of Israelites approached the borders of Canaan.

Balak, king of Moab, saw the Israelites moving through the desert. He was frightened by their numbers and he wanted to stop them.

'Give a message to Balaam, the sorcerer,' he ordered. 'Tell him to come and put a curse on the Israelites, so that I can defeat them. Promise him great wealth if he does this for me.'

Balak's messengers found Balaam, and told him what their king had said.

'Do not go,' God told Balaam that night. 'You must not curse these people, because I have blessed them.'

Balaam listened to God, but with the promise of more money, agreed to go. He saddled his donkey, and set off on his journey.

But God was angry with Balaam. He sent an angel to stand in his path. Balaam did not see the angel, but his donkey did. She veered off the road, and into the field. Balaam beat her severely. Balaam rode on. Suddenly the angel appeared again. The donkey squeezed against a wall, and crushed Balaam's foot. He beat her on.

The angel blocked Balaam's path. The donkey lay down, and Balaam beat her again. Then God opened the donkey's mouth.

'Why do you beat me?' said the donkey.

Suddenly Balaam saw the angel.

'Your donkey has saved your life!' said the angel. 'Continue your journey, but only say what I tell you.'

When Balaam met the king, he told him that he could only speak God's words. Three times Balaam prepared to curse the Israelites, but three times God put words of blessing into his mouth.

68 New ways to live

As the Israelites camped on the border of Canaan, Moses spoke to the people. He reminded them of all that had happened since their parents and grandparents left Egypt. He reminded them of God's laws and warned them not to be disobedient, but to live in a way that pleased God.

'When you enter Canaan, you must help those among you who are poor. If you lend or borrow money, after seven years the debt will be cancelled,' said Moses. 'No one should be poor. Be generous to one another, and God will bless you.'

67 Numbers chapters 22 to 24.

Moab
Moab was on the east side of the Dead Sea. The people who lived there were descendants of Abraham's nephew, Lot (see story 99).

Balaam the sorcerer
A sorcerer is a magician or wizard who tries to control people and events by using magic. When sorcerers curse people they are asking God's enemy, Satan, to bring harm to someone.

Angels
Angels are God's messengers who live in heaven. They cannot usually be seen by people. However, when they are seen they usually look like ordinary people (story 15) or sometimes as unusual beings shining with God's glory (story 224).

Balaam's blindness
The angel was invisible. The donkey was simple and obedient, and could sense the angel was there. Balaam had lost his simple trust in God and so wasn't able to 'see' God's activity or 'hear' God's voice very well.

Blessing
God is the source of all good things; to be blessed is to receive something good from God. A blessing is the opposite to a curse.

68 Deuteronomy chapter 15, verses 1-14.

Seven years
According to Jewish law poor Israelites who had become slaves should be released after seven years. This law helped to stop whole families being kept in poverty all their lives.

69 Deuteronomy chapter 28, verses 1-11.

The covenant
Before they enter the land of Canaan, Moses reminds the people of the covenant (God's promise and his people's response of obedience) and urges them to keep God's laws.

See Feature pages 12-13.

70 Numbers chapter 27, verses 12-23.

Mount Nebo
This is one of the Abarim range of mountains at the northern end of the Dead Sea.

Joshua
Moses 'laid his hands' on Joshua to show the people that God had chosen him as leader, and had given him God's Spirit and authority.

71 Deuteronomy chapter 34.

Moses' long life
Moses was said to be 120 years old when he died. He had led the Israelites for about 40 years. Under him, they had left the slavery of Egypt, received God's Law, and been prepared for their new life in Canaan.

Moses is buried
No one has ever found a tomb or remembered where Moses was buried.

69 'You will be a great nation'

'If you obey God and follow everything he has said, God will bless you,' said Moses to the people.

'You will be a great nation, and your enemies will be defeated,' he continued. 'You will have bumper harvests, plenty of water, and many children. Other countries will see that God is with you.'

'But,' warned Moses, 'God will make you a special and holy nation, only if you keep his commandments and walk in his ways.'

70 God chooses Joshua

'Climb up Mount Nebo,' God told Moses. 'From there you will be able to see the Promised Land. But, because of your disobedience you will not be able to go there yourself. When you have seen it, it will be time for you to die.'

'Lord God,' said Moses. 'Do not leave the people without a leader.'

'I have chosen Joshua to be your successor,' God told him. 'Show him to the people.'

Moses stood with Joshua before the people, and he laid his hands on him. The people knew that Joshua was God's chosen leader.

71 The death of Moses

Moses climbed the mountain, and saw the Promised Land, but he knew he would never go there himself.

Then Moses died, and he was buried.

The Israelites mourned his death. They knew that there would never be another man like him. He had spoken to God, face to face. He had performed wonderful and amazing things, and he had spoken God's words to his people.

But God's Spirit came to Joshua. He was wise and obedient. And the Israelites listened to him.

LEADERS AND JUDGES

The story continues from the books of Joshua and Judges. Joshua was the
leader who took over from Moses and led the Israelites into Canaan.
The judges were local leaders who helped sort out disputes
and who taught people to obey God's Law.
Sometimes they also united all the tribes to defeat an enemy.

Moses had led God's people for over forty years.
He had led them out of Egypt, given them God's
Law and taught them how to worship God.
When he died, Joshua took over. His job was to
take the Israelites across the River Jordan and into
Canaan, the land God had promised them.
Joshua had always believed that God would
help them make a home there.
When they arrived in Canaan, the
Israelites faced many battles, but
at last the land was divided
up between the twelve
tribes. Then Joshua died.

The people began to
forget God and to follow
the customs of the people
around them which God's
Law did not allow. Each

time this happened, they were attacked by other
tribes and, each time, a 'judge' was called by
God to bring the people back to their faith and
to rescue them from their attackers.

The judges we read about in the Bible were
a mixed bunch of people. Gideon was an
unknown person whose tiny army chased away
a much larger one. Deborah was
a prophet who advised Barak,
the army commander. Samson
was a strong man who amazed
everyone with his strength but
whose own faults led to his
downfall. These stories show
how God continued to love
and guide his people, and
how he worked through a
variety of leaders.

72 Joshua, the new leader

Joshua was the new leader of the Israelites. He was a good man and
a strong leader. He listened to God and obeyed him.

'Get ready!' said God to Joshua. 'Now you can lead the Israelites
across the River Jordan and enter Canaan, the land I promised to
give you. Be strong and brave. I will be with you, just as I was with
Moses.'

But God gave Joshua a warning. 'Remember the laws I gave to
Moses, and do not forget them. If you obey them, you will be
successful.'

So Joshua sent the leaders of the people
through the Israelite camp.
'Get everything you need,'
they said. 'In three
days' time we will
enter the Promised
Land.'

The Israelites
had waited for this
moment. At long
last, here was the
land that God had
promised them.

72 Joshua chapter 1.

The River Jordan
This is a very long river
which begins north of the
Sea of Galilee and winds
through the Jordan Valley
for 100km/62 miles until it
reaches the Dead Sea (the
lowest point on the earth's
surface). The Israelites had to
cross it at some point in
order to enter Canaan.

📖 See Feature pages 44-45.

Provisions for the journey
The people had to prepare
food to take with them. They
would not be able to turn
grain into bread when they
were walking all day.

73 Joshua chapter 2, verses 1-21.

Jericho
A city on the west of the River Jordan, Jericho had high stone walls which protected the houses and people inside. It is possible that the walls of the city were so thick that houses were built inside them. Jericho seemed an impossible place for the Israelites to capture.

Rahab
When Rahab protected the spies it was not just because she was afraid, but also because she believed Israel's God was the true God. Rahab was an ancestor of King David and of Jesus.

Flax
This plant has blue flowers and grows to 1m/3ft high. Its stalks are stringy and when dried can be spun into thread for making clothes.

74 Joshua chapter 3, verse 1 to chapter 4, verse 18.

The dry river bed
The River Jordan stopped flowing because the water was dammed upstream at a place called Adam. This could have been caused by a God-given earthquake or landslide. The Israelites were able to cross the river very close to Jericho.

The Promised Land
At last the Israelites stepped into the land which God had promised Abraham centuries before.

73 Rahab and the spies

Joshua secretly sent two spies to find information about the city of Jericho.

The spies noticed a house within the city walls and thought it would be a good place from which to start. It belonged to a woman called Rahab.

But the king of Jericho had his own informants. He knew what the Israelites planned, and that his own people were afraid. He was told where the spies were, and sent a message to Rahab, with some of his own men, demanding she hand them over.

But Rahab hid the spies on her roof under some drying flax and told the king's men that they had left the city. She knew that the Israelites had the living God on their side.

'I know that God will give you Canaan,' she said, as she spoke to the spies that night. 'But promise me you will be kind to my family.'

'Agreed!' said the spies.

Rahab led them to a window. It was in the city wall. 'Climb down, and hide!' she said.

'Tie a scarlet cord in this window,' said the spies, 'and bring your family here. When we capture Jericho, everyone inside this house will be safe.'

The spies left. Rahab tied the scarlet cord in the window.

74 Crossing the River Jordan

Joshua sent the leaders of the people into the Israelite camp. 'Follow the ark of the covenant,' they told the people.

At Joshua's command the priests carried the ark, and the people followed it. 'Today, everyone will know that I am with you, just as I was with Moses,' said God, and he told Joshua how he would lead the people into the Promised Land.

The priests started to walk into the River Jordan, still carrying the ark. Immediately, the waters which ran downstream stopped flowing. The priests stayed in the middle of the river, and the Israelites filed past. The waters piled up, and the people crossed on dry land.

'Choose one man from each of the twelve tribes,' said God to Joshua. 'Tell them to take one stone each from the middle of the river bed, and to place them near where you camp tonight. Then your children and grandchildren will know what I have done for you.'

Joshua chose the men, and they did as God asked. The ark and the priests remained in the middle of the river until everything was completed. As soon as the priests stood on the land, the waters started to flow again.

Everyone who lived in Canaan heard what God had done for the Israelites. No one wanted to fight against them.

75 Victory in Jericho

Joshua gathered his army and advanced towards Jericho. As they approached, they saw that the gates of the city were closed.

Suddenly a man stood in Joshua's path. He had a sword in his hand.

'Are you for us, or against us?' Joshua asked.

'I am the commander of God's army,' replied the man. Joshua knew that God was with him.

'Ask seven priests to lead you in a march around the city walls,' said God. 'The priests must walk in front of the ark. They must each carry a trumpet. Do this for six days. On the seventh day, march around the city walls seven times. This time the priests must blow their trumpets. When you hear a long trumpet blast, signal the people to shout. Then the city walls will collapse.'

Joshua gave the people God's instructions. For six days they did as God had told them. On the seventh day, at the sound of the long trumpet blast, the people shouted. Immediately the strong walls of Jericho began to crack and crumble. They toppled over and collapsed, and the city was destroyed. Only Rahab and her family were saved.

God was with Joshua, and news of his victory quickly spread throughout Canaan.

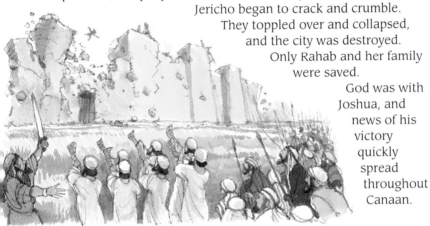

76 Achan disobeys

'Don't take anything for yourselves!' Joshua had warned his troops as they entered Jericho. 'Everything belongs to God.'

But Achan ignored Joshua's warning. Secretly, he took an expensive robe, some silver and some gold, and hid them under his tent. No one knew what he had done.

'Go and spy out the city of Ai,' Joshua said to some of his men. They returned with good news. 'Not many people live there,' they said. 'We will only need a small army to defeat them.'

Joshua took their advice. But the Israelites were defeated.

'Why have you done this?' Joshua asked God.

'Because someone has disobeyed me,' God replied. 'They have stolen, and they have lied.'

Joshua gathered the people together. When he saw Achan, he knew that he was guilty.

'What have you done?' Joshua said to him.

'I took some things from Jericho and hid them,' he said.

'Find them,' Joshua said to his men.

'Achan must be punished,' said God. 'He must die.'

75 Joshua chapter 5, verse 13 to chapter 6, verse 27.

Lots of sevens
The number seven in the Bible stands for something complete or whole. Seven priests, seven days and seven circuits of the city all reminded the people that God would fully keep his promise to give them the land.

Trumpets
The Israelites used rams' horns to make trumpets. They used to steam each horn to soften it, then bend the end round to form a trumpet shape. The horn was called a shofor and made a deep, sad sound.

76 Joshua chapter 7.

The city of Ai
Ai was in an important position, at the main entrance to Canaan from the west. Ai was close to Bethel, where Jacob had his dream (story 24).

Achan's sin
Because he lied and stole, Achan caused the death of thirty-six Israelites in the battle. He was stoned to death and his body and possessions were burned. It reminded the people that everyone had to obey God and that they relied on each other to do what was right. God had reminded Joshua of this before they crossed the River Jordan (story 72).

77 Joshua chapter 8.

Plunder

Loot or valuables stolen from people's homes by the conquering armies during a battle or war are called plunder. God had forbidden the Israelites to take plunder in previous battles to test their obedience. Now he allows them to do so.

78 Joshua chapter 9, verse 1 to chapter 10, verse 15.

Wineskins

Wine was carried in goatskins. New wine was always put into new skins. Cracked wineskins showed they were old and well used, which made it look as if the Gibeonites were poor.

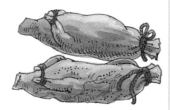

Gibeon

Not far from Jerusalem, this was a large city which controlled the chief road to the western plains.

The 'sun stood still'

It is not likely that the earth stopped rotating and the sun shone for twenty-four hours. The weather conditions and light may have been confusing because of the hailstorm or an eclipse of the sun. But it is more likely that the battle should have taken at least a day but was won more quickly. Joshua prayed that the sun would not set until they had finished. It didn't, because God helped the Israelites to fight more effectively than usual.

77 Joshua destroys Ai

'Attack Ai again,' said God to Joshua. 'This time, you will win, and you may take some plunder.'

Joshua carefully chose his army. 'When it is dark, half of you go to the far side of the city and hide,' he said. 'In the morning, the rest of us will attack the city gates. The king of Ai will chase us, and we will lead his army away from the city. Then we can take Ai.'

Joshua and his army advanced. The king and his troops ran out to meet the Israelites. He chased them as far as the desert. He did not know that half of the Israelite army lay hidden.

'Hold up your spear towards Ai!' God told Joshua. Joshua obeyed. The soldiers who had been lying in wait rushed through the open city gates. The Israelites had won another victory.

78 The sun stands still

The Israelites progressed through Canaan. The kings of all the different tribes grew alarmed. They knew that God had promised to give Canaan to the Israelites. They met and thought of a way to join together to fight the Israelites.

But the people of Gibeon wanted to make a pact with Israel. They dressed in old clothes and loaded their donkeys with cracked wineskins and stale bread.

'We have come from a distant place,' they lied. 'We want to make a peace treaty with you.'

Joshua and his leaders promised peace. They did not ask God what to do. When they found out that the men were from Gibeon, they were angry but they did not break their promise.

When the other kings heard about the pact, they joined forces and decided to attack Gibeon.

The Gibeonites sent a message to Joshua. 'Come and save us!'

Joshua marched towards Gibeon and surprised the enemy. As the enemy armies fled, God sent huge hailstones from the sky, which battered the enemy soldiers to death.

Then, in the middle of the day Joshua prayed to God in a loud voice, 'Do not let the sun go down!'

The sun stood still in the sky. It did not set. It shone for a whole day until the battle was won. God was fighting with Israel.

79 Joshua fights on

Joshua led the Israelites on through Canaan. As he marched northwards, King Jabin of Hazor watched Joshua's progress.

'Come and fight these Israelites with me!' he said to some of his allies. They gathered a huge army, with horses and chariots, and set out to confront the Israelites.

'Do not be afraid,' said God to Joshua. 'By this time tomorrow you will have defeated them.'

As the two armies fought, the enemy army was quickly defeated. There were no survivors.

Joshua led the Israelites in victory over thirty-one kings. Canaan had been captured. Now the Israelites could enjoy the land God had given them.

80 Dividing the Promised Land

Joshua was an old man, but God still had work for him to do. 'Divide up the land between all the tribes of Israel,' God told Joshua.

So Joshua, together with a priest and some of Israel's leaders, set about allocating portions of land to the different tribes. Each tribe was descended from Jacob's twelve sons. Now, at last, they could receive their inheritance, just as Jacob and Moses had predicted.

81 Caleb's special present

A long time had passed since Caleb had been sent by Moses to spy out the land of Canaan. He and Joshua had known that God would help them conquer their enemies but the other spies had told the people frightening stories. Because Caleb had believed God, Moses had promised that Caleb would be rewarded.

One day, Caleb went to see Joshua. 'Forty-five years ago, Moses made me a promise,' he said. 'Now I am eighty-five! Please give me the land I was promised, so that I can pass it on to my children and grandchildren.'

Joshua blessed his old friend, Caleb. He knew how much he loved God. He gave Caleb the area of Hebron as his special reward.

82 Cities of refuge

As the people settled into the new land of Canaan, they established themselves as a nation. Years before, Moses had received God's laws for his people. Now was the time to put them into action.

'Tell the Israelites to choose special cities, which can be cities of refuge,' said God. 'If anyone accidentally kills someone, they can run to one of these cities, and be sure to get a fair trial.'

The people chose cities which were scattered throughout the whole land. No one lived more than a day's journey from a city of refuge.

---

79 Joshua chapter 11, verses 1-20.

Hazor
This was a large city of up to 40,000 people. Its king, Jabin, was very powerful.

80 Joshua chapters 13 to 21.

Dividing the land
The nation of Israel was like a country with twelve states which organized themselves separately. The land was divided between the twelve tribes.

📖 See Feature pages 44-45.

The twelve tribes of Israel
The tribes were: Judah, Reuben, Gad, Simeon, Issachar, Zebulun, Dan, Asher, Naphtali, Ephraim, Manasseh, Benjamin. Israel, or Jacob's, other two sons were Joseph and Levi. Joseph's territory was divided between his two sons, Manasseh and Ephraim. The Levites were scattered throughout Israel so that each area had its own religious leaders.

81 Joshua chapter 14, verses 6-15.

Caleb
Caleb had spied out the land of Canaan with Joshua and had remained loyal to God and to Moses (story 63).

82 Joshua chapter 20, verses 1-9.

Cities of refuge
If a person was killed, even accidentally, their family would find out who did it and try to kill them as a punishment. At one of the cities of refuge, they would be safe from the angry relatives.

📖FOOD

In Bible times most people grew and prepared their own food. Bread was the most important part of any meal, with fresh or dried fruit, vegetables, some cheese or milk, and perhaps a stew made from beans or lentils. Most people only ate meat on special occasions.

Sharing a meal together was a very important part of family life; and inviting visitors or people who were journeying to stay at your house and share a meal was a strong tradition carried out by all God's people, however poor.

Meat

Flocks of sheep and goats were kept for their milk (for drinking and to make cheese and yogurt) as well as for their meat. Richer people kept cattle. For most people, meat was for special occasions only. It was usually boiled or stewed except for the Passover meal. Only rich people ate meat every day. It is said that in the time of King Solomon, 1000 sheep a day were eaten at his palace.

Bread

In Bible times 'to eat bread' meant 'to have a meal'. Bread was the most important food for most people and they baked it fresh every day. Poor people used the coarse flour made from barley, and those with more money baked with flour from wheat.

The women ground the grain into flour, adding salt and water to make a dough. They added some fermented dough (leaven) from a previous batch, and left it in the sun to rise. When the Israelites left Egypt in a hurry they took 'unleavened' bread with them because they did not have time to wait for it to rise.

Sometimes dough was shaped into rolls or it was cooked flat.

Bread could be made by putting it on flat stones which were heated by an open fire; there were also simple ovens made by sinking a large earthenware jar into the ground. First, a fire was lit inside the jar. Then, when the flames had died down and the sides of the jar were hot, balls of dough were placed inside or outside the walls to cook.

Wine

Most water was not safe to drink, so wine was the everyday drink for adults, and milk for children. Most people grew grapevines. After harvesting the grapes they were trodden down into pulp in a wine press. The juice ran down a channel and into a basin cut in the rock. The juice was put into new goatskins and left to ferment for six weeks.

Mealtimes

The first meal of the day for many people was the midday meal – something simple like bread, olives and dried fruit. The main meal was eaten in the evening.

In New Testament times rich people held dinner parties and the guests were seated according to their importance. To sit on the right hand side of the host showed that you had the most honour. As the weather was hot and the roads dusty, people's feet were often dirty by the time they arrived so a servant took off their sandals and washed their feet for them. People ate with their fingers, and washed them between courses.

Fish In New Testament times, people who lived near the Sea of Galilee, like Jesus and his friends, ate fresh fish. Some of the fish were salted to preserve them and then dried. This meant that they could be kept for longer.

Vegetables Lentils, beans, onions, leeks, garlic and cucumbers were cooked before eating.

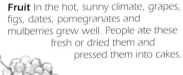

Fruit In the hot, sunny climate, grapes, figs, dates, pomegranates and mulberries grew well. People ate these fresh or dried them and pressed them into cakes.

Olives This was one of the most important crops. Olives were eaten for food, but the oil was used for lighting, cooking, medicine and skin care.

THE PASSOVER MEAL

A meal of roast lamb, bitter herbs, sauce and unleavened bread is still eaten once a year by Jews the world over. It recalls the meal that the Israelites ate together in haste before Moses led them out of Egypt, where they were slaves.

FOOD LAWS

God gave the Israelites rules about what they should not eat. These protected people's health in a hot country where food goes rotten very quickly. They could eat cattle, sheep and goats, but not pigs or shellfish which were 'unclean'. There was also a law about making food with meat and milk together.

When both Jews and Gentiles became Christians there was sometimes a problem about eating together because of the food laws.

83 *Joshua chapters 23 and 24.*

The covenant
Joshua called the Israelites together at Shechem to renew the agreement God had made with them when he gave them the Ten Commandments. God promised to protect them if they kept his laws.

Oak tree
During Bible times oak trees grew on the mountains of Israel. It was common for a well-respected person to be buried under an oak tree.

84 *Judges chapter 3, verses 7-11.*

The judges
Othniel was the first of the judges chosen to lead Israel. Many were gifted by God to deal with legal and religious matters, and to lead the army in battle.

85 *Judges chapter 3, verses 12-30.*

Ehud
Ehud was from the tribe of Benjamin. Many of this tribe could use left and right hands equally well. As most warriors were righthanded, King Eglon was not suspicious when Ehud put his left hand into his cloak to grab his sword.

Tribute
A 'tribute' was a gift of money or goods which conquerors demanded from their victims. If the victims paid the tribute, they would be left in peace.

83 Joshua says goodbye

Finally, after years of peace, when Joshua was a very old man, he called all the people together. He knew that he did not have long to live. He reminded them of God's goodness.

'I want you to remember everything God has done for us,' he said. 'He has kept every one of his promises. But if you disobey him, disaster will follow. You have the choice – to serve him or not.'

'We will obey God and serve him,' the people replied.

Joshua took a large stone and placed it under an oak tree. 'This stone has heard what you have said! Let it be a reminder to you of your promise to serve the living God.'

84 The rescue of the judges

Joshua died, and the people buried him. But before long, they had forgotten the things that Joshua had told them. They did not remember the promise they had made. They chose to worship other gods and failed to obey God's laws.

God was angry. He allowed a foreign king to defeat Israel. But when the people asked God to help them, he chose Caleb's nephew, Othniel, to be their leader. Othniel returned Israel to peace, and reminded them to love and serve God.

85 Ehud

When Othniel died, the Israelites disobeyed God again. So God allowed Eglon, king of Moab, to make a pact with Israel's enemies. Eglon gathered an army and captured Jericho. The Israelites cried out to God to help them and he chose Ehud to rescue them.

When King Eglon demanded a tribute from the Israelites, Ehud was sent to take it to the king. Ehud was left-handed and had a double-edged sword. As he prepared to visit the king, he carefully strapped the sword to his right thigh, and hid it underneath his tunic.

Ehud bowed before the king, and gave him the tribute. He dismissed the men who had helped him carry the gifts and whispered, 'I have a secret message for you, your majesty.'

Eglon was intrigued. He sent his attendants away.

Ehud approached the king. 'I have a message from God for you,' he said. He reached for his sword and plunged it into the king. Eglon sank to the ground. Quietly, Ehud left the room, locked the doors behind him, and made his escape.

When Ehud reached the hill country, he blew his trumpet. The Israelites rushed down the hills.

'Follow me!' cried Ehud as he led the people into battle. 'God has helped us defeat our enemies!'

86 Deborah and Barak

After Ehud died, the Israelites stopped following God's ways.

One of the kings who lived in Canaan was called Jabin. He had a large and fierce army under the command of a man called Sisera. He equipped his troops with 900 iron chariots, and for twenty years he oppressed Israel. The Israelites suffered and cried out to God.

Deborah, a prophet who served the living God, led Israel at this time. One day Deborah sent for a warrior called Barak.

'I have a message to you from God,' she said. 'Take 10,000 troops and march to Mount Tabor. Meanwhile, I will lure Sisera and King Jabin's army toward the River Kishon. Then they will be trapped, and you can defeat them.'

But Barak was scared. 'You must come with me,' he said.

Deborah was disappointed by Barak's response, but she agreed. 'But be warned!' she said. 'Because you have not acted on God's instructions, a woman will have the honour of defeating Sisera.'

87 Victory for Deborah

When Sisera heard that Barak was leading an attack, he gathered his army and waited.

'Go!' signalled Deborah to Barak. 'Attack! This is God's plan. Today we will defeat our enemies.'

Barak led his troops and charged down the hillside. They attacked Sisera's army, slashing with their swords.

Sisera abandoned his chariot and ran away from the battle. He knew that his army had lost. He ran towards some tents belonging to a man called Heber. 'I'll be safe here,' thought Sisera. 'Heber and King Jabin are friends.'

Heber's wife, Jael, saw Sisera. She knew who he was. 'Don't be afraid,' she said. 'Come and hide in my tent.'

Gratefully, Sisera went inside. Jael hid him under some covers.

'Keep watch!' he pleaded. 'If someone comes looking for me, don't tell them I am here!' He was exhausted, and fell fast asleep.

But Jael did not keep watch. Instead, she made sure Sisera was asleep, and she killed him.

Barak charged through Heber's camp. He was looking for Sisera.

'I'll show him to you,' offered Jael, and she showed him Sisera's body. King Jabin had been defeated.

'Praise the Lord!' sang Deborah and Barak. 'He has defeated our enemies.'

86 Judges chapter 4, verses 1-10.

Deborah

She was the fourth judge to lead Israel. In Israelite society, it was very unusual for a woman to be a leader. Men were usually regarded as leaders, especially in battles.

Mount Tabor

This cone-shaped hill has a flat summit. It was an ideal place for the Israelites to gather before charging down on to the plains.

Iron chariots

The Egyptians had introduced chariots into Canaan. They were ideal for warfare on the open plains, but terrifying for the Israelites who did not have them. The 900 probably came from several of Jabin's allies.

87 Judges chapter 4, verse 11 to chapter 5, verse 31.

The victory

Besides the strong Israelite attack, the River Kishon flooded and many of the enemy chariots were swept away or became bogged down in the mud.

The death of Sisera

Jael killed Sisera by hammering a tent-peg through his head. It was women's work to pitch the tents so Jael would have been skilled at using a hammer.

88 Judges chapter 6, verses 1-24.

The Midianites
These were a fierce camel-riding desert people who terrorized the Israelites for years, raiding their crops and carrying off their animals.

Threshing wheat
Gideon was trying to outwit the Midianites by growing his wheat in secret and threshing it in a winepress, a shallow pit in the ground.

Flames
God often used fire to show his presence (see stories 41, 47).

89 Judges chapter 6, verses 25-40.

Sheepskin and dew
The wool on a sheepskin holds moisture for a long time. Dew can come from moisture in the air. On the first night dew soaked into the wool but not the hard ground. But dew can also be held in the soil and come to the surface at night; this is what happened the second time. The sheepskin stopped the moisture from getting into the wool. They were natural events, but the timing of them was God's miracle in answer to prayer.

88 A mighty hero

The Israelites enjoyed peace for a while. But then they forgot all the things that God had done for them.

The Midianites attacked. They destroyed the Israelite crops and killed the livestock. The Israelites were too weak to fight back. They hid in the mountains, and because they were so afraid they cried out to God for help.

'We have disobeyed God!' a prophet warned the people. 'That is why we are being attacked by our enemies.'

Meanwhile a man called Gideon was trying to thresh wheat in secret, out of sight of his enemies.

Suddenly a stranger appeared.

'God is with you, mighty warrior!' he said.

'Is he?' asked Gideon. 'Then why are we in so much trouble? God has forgotten all about us!'

'You can save Israel from the Midianites,' said the stranger.

'Me? How can I save Israel?' asked Gideon.

'I will be with you,' said the stranger. 'We will save Israel together.'

Gideon was amazed. 'I need a sign to show that what you are saying is right,' said Gideon, and he rushed home.

The stranger waited. Gideon returned with some food. 'Put the food on a rock,' ordered the stranger, and he touched it with his stick. Immediately it burst into flames, and the stranger vanished.

Then Gideon knew that he had been talking to God.

89 Gideon and the sheepskin

That night, Gideon destroyed the foreign gods that belonged to his father, and built an altar to the living God.

In the morning, when the local men saw what had happened they were angry with Gideon. 'Hand him over!' they demanded of Gideon's father. 'Your son must die!'

'Whose side are you on?' asked Gideon's father. 'Why are you defending foreign gods?'

The mob left Gideon alone.

The Midianites joined forces with the Amalekites. They crossed over the Jordan and made camp.

At the same time, Gideon was filled with God's Spirit. He blew his trumpet and summoned the Israelite men from every tribe to come and fight.

'I need to be sure that you will use me to save Israel,' said Gideon to God. 'I will put a sheepskin on the ground this evening. In the morning, if the sheepskin is wet and the ground dry, I will know that you want me to lead Israel.'

In the morning Gideon squeezed the sheepskin. It was wet, but the ground was dry.

'Don't be angry, but I need to be absolutely certain,' said Gideon to God. 'Let me put the sheepskin out again, only this time let the ground be wet and the skin dry.'

In the morning the ground was covered with dew, and the sheepskin was dry.

90 Gideon's small army

The Israelite army gathered together and made camp.

'You have too many soldiers,' said God to Gideon. 'When the battle is won, I don't want there to be any doubt that I was the one who saved Israel. Tell everyone who trembles with fear to go home.' Twenty-two thousand men went home. Ten thousand remained.

'There are still too many,' said God. 'Ask the men to go to the river and drink.'

The men drank. Some knelt down to drink, while others stood up and lapped the water out of their hands like dogs.

'I will use the men who stood up and lapped the water,' said God. 'Send the others away.'

Gideon obeyed God. He had an army of 300 men.

91 Battle by night

'Get up!' said God to Gideon during the night. 'Now is the time to defeat your enemies!'

Gideon was afraid. 'Don't be frightened,' said God. 'Go down to the enemy camp. Listen to what is said, and you will know that it is right to attack.'

Gideon woke his servant. Silently they moved towards the enemy camp. Two men were sitting talking together.

'I've had a terrible dream!' said one. 'A huge, round barley loaf rolled into our camp, and hit the tent so violently it collapsed!'

'I know what that means,' said the other. 'God is on the side of Gideon's army. They will win.'

Gideon thanked God for what he had heard.

'Wake up!' he said to his men. 'God has already won the battle!'

He divided the men into small groups, and gave each man a trumpet and a burning torch, covered by an empty jar. In the darkness, the Israelites surrounded the enemy camp. Gideon gave the signal. He and his men blew their trumpets and smashed the jars. 'For the Lord and for Gideon!' they cried.

The Midianites and the Amalekites were terrified. They stumbled and fell upon each other in the darkness. They killed each other with their swords, and fled to the hills. God had rescued the Israelites once again.

90 Judges chapter 7, verses 1-8.

God on their side
Gideon was to go into battle with only a few men against the might of the enemy so that the Israelites could see that victory was a miracle brought about by God.

Men of action
It seems God chose the men who lapped the water like dogs because they had not dropped their guard; they were alert, ready for action.

91 Judges chapter 7, verses 8-25.

Burning torch
This was a wooden pole with rags tied round one end. The rags were soaked in oil and set alight. The jars hid the lights until they were needed so Gideon's men could creep up unseen.

Trumpets
These would have been made from rams' horns (see story 75).

The enemy panics
The sleeping enemy woke up to find themselves surrounded by light and noise and thought a huge army had come against them.

92 Judges chapter 9, verses 1-25.

Abimelech's mother
In Old Testament times it was the custom for men to have more than one wife (see story 14).

📖 See Feature pages 22-23.

Shechem
This is where Abraham first built an altar to God (story 11). It was one of the six cities of refuge (story 82) and where Joshua renewed the covenant with God (story 83). Shechem had always been a special place for the Israelites but at the time of Abimelech they were so disobedient they had even set up a temple to the pagan god, Baal.

93 Judges chapter 9, verses 26-57.

Millstones
These were very large, round stones which were used to grind corn into flour. They were often so heavy they were pulled around by an ox.

📖 See Feature pages 54-55.

Servant
A young man would travel with a military leader into battle to carry his shield and spear. Abimelech asked his servant to kill him because he was ashamed to have been killed by a woman.

92 Abimelech takes power

Now Gideon had lots of wives and many children. One son was called Abimelech. His mother was a slave.

After Gideon died, Abimelech went to his mother's home town of Shechem and spoke to his relatives.

'Now that my father is dead, choose me as your leader, instead of one of my father's seventy sons, my half-brothers.'

Abimelech's relatives agreed and Abimelech hired a band of men to follow him. Then he went to his father's home town, and killed all his half-brothers. Only the youngest, Jotham, escaped. Then Abimelech returned to Shechem and the people crowned him king.

When Jotham heard this he went to Shechem and climbed to the top of Mount Gerizim. 'Remember what my father did for you!' he cried. 'Now think about what you have done to his family!'

Abimelech ruled Israel, but God had seen what he had done.

93 Abimelech's punishment

A newcomer called Gaal came to Shechem. He was popular and started to stir up trouble.

'What is so special about Abimelech?' he asked. 'If you followed me, I would easily defeat Abimelech and his whole army.'

Zebul, the governor of Shechem, heard of Gaal's boasting.

'Gaal is stirring up trouble,' he warned Abimelech. 'Make a surprise dawn attack and get rid of him and his followers.'

As Abimelech approached Shechem, Zebul went to Gaal. 'So, you think you can destroy Abimelech's entire army,' he sneered. 'Well, now's your chance!' Gaal and the citizens of Shechem fought Abimelech, but they were driven out of the city.

The next day, Abimelech attacked Shechem again. Then he marched on to Thebez. The people fled from their homes and locked themselves in a strong tower. Abimelech made his way towards the entrance to set it on fire.

A woman saw what Abimelech was trying to do so she lifted a heavy millstone, and flung it down. It landed on Abimelech's head and cracked his skull.

'Kill me with your sword,' Abimelech begged his servant. The man obeyed. When the Israelites saw what had happened, they left the city. God had punished Abimelech for what he had done.

94 Jephthah the leader

Then the Ammonites attacked the Israelites. The elders of Gilead went to Jephthah. 'Be our leader,' they said, 'and help us fight.'

'If God helps me defeat the Ammonites, will I still be your leader?' asked Jephthah.

'We promise before God,' they replied.

Jephthah sent a peace message to the Ammonite king, which he ignored. Then Jephthah knew that God was leading him into battle.

'I will make a bargain with you,' Jephthah foolishly said to God. 'If you make me victorious, I will sacrifice the first thing I see when I return home in triumph!'

Jephthah led the Israelite army into victory. Then he went home. The first thing he saw was his only daughter, dancing. When Jephthah saw her, he remembered what he had said to God. He tore his clothes and wept. He knew that he had made a promise to God that he could not break.

95 The birth of Samson

After Jephthah died, the people returned to their old ways and the Philistines attacked and ruled over the Israelites.

One day an angel appeared to the wife of a man called Manoah. 'I know that you are unable to have children,' said the angel, 'but you will have a son. He has been specially chosen by God to save Israel from the Philistines. To show that he is special, make sure that you never cut his hair.'

Some months later, the woman gave birth to a son called Samson.

96 Samson's riddle

When Samson grew up he wanted to marry a Philistine woman. His parents set off to make the wedding arrangements and Samson followed. Suddenly, as Samson walked through a vineyard, a young lion bounded towards him. God filled Samson with his Spirit and gave him amazing strength. He grappled with the lion, killing it with his bare hands. He did not tell anyone.

Some time later, Samson returned to the vineyard. Some bees had made a nest within the lion's carcass. There was honey inside.

During the wedding feast, Samson told his Philistine companions a riddle: 'Out of the eater, something to eat; out of the strong, something sweet,' he said. 'Tell me the answer within seven days, and I will give you a prize. If not, you must reward me.'

The Philistines were clueless, but they had no intention of giving Samson a prize. Instead, they begged Samson's wife to find the answer. She nagged him until finally, he gave in.

'What is sweeter than honey? What is stronger than a lion?' they cried.

Samson was angry. He wanted revenge.

94 Judges chapter 11, verse 4 to chapter 12, verse 7.

Bargaining with God
Having made a promise to God, Jephthah felt he had to fulfil it. In Old Testament times it was quite common for worshippers of other gods to sacrifice children to them. But the true God did not ask Jephthah to kill his little girl. Jephthah let her have two months to say goodbye to her friends before she died.

95 Judges chapter 13, verses 1-25.

Philistines
These were one of the most dreaded and powerful enemies of the Israelites. Their land, called Philistia, was between the coast and Israelite territory.

📖 See Feature pages 44-45.

Long hair
Samson was a Nazirite. These were Israelites who dedicated themselves to God and had to promise never to cut their hair or drink alcohol. Samson probably wore his long hair in braids.

96 Judges chapter 14.

Samson's wife
Samson was doing wrong in choosing a wife from among the Philistines instead of the Israelites. But God used him to start to defeat the Philistines as a result (see also story 113).

Lions
In Old Testament times lions lived in Canaan. They roamed wild in the forests and scrubland. They do not exist there today.

97 Judges chapter 15, verse 1 to chapter 16, verse 22.

Samson's weakness
Instead of obeying God, Samson listened to both his wife and Delilah. His stupidity caused him to lose the strength God had given him.

Bowstrings
These were made from twisted animal gut. They were very strong and springy, used to fire arrows from bows.

Ropes
These were woven from plant fibres such as papyrus or flax (see note to story 73).

Loom
A loom is a frame on which cloth is woven from threads of wool or other material. In Samson's time some looms had heavy wooden posts fixed to the floor, and wooden beams joining them across the top.

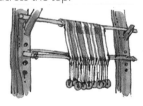

98 Judges chapter 16, verses 23-31.

Dagon
This was the chief god of the Philistines. It was the god of grain (which meant food). Some people think Dagon was a fish-god.

97 Samson is betrayed

Samson hated the Philistines. But they could not touch him, because of his amazing strength.

Time passed, and Samson fell in love with a woman called Delilah. The Philistine leaders seized their chance. 'Find out the secret of Samson's strength,' they said to her, 'and silver will be yours.'

Delilah was determined to find out the secret.

'Tell me the secret of your strength,' she whispered.

'Tie me with seven new bowstrings, and I will lose my strength,' Samson replied.

Delilah got the bowstrings, and tied Samson. 'The Philistines are here,' she screamed. Samson leapt up, and snapped the strings.

'You lied to me,' said Delilah, some time later. 'Tell me your secret.'

'New ropes will make me weak,' he replied.

Delilah tried the same trick again, but Samson ripped the ropes.

'Weave my hair on the loom,' said Samson the next time. He broke the loom.

Determined not to give up, Delilah continued to nag Samson. Eventually he could stand it no longer. 'If I cut my hair,' he told her, 'I will lose my strength.'

Delilah made sure that Samson was asleep. Then one of the Philistines cut off his hair. His strength vanished. They overpowered him, then blinded him and put him in prison. He could not fight back. His strength had gone.

98 The final victory

The Philistines were delighted. They organized a celebration to thank their god Dagon for letting them capture Samson. 'Let him entertain us!' cried the people.

So Samson was brought out from prison to amuse the people. When they had had enough, they stood him between the temple pillars. They had not noticed that Samson's hair had begun to grow.

'Let me feel the pillars while I rest,' said Samson to his guide, and stretched out his arms.

'Do not forget me, Lord God,' prayed Samson. 'Punish the Philistines, and let me die too.'

Samson stretched and pushed at the pillars as hard as he could. God gave him back his strength, and the giant pillars toppled over. The walls caved inwards and the roof crashed to the ground. The building was destroyed. Everyone in it, including Samson, was dead.

THE STORY OF RUTH

This is a simple story about the love and loyalty of its main character, Ruth, and is set during the time of the judges. Ruth became the great-grandmother of King David, and an ancestor of Jesus.

The story of Ruth is about everyday life during the time when the judges led the Israelites (about 1150-1000 BC). It is important because it shows the customs and way of life of ordinary people living at that time. It is also a reminder that all the battles and the people's failings recorded in the books of Joshua and Judges were not the whole story. People lived normal lives for most of the time, and many tried to follow God's Law.

Ruth came from Moab, on the east side of the Dead Sea. Moabites were descended from Lot, Abraham's nephew. She had married an Israelite man, whose mother was Naomi. Both Ruth and Naomi became widows and, when Naomi decided to return to Israel, Ruth went with her instead of staying in her home in Moab. In Israel, Ruth met Boaz, a relative of Naomi, who admired Ruth's kindness and so married her. The remarkable thing about this book is that God is hardly mentioned. But the people's trust in him, and his help for them in their daily lives, is still clearly seen.

99 Famine in Israel

During the time when the judges led Israel, there was a terrible famine. Elimelech left his home town of Bethlehem and took Naomi, his wife, and his two sons, to Moab, in search of food.

Elimelech died in Moab. His two sons married Moabite women, but soon both the sons died too. Naomi was left all alone, with no one to care for her.

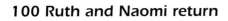

100 Ruth and Naomi return

When Naomi heard that the famine in Bethlehem was over, she decided to return home.

'Don't come with me,' she said to her daughters-in-law. 'Go back to your own mothers.' But Ruth and Orpah did not want to leave Naomi.

'We'll stay with you,' they said.

'No!' urged Naomi. 'I have nothing to offer you.'

Orpah turned back but Ruth would not leave.

'Don't tell me to go!' she begged. 'I will never leave you. I will go with you to your country, and your God will become my God.'

So the two women made their way towards Bethlehem.

99 Ruth chapter 1, verses 1-5.

Bethlehem
This small Israelite town was high up on a hill usually surrounded by fertile land with plenty of crops. It was 80km/50 miles from Moab, which was east of the Dead Sea and therefore not in Israel. Bethlehem was later the birthplace of King David and Jesus.

Naomi's sons
Naomi's sons were Mahlon and Kilion. They probably died of disease. People often died young in biblical times.

100 Ruth chapter 1, verses 6-22.

Widows
In those days if a woman's husband died and she had no grown-up sons to look after her, she was usually very poor. It was important for young widows to try to marry again.

101 Ruth chapter 2.

Barley
This was the cereal crop that grew most easily in the soil and weather conditions of Canaan. Barley was therefore made into the cheapest flour and was eaten by the poor.

See Feature pages 54-55.

Food for the poor
Poor people were allowed to pick up the remains of the barley after the harvest. This was called 'gleaning'. The law said that reapers should leave some corn at the edges of fields for them.

Boaz
Boaz asked Ruth to stay in his field because he wanted her to collect more barley, but also because he wanted to make sure that no harm came to her.

102 Ruth chapters 3 and 4.

Ruth's relative
By Jewish law if a man died without leaving a child, his brother or closest male relative was supposed to make the widow one of his wives so that she could have a baby and the family name would not die out. Boaz and the other relative swapped sandals to show that they had agreed who would marry her.

101 Ruth meets Boaz

It was the time of the barley harvest.

'Let me go and see how much grain I can pick up,' Ruth said to Naomi, for they had nothing to eat.

Ruth worked hard, picking up any grain that was left. The owner of the fields noticed Ruth. 'Who is that woman?' he asked one of his men.

'She is Naomi's daughter-in-law,' the man replied.

The owner went over to talk to Ruth. 'Stay and gather grain in my fields,' he said, 'and take some water whenever you are thirsty.'

Ruth was surprised. 'Why are you being so kind?' she asked.

'Because I have heard of your kindness to Naomi,' he replied.

When it was time to eat, the man offered Ruth some food.

'Make sure that Ruth gathers plenty of grain,' the man said to his harvesters. 'Drop some for her to pick up.'

In the evening Ruth threshed the barley, and walked home. Naomi was amazed at the amount she had gathered. 'Which field did you go to?' she asked.

Ruth explained, and she told Naomi about the kindness of the landowner. 'His name is Boaz,' she added.

'But he is a relative of ours!' exclaimed Naomi. 'Work in his fields again. May God bless him for his kindness!'

102 Naomi's plan

Naomi had a plan. 'Boaz has been kind to you,' she said. 'We are also related to him. Ask him to look after us. That's the custom.'

Ruth found Boaz asleep. She lay down at his feet, and waited. Suddenly he stirred. 'Who's there?' he asked.

Ruth told him why she had come.

'I will look after you,' said Boaz kindly, 'but there is a man who is a closer relative of yours than I am. Before I can care for you, I must ask his permission.'

'What happened?' asked Naomi anxiously when Ruth returned.

Ruth told her everything.

'Now we must wait,' said Naomi.

Boaz went to the town gate. He found Ruth's relative and asked him if he wanted to take Ruth into his household. The man did not.

So Boaz married Ruth and before long she gave birth to a son, Obed. There was great rejoicing in the household.

'Praise God!' said the women to Naomi, as she held her first grandchild in her arms.

KINGS OF ISRAEL

In about 1100BC, God's people asked for a king to rule over them. Samuel, the last of the judges, was a good, wise and holy man. Samuel told the people that having a king would lead them away from God and cause much suffering.

The Israelites took no notice of Samuel's warning. Until then, God had been their king. Now they wanted to be like the other people who lived around them. They were insistent, so God told Samuel to give the people what they wanted. He made Saul the first king of Israel.

The people thought Saul a good king until he stopped listening to God. Saul was followed by David who obeyed God but made some bad mistakes. Under David's son, Solomon, Israel's first temple was built in Jerusalem and the country became very wealthy. But Samuel's prophecy started to come true. Solomon forced the people to pay high taxes to finance his buildings and his luxury lifestyle. He sometimes treated his people badly.

When Solomon died, there was a civil war and the country was split into two: Israel (the ten northern tribes) and Judah (the two southern tribes). Each kingdom had a king. Things went from bad to worse. Eventually Israel was destroyed by the Assyrians in about 722BC. Later Judah was destroyed by the Babylonians in about 597BC.

Alongside the kings there were also prophets, such as Elijah and Elisha. These were brave and holy people who were not afraid to tell people, and even kings, when they were disobeying God's laws.

All the stories in this section are from the books of 1 and 2 Samuel, and 1 and 2 Kings (most of which are also recorded in 1 and 2 Chronicles).

103 Hannah's prayer

103 1 Samuel chapter 1, verses 1-20.

Every year Hannah and her husband, Elkanah, went to Shiloh to worship God and make a special sacrifice. Elkanah's other wife, Peninnah, went with them. She had lots of children, but though Hannah longed to have a baby of her own, she had none. Peninnah taunted Hannah, until Hannah cried so much she could not eat.

One day, while they were visiting Shiloh, Hannah went to the place of worship to pray.

'Lord God,' she sobbed, 'please give me a son. I promise that if you answer my prayer, I will give my boy back to you, so that he can work for you all his life.'

Eli, the priest, saw Hannah's unhappiness. 'May God answer your prayer,' he said.

Hannah returned home. Before long she found that she was pregnant, and when she gave birth to a son, she called him Samuel.

Sacrifices

At this time Israelites were supposed to go to Shiloh three times a year to worship God. They would offer sacrifices, usually an animal, as part of their worship.

See Feature pages 82-83.

Two wives

It was quite common for men to have two wives at this time. This was not God's original plan, however, and it often caused family arguments.

See Feature pages 22-23.

104 1 Samuel chapter 1, verse 21 to chapter 2, verse 11.

Places for worship
At this time, Israel did not have one central temple. The tent of meeting had been put in Shiloh, and they may have built a solid wall around it or built a stone building like it. Some Bible versions call this shrine a 'temple'. There may have been other places for worship too.

See Feature pages 82-83.

105 1 Samuel chapter 2, verses 22-36.

Priests
Priests were men who could trace their family back to Aaron, Moses' brother. They looked after the shrine where people came to worship God and offer sacrifices. They were meant to be good and kind. Priests such as Eli lived at the shrine so that they could serve God and the needs of his people at any time.

106 1 Samuel chapter 3.

Oil lamp
This simple light burned through the night, only running out of olive oil at dawn. A lamp like this lit Samuel's way to Eli when God called to him in the middle of the night.

See Feature pages 54-55.

104 Hannah keeps her promise

When Samuel was no longer a baby, Hannah took him to the place of worship in Shiloh. Eli the priest was there.

'I came here once, and I prayed a special prayer which God has answered,' said Hannah to Eli. 'God has given me a son. Now I will keep my promise and let my son live here, with you, so that he will work for God.'

So Samuel stayed with Eli, and became his helper. And God watched over Samuel as he grew up.

105 Eli's wicked sons

Eli had two sons. Their names were Hophni and Phinehas. Both of them were priests like their father.

But Hophni and Phinehas were selfish men. They broke God's rules and did not take their work for God seriously.

Eli heard what his sons were doing. 'Why are you being so disobedient?' he asked. 'You will make God angry, and he will punish you.'

But Hophni and Phinehas ignored their father's warning. They did not listen.

106 God speaks to Samuel

Samuel stayed with Eli in the place of worship. Every year Hannah came to visit him and brought him a little coat that she had made.

One night, when Samuel was asleep, he heard a voice. 'Samuel! Samuel!' called the voice.

Samuel went to where Eli slept. 'Here I am!' said Samuel. 'You called me!'

'No, I didn't!' said Eli. 'Go back to sleep.'

Before long Samuel heard the voice calling him again. He went again to Eli, but the old man had not called him, and he told Samuel to go back to sleep again.

Then Samuel heard the voice for a third time. 'God is calling you,' said Eli. 'Go back to bed. But this time, if the voice calls your name, reply, "Please speak, Lord. I am listening."'

God spoke to Samuel. He told him of his plans for the future of Israel and for the future of Eli and his family. And Samuel learned to listen to God as he grew up.

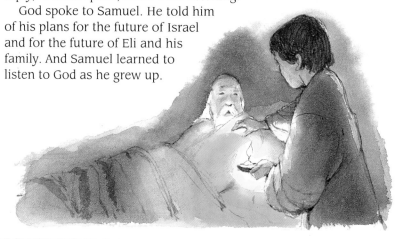

107 Samuel leads Israel

There was trouble in Israel. The people disobeyed God's laws. The Philistines captured the ark of the covenant. Eli's sons were killed in the battle, and Eli died when he heard of their death.

Eventually, the Philistines returned the ark, fearing that they had angered their own god. Gradually, the Israelites began to think about the living God again. They were sorry they had worshipped other gods. They were sorry they had been disobedient.

Samuel seized the moment. He told the whole of Israel to meet together at Mizpah. 'I will pray to God with you,' he said. 'Let us show him we are sorry. Let us tell him we have sinned.'

So Samuel led the people in prayer. He offered sacrifices to God, and along with all the people, he fasted.

The Philistines threatened to attack the Israelites at Mizpah. But Samuel kept on praying.

God heard the prayers of his people. He sent a huge blast of thunder, which frightened the Philistines and gave the Israelites the opportunity to attack and defeat their enemy.

From this time on, Samuel became Israel's leader, and he judged the people wisely.

108 The first king of Israel

'We want a king!' cried Israel's elders as they stood before Samuel. 'You are too old now, and your sons do not obey God's laws.'

Samuel was angry. He prayed to God.

'I am Israel's king,' said God. 'They have rejected me. I shall let them have a king but he will bring them great unhappiness.'

Samuel repeated God's warning, but the people ignored it.

One day, a man called Kish had lost his donkeys in the hills. 'Go and find them for me,' he said to his son, Saul.

After many days, Saul and his servants could not find the donkeys. They heard that Samuel was nearby, and went to ask him for help.

God had already told Samuel that he would meet Israel's future king. When Samuel saw Saul, he knew that this man was God's choice. He took some oil and anointed Saul, the first king of Israel.

107 1 Samuel chapters 5, 6 and 7.

The ark of the covenant
This was Israel's most precious possession. The ark was a large, ornate box which contained the commandments given to Moses by God on Mount Sinai (see story 59). It was the sign that God was with them. When the ark was stolen it seemed to the Israelites that God himself had gone away.

Fasting
To fast is to go without food for a time (perhaps just a day or part of a day). People fast in order to spend longer praying instead of preparing and eating food. It is a sign that the person really means what they are praying, and that God is more important to them than anything else.

108 1 Samuel chapter 8, verse 1 to chapter 10, verse 1.

Anointing horn and oil
When people were set aside to do something special, such as being a king or a priest, they were 'anointed' by having oil poured over their heads.

Olive oil was mixed with spices to make it smell sweet. It was often stored in an animal's horn attached to the priest's belt.

109 1 Samuel chapters 10, 11 and 13.

Ammonites
These were a tribe of people who often fought battles with Israel, usually about who should own the land to the east of the River Jordan.

110 1 Samuel chapter 13, verse 16 to chapter 14, verse 47.

The Philistines
The Philistines had helmets, shields and chain mail to protect their bodies. They fought with huge sharp swords and spears. They were skilled iron workers and lived near the coast.

111 1 Samuel chapter 15, verse 1 to chapter 16, verse 13.

Shepherds
A shepherd lived outdoors, looking after flocks of sheep and goats. He carried a staff with a crook on the end to help walk up steep cliffs and to rescue stray animals. David was young, fit and healthy-looking from his work with the animals, but he seemed too young to be the next king of Israel.

109 Saul, the warrior king

'Long live the king!' shouted God's people when Samuel presented their new leader to them. Saul was a strong, fine-looking man.

Meanwhile, the Ammonites attacked the Israelite city of Jabesh. The people of Jabesh wanted to make peace with them.

'On one condition,' agreed the Ammonites. 'We will blind all the inhabitants in one eye.'

When the Israelites heard this, they were afraid. But Saul gathered his army together and marched to Jabesh. He surprised the Ammonites with the ferocity of his attack.

At first Saul asked Samuel to tell him God's plans and wishes. But as Saul grew in confidence and power, he started to take control and he no longer waited for what God had to say.

'You have been stupid!' Samuel told Saul. 'You have disobeyed God. Now he will look for another king, a man who listens to him and obeys him.'

110 Jonathan's bravery

The Philistines continued to raid Israel. One day King Saul and his army were preparing themselves for the next battle. Saul's son, Jonathan, left the group unnoticed, taking his servant with him.

'Let's find out what the Philistines are doing,' Jonathan said to his servant. 'Perhaps God will give us a victory over them.'

They climbed up into the rocky mountains.

Jonathan thought of a plan. 'We'll let the enemy see us. If they say, "We're coming to get you!" we'll stay here. But if they say, "Come here and get us!" we'll know God will help us defeat them.'

As soon as the Philistines saw Jonathan, they dared him to come and fight. Jonathan knew that God was with him. He climbed over the rocks, his servant following behind. The Philistine army panicked as Jonathan approached. They killed each other with their own swords.

God had rescued Israel.

111 Jesse's youngest son

After King Saul disobeyed God, the prophet Samuel was told by God to go to Bethlehem.

'One of Jesse's sons will be the next king,' said God.

So Samuel went to Bethlehem and held a feast for all the people.

When Samuel saw Jesse's eldest son, he felt sure that he must be God's choice. But God said, 'I have not chosen him. You see what a person looks like on the outside, but I see what they think and feel.'

When Samuel had met seven of Jesse's sons, he asked, 'Do you have another son?'

'My youngest son is looking after the sheep,' replied Jesse.

When Samuel saw David, God spoke: 'I have chosen him!'

So Samuel anointed him with oil, and God's Spirit filled him.

112 The king's unhappy moods

King Saul suffered from depression. His mind was full of bad, unhappy thoughts. While he was feeling like this Saul wanted to hear music.

'Find me someone who plays the harp,' he snapped.

'One of Jesse's sons plays well,' suggested a servant. 'He is a fine young man, and he loves the living God.'

'Bring him to me,' ordered Saul.

From that time on, David played to Saul. It soothed the king's unhappy moods. Saul liked David very much. He made him one of his most important servants.

113 The giant's challenge

The Israelite army was terrified. The Philistines had a champion who was more than three metres tall. His name was Goliath.

One day David visited the Israelite camp. He saw Goliath. He heard him shout. And he watched while the Israelites ran away.

Every morning and evening Goliath challenged the Israelites. But nobody wanted to fight.

'How dare he challenge us!' said David to the men around him. 'We have the living God on our side.'

David went to King Saul. 'I will fight him!' he said.

'But you are just a boy,' said the king.

'When I look after my father's sheep,' said David, 'I have to fight wild animals. God has always looked after me.'

David took his sling. He chose five small stones from the stream, and went out to face Goliath. When Goliath saw him, he sneered. But David shouted back. 'I have the living God on my side!'

As Goliath lunged forwards, David slipped a stone into his sling and whirled it around his head. The stone shot through the air and crashed into Goliath's forehead. He sank to the ground. The enemy champion was dead!

112 1 Samuel chapter 16, verses 14-23.

David's harp
The harp which David played was called a 'kinnor'. It was made from the wood of the cypress trees which grew all around. It probably had eight or ten strings. The sound made by the gentle plucking of the strings would be comforting to someone who was tense and worried.

David the musician
People have always enjoyed making and listening to music. David was a composer as well as a singer and harpist. He wrote many religious songs called psalms, some of which are included with others in the Bible's Book of Psalms. They express his feelings about God and the things which happened in his life.

113 1 Samuel chapter 17.

Sling and stones
Shepherds used these simple weapons to kill wild beasts which attacked their flocks.

The shepherd spun the leather sling around and around above his head. When he let one end go free, the small stone inside the sling shot through the air, hitting its target with great force.

114 1 Samuel chapter 18, verses 1-16.

115 1 Samuel chapter 18, verses 1-4; chapter 19, verses 1-10; chapter 20.

Friends
Friends were very important in Bible times. They were supposed to love and care for each other as if they were brothers or sisters.

David's promise
David and Jonathan swapped gifts as a sign of their friendship. It was like a covenant in the Bible, which is a promise each person must keep.

Weapons
Israelite soldiers in David's time used four main weapons. Archers had bows and arrows; they carried about 20 arrows in a quiver slung over their shoulder.

Some soldiers used slings to fire stones. Most carried a short sword, kept in a sheath fixed to their belt.

Spearmen had long javelins which they might throw, or use to stab people. Most fighting was close hand-to-hand combat.

114 Saul, the jealous king

After David defeated Goliath, Saul promoted him to a position of great authority in his army. David led his men in a succession of victories. Everyone liked David.

The people were delighted to have defeated the Philistines. They came out of their houses to welcome the returning army. 'Saul has killed thousands!' they sang. 'David has killed tens of thousands!'

This song angered Saul. David was successful at everything, and Saul no longer liked him. Now he was jealous of him.

One day David was playing his harp when suddenly Saul picked up his spear. He hurled it at David, hoping to kill him. But David escaped. He was not afraid of him.

115 Jonathan warns his friend

King Saul's son, Jonathan, was David's closest friend.

'Let us promise always to be friends,' said Jonathan to David, and he gave him his sword and his bow.

But it was difficult. King Saul told his son everything. He told Jonathan he was going to kill David.

'David, you must hide,' warned Jonathan. 'I will speak to my father. If he changes his mind, I will tell you.'

King Saul promised not to kill David. But at the next opportunity, he threw his spear at him. Once more David escaped.

'I don't understand why your father wants to kill me,' said David at one of their secret meetings. 'When can I come out of hiding?'

'I will find out,' promised Jonathan.

When Saul burst into a furious rage because David did not attend a special celebration, Jonathan knew that David's life was in danger.

He went into the field to fire some arrows, and ordered a boy to fetch them. He fired an arrow into the distance. 'The arrow is ahead of you,' he said to the boy. David was listening. He knew that Jonathan had given him a signal. He must run from the king. Jonathan had saved his life.

116 David, the outlaw

David could only think of one place in which to hide from King Saul. He went to the priests who lived at Nob.

'I'm here on a secret mission from the king,' David said. 'I need something to eat, and a weapon, if you have one.'

Ahimelech gave David some special, holy bread. He also gave David Goliath's sword.

David moved on. But he had been noticed by one of Saul's men. 'I will have all the priests killed for helping David,' snarled Saul.

117 Saul's life is spared

One day Saul and his men were searching for David. David and his friends hid at the back of a cave. Saul came into the cave, but he did not know they were there. 'Now you can kill the king,' whispered David's companions.

David refused. He crept up behind Saul and cut off a piece of his robe. As Saul left the cave, David showed him the torn cloth.

'Now do you believe that I don't want to kill you?' asked David.

Saul felt sorry. But it did not last long. He just waited for another opportunity to kill David.

118 Abigail's kindness

The prophet Samuel died and all God's people were sad. David and his men were living rough in the countryside, hiding from King Saul.

One day, a rich shepherd called Nabal gave a feast. David sent him a message, asking for food for his men. He reminded Nabal that he had kept a watchful eye over his shepherds and their sheep. Nabal refused. 'Why should I give David food?' he sneered. He had a reputation for being rude and mean.

David was angry. He told his men to arm themselves to fight.

But a servant warned Nabal's wife, Abigail, what her husband had said. Abigail quickly prepared some food for David's men, and without telling her husband, went out to meet him.

'Don't take any notice of my husband,' she begged. 'Forgive us.'

David accepted her gift. 'Go home,' he said to Abigail.

Abigail went home. When she told Nabal what she had done, he became ill and died.

David did not forget Abigail. Later he asked her to be his wife.

116 1 Samuel chapters 21 and 22.

Special bread
The only bread which the priests had was specially baked. Once a week they put twelve loaves (one for each tribe of Israel) on a table in the shrine as an offering to God. Only the priests were supposed to eat it.

Goliath's sword
After David had killed the giant, it was kept by the priests as a souvenir. David was now big and strong enough to use it – but it must still have been heavy for him.

117 1 Samuel chapter 24.

David's decision
David knew he would be king one day. Now here was his chance to become king by killing Saul and taking his place. But David knew that it was wrong to kill. He let Saul go, and trusted God to work things out.

118 1 Samuel chapter 25.

Abigail
David had already married Michal, Saul's daughter. But because he had run away, Saul had given Michal to someone else as a wife.

Abigail's provisions
These amounted to 200 loaves of bread, 2 skins of wine, 5 roasted sheep, 36 litres of roasted grain, 100 cakes of raisins and 200 cakes of pressed figs!

119 1 Samuel chapter 26.

Secret mission

Saul's camp was a group of tents in an open field with a few sentries on duty. David and Abishai could easily have slipped past them in the dark. Armies did not fight at night.

120 1 Samuel chapter 27.

Double agent

David pretended that he had become a traitor to Israel by joining the Philistines. But his raids were all on Israel's other enemies, so he never fought against his own people, and did nothing to really help the Philistines.

121 1 Samuel chapter 28.

Calling on the dead

The woman was a 'medium' who claimed she could bring messages from dead people. The Bible tells us not to try to do this, because dead people cannot really send messages. They are in a new world which is controlled by God. The 'messages' come either from people's own minds, or from evil spirits who deceive them.

Samuel's 'ghost'

The Bible doesn't tell us what really happened. Perhaps both the woman and Saul had a vivid mental picture of Samuel. The message repeated what God had already told Saul. He had done wrong by seeing the woman, and what he heard only frightened him still more.

119 David's night raid

Saul took 3,000 men and went to look for David, who was hiding in the hills.

David's spies watched while Saul and his army made camp. Saul was surrounded by his troops and Abner, the commander of Saul's army, was by his side.

'Who will come with me to see Saul?' David asked his friends.

'I will,' offered Abishai.

The two men waited until it was dark. Then they crept down to Saul's camp. Everyone was asleep. Saul slept soundly, his spear stuck in the ground, close to his head, and a water jug by his side.

'What luck!' whispered Abishai to David. 'Let me kill Saul while we have the chance.'

'Don't touch him!' ordered David. 'He is still God's chosen king,' and he told Abishai to pick up the spear and water jug, and they left the camp.

'Speak to me, Abner!' called David, from a safe distance. 'You haven't done your job properly! Where is your master's spear and water jug?'

Saul recognized David's voice. He realized what had happened. He knew that David had spared his life again.

'I'm sorry!' cried the king. 'I promise not to harm you.'

120 Living with the enemy

David did not believe that King Saul was sorry. He knew how quickly he changed his mind.

'Before long he will want to kill me,' thought David.

He took 600 of his men and escaped to the land of the Philistines. The Philistine King Achish knew that Saul and David had become enemies. He let David settle in his land, and gave him a town to live in. From time to time David raided nearby lands, and brought back the plunder to King Achish.

Achish trusted David. He preferred to have him as a friend rather than an enemy. 'Now David is living here, his own people hate him,' thought Achish. 'He will never return home.'

121 Victory for the Philistines

King Achish of the Philistines gathered his army to fight the Israelites. 'You will fight with me,' he said to David.

Meanwhile Saul prepared to lead the Israelite army. His greatest friend, Samuel, the prophet, was dead and could no longer advise him. Saul tried to talk to God, but it was no use. In desperation he disguised himself and went to Endor to find a woman who could speak to the dead. 'I must talk to Samuel,' he told her.

As soon as Samuel appeared, the woman recognized King Saul. 'Is this a trick?' she screamed. She knew it was against God's Law to speak to the dead.

'Because you have been disobedient, God has left you!' Samuel said. 'Tomorrow, when you fight the Philistines you will be defeated. Your sons will be killed and you will die.'

Meanwhile, the Philistine commanders were unhappy. 'We do not want David to fight with us!' they said to King Achish. Reluctantly, Achish sent David back to the land of the Philistines.

The next day the Philistines fought the Israelites and defeated them. Both Saul and Jonathan were killed.

When David heard the news he was very sad. Israel had lost a king, and he had lost a special friend.

122 David, king of Judah

After Saul's death, David wanted to return to his own land.

'Shall I go to one of the towns in my home province of Judah?' he asked God.

'Yes,' said God. 'Go to Hebron.'

Men from the southern tribe of Judah came to Hebron to anoint David king. But in the north Israel did not accept David as king. Saul's only surviving son, Ish-Bosheth, fled north with Abner, the commander of Saul's army. Abner made Ish-Bosheth king of Israel.

123 Abner changes sides

The two armies sat on opposite sides of the pool of Gibeon. Abner was the leader of Ish-Bosheth's army. Joab was the leader of David's army.

'Let us have a contest!' said Abner. 'We'll each choose twelve of our strongest men, and whichever side wins will be declared the champions!' Joab agreed.

When all the soldiers died in the struggle, war was declared. The armies fought one another but David's men were stronger. Ish-Bosheth's army was defeated.

Abner ran. Asahel, Joab's brother, chased after him. 'Stop!' shouted Abner. 'I don't want to kill you!' But Asahel would not give up. At last, Abner threw his spear at Asahel. He died instantly.

'Let us stop fighting one another,' shouted Abner to Joab.

So Joab called an end to the battle, but he did not forget what Abner had done to his brother.

As the war continued, David's side got stronger. Abner did not respect King Ish-Bosheth so he decided to join David's army.

But Joab was not pleased that Abner had changed sides. He still hated him for killing Asahel and found an opportunity to take his life. David was sad when he heard that Abner had been murdered. He knew that he had been a brave soldier.

122 2 Samuel chapter 2, verses 1-9.

Judah and Israel
Israel was made up of twelve tribes. When Saul died, there was no obvious person to lead them all. So some of the tribes in the north called 'Israel' crowned Ish-Bosheth, and the southern tribe of Judah crowned David.

123 2 Samuel chapter 2, verse 12 to chapter 3, verse 39.

Gibeon
This important city was 9km/5.5 miles north-west of Jerusalem. Its people were Canaanites who had tricked Joshua into making a peace treaty when Israel invaded Canaan (see story 78).

Contests
When tribes were at war, they sometimes chose a few men to fight each other in a contest which saved many people being killed. Whoever won the contest was declared winner of the war. The challenge of Goliath (story 113) was another such contest.

Civil war
There was no clear winner in the contest, so the war between the tribes continued. Both sides wanted their king to rule all twelve tribes of Israel.

Abner's spear
Abner threw the butt end of his spear at Asahel, only intending to wound him. But the end was sharp enough to stand in the ground and so killed him.

Joab and Abner
Joab was probably afraid that Abner would turn against David.

124 2 Samuel chapter 4.

Revenge
The men who killed Ish-Bosheth believed God wanted to get his own back on David's enemies. But David knew that God did not want people to kill each other out of revenge. So he executed the men as murderers.

125 2 Samuel chapter 5, verses 1-12.

Jerusalem
This was a small hill-top fortress, very hard to capture. The Jebusites had dug a tunnel to bring water to a well inside the city from a spring outside it. The tunnel still exists today.

126 2 Samuel chapter 6.

The ark and Uzzah
The ark of the covenant contained the Ten Commandments (story 60). It was a sign that God was with the Israelites. Only priests were allowed to touch it. Uzzah's death showed that God's rules should not be broken even when it seemed sensible to do so.

📖 *See Feature pages 82-83.*

124 The murder of Ish-Bosheth

When Ish-Bosheth heard that Abner was dead, he was terrified. The whole of Israel was afraid.

Then one day, two of David's men set out for Ish-Bosheth's house. It was midday when they arrived and the place was quiet and unguarded. Ish-Bosheth was asleep on his bed.

They crept inside the house and found Ish-Bosheth's bedroom. There they stabbed him and cut off his head.

Quickly, they escaped to Hebron.

'We have brought you Ish-Bosheth's head,' they told David.

But David was angry. 'How dare you murder an innocent man in his own bed!' he cried, and called for their immediate execution.

Now there was no one left alive from Saul's family who could threaten David. The way was clear for him to be king of all Israel.

125 Surprise attack on Jerusalem

Israel's leaders wanted to make a pact. They came to see David at Hebron. 'Years ago we were one nation, and you used to fight with us,' they said. 'God promised that you would be our leader.' Then they anointed David with oil, and proclaimed him king of all Israel.

Knowing that he had the support of the whole nation, David gathered an army and marched towards Jerusalem. He wanted to make it his capital. The city was occupied by a Canaanite tribe, called the Jebusites, who thought that they were safe behind Jerusalem's strong walls. 'Not even David will be able to get us here!' they boasted.

But David surprised the Jebusites by entering the city through the water tunnel. He captured Jerusalem and called it the City of David.

David's reign had begun, and God was with him.

126 Dancing in the streets

David wanted to bring the ark of the covenant to Jerusalem, the capital city, as a sign of God's presence. So the ark was placed on a new cart, and carefully guided along the road. Everyone rejoiced.

Suddenly one of the oxen stumbled. Uzzah put out his hand and touched the ark. He died instantly.

David was angry. He knew that the ark was holy, and that Uzzah should not have touched it, but what had happened seemed unfair.

'I can't bring the ark back to Jerusalem,' said David. So he left it in Obed-Edom's house.

'God has blessed Obed-Edom because he has the ark,' said someone one day. David knew he had to bring the ark back to Jerusalem. Then God would bless the whole nation.

Everyone gathered as the ark was carried into Jerusalem. They shouted and sang to God. David joined the people and danced before God.

Michal, David's wife, saw him dance. 'What a fool!' she thought.

When the celebrations were over, Michal went out to meet David.

'I saw you today!' she sneered. 'You didn't behave like a king.'

'I don't care how stupid I looked,' said David to his wife. 'I was dancing for God. I was praising him.'

127 God's plans for David

David built a palace in Jerusalem. His enemies knew that God was with him and so they left Israel alone.

One day David asked to see Nathan, who was a prophet. He wanted some advice.

'It does not seem right that God's ark lives in a tent,' said David. 'I think I should build a temple.'

That night Nathan heard God speaking to him. 'I don't want David to build a temple,' said God. 'I want him to make Israel into a great nation. I promise that I will make him a great king and I will never stop loving him. One of David's sons will be a great king as well, and I have chosen him to build a temple.'

Nathan told David everything that God had said. David was amazed. He spent time talking to God.

'I don't know why you have chosen me or looked after me,' said David, 'or why you have told me your plans. But I do know that you are a great God, and you always keep your promises.'

128 David and Mephibosheth

'Does Saul have any relatives still alive?' David inquired one day, remembering his friend Jonathan.

'One of Jonathan's sons, called Mephibosheth, is still alive,' Ziba told the king. 'But both of his feet have been injured, and he cannot walk well.'

'Bring him here,' said David.

Mephibosheth was frightened. He thought David would kill him.

'Your father was my greatest friend,' David told him, 'and I promised to look after his family. Come and live in the palace with me and I will give you the land that belonged to your family.'

Mephibosheth was amazed that a great king like David should keep his promise and take such care of him.

Singing and dancing
Music and dancing were part of worship in Bible times. Some of the Psalms (for example, 24 and 47) were written for joyful processions such as this. Instruments used included the kinnor and nebel, which were stringed instruments with variable numbers of strings; tambourines; trumpets made of metal or rams' horns; and cup-shaped cymbals.

127 2 Samuel chapter 7.

God's tent
David put the ark into the tent of meeting, the chief place for worship.

David's reaction
David wanted to build a temple very much. But he was willing to obey God, even though that meant not doing what he really wanted. David felt humble that God should share his plans with him. David wrote something like these words in Psalm 8: 'When I look up at the stars, the people you've made seem so small! Yet you've made them almost like angels, and given them more honour than anything else.'

128 2 Samuel chapter 9.

Keeping promises
David had made a covenant or pact with Saul's son, Jonathan (story 115). Helping Mephibosheth was a way of showing the friendship was still important, even though Jonathan had been killed.

129 2 Samuel chapter 11, verses 1-5.

130 2 Samuel chapter 11, verses 6-27.

Outdoor bathing
Taking a bath usually meant pouring water over your body from a jug, or standing in a pottery container of water. Bathsheba was washing in the open inner courtyard of her house.

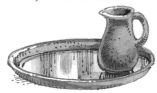

📖 See Feature pages 140-41.

David's sin
David thought that now he was king he could steal someone's wife and arrange for her husband to be killed. But he was wrong. He still had to keep God's rules.

131 2 Samuel chapter 12.

David's confession
Nathan was clever. His story (or parable) awoke David's sense of right and wrong. If he had simply told David off, the king might not have listened.

David's sorrow
After he realized how wrong he was, David wrote about his deep sorrow in Psalm 51. He said something like this: 'I've sinned against you, O Lord, and done what you say is wrong. I've been a sinner since I was born, so teach me to be wise and good.' David knew that by hurting someone else, he had hurt God even more. He saw that everyone does wrong things in their lives, but God wants people to be sorry and to try to do good things.

129 David's mistake

It was a lovely evening in spring. The Israelite army were away fighting but David remained at his palace in Jerusalem. He got up and went out on to the roof. From where he was standing he could see across the city and he noticed a woman in the courtyard of a nearby house. She did not know she was being watched. She was bathing. David thought she was very beautiful.

'Who is that woman?' David asked a servant.

'That's Bathsheba,' the servant replied. 'She's Uriah's wife.'

David knew Uriah. He was a soldier in his army. But David was not thinking clearly. He did not care whose wife she was. He wanted Bathsheba for himself.

'Bring her to me!' he ordered. So Bathsheba came to the palace, and David treated her as his wife.

But after a time, Bathsheba sent a message to David. 'I'm pregnant,' she said. 'I am going to have your baby.'

130 Uriah is killed

David was in trouble. He knew he had disobeyed God's Law. He tried to cover up what he had done. So he sent a message to Joab at the battlefront, asking him to send Uriah home.

Uriah came back to Jerusalem. He spent time talking with David about the state of the army, but he did not go home to Bathsheba. Exasperated, David let him return to fight.

Then David had an idea. He wrote a letter to Joab, in charge of the army. 'Make sure Uriah fights on the front line, and then leave him undefended. Make sure that he dies.'

Before long a messenger came from the battlefront. Uriah was dead. David felt relieved. Now no one would know what he had done.

But God knew. He was angry with David.

131 Nathan's message

After a while David married Bathsheba and she had a son. But God had not forgotten what David had done. He sent Nathan the prophet to speak to him. He told him a story.

'There were once two men,' said Nathan. 'One of them was a wealthy sheep owner, and the other man was poor. He just had one little ewe lamb. She meant everything to him. One day the rich man had a guest. Instead of killing one of his own sheep, he stole the little ewe from the poor man.'

David was furious. 'That rich man must be punished!' he said.

'But you are the rich man,' said Nathan. 'God has given you so much and yet you took another man's wife. He will punish you.'

David knew that what Nathan said was true. 'I am so sorry,' said David. 'I have sinned against God.'

'He forgives you,' said Nathan. 'But you may still have to face the consequences of what you have done.'

132 Absalom's revenge

David had many wives and lots of sons. His sons were jealous of one another. Amnon was David's eldest son. One day he violently attacked his half-sister, Tamar. Absalom, Tamar's brother, was angry. He hated Amnon. David was also angry with Amnon, but he did not punish him.

Two years passed, and Absalom had still not forgotten what Amnon had done. He took matters into his own hands. He organized a family feast, made sure Amnon drank too much wine, and then ordered him to be killed.

When David heard what had happened to his eldest son he was grief-stricken. Quickly Absalom left the country. David missed Absalom. But he vowed never to see him again.

133 Absalom returns

As the years went by, Joab saw how much the king missed his son. He found a way to ask the king to bring Absalom home.

'Absalom may come and live in Jerusalem,' said David.

But after two years, Absalom still had not seen his father. 'What was the point of me coming back, if I cannot see the king?' he complained to Joab. 'I am an innocent man.'

David loved Absalom, and so eventually he agreed to see him. But Absalom dreamed of being king. He knew that he was strong and handsome and popular with the people. He asked his father for permission to go to Hebron.

Before long a messenger came to David in Jerusalem. 'Absalom has been proclaimed king in Hebron,' he announced.

'Quick! We must escape from here,' said David to his men, 'or Absalom will kill us all.' They fled from Jerusalem.

Another messenger came to find them. 'Your friend Ahithophel has joined Absalom,' he said.

David cried, and then he prayed. 'Oh, God, please may he give Absalom bad advice.'

Then David turned to Hushai. 'Go back to Jerusalem and pretend to join Absalom. Then advise against any plans Ahithophel may have.'

So Hushai returned to Jerusalem.

132 2 Samuel chapter 13.

David's sons
Amnon was David's eldest son and would become king when David died. Absalom was David's third son but he wanted to be king one day.

Feasts
Special meals probably had meat, which people did not eat often. It might be lamb or veal, or possibly venison, stewed or boiled with herbs and spices. There would be bread to soak up the gravy, and vegetables such as onions and leeks. For dessert there might be melon, pomegranates, grapes and figs, and honey. Everyone would drink wine.

See Feature pages 54-55.

Revenge
There was no police force in David's time. When a crime was committed, the victim's relatives had a duty to punish the criminal. But the penalty for Amnon's crime was a fine, not death. Absalom went too far.

133 2 Samuel chapters 14 and 15.

Joab
He was commander of David's army and also David's nephew.

David and Absalom
Psalm 3 tells us how David felt when he ran away from Absalom's rebellion: 'Lord, my enemies are rising around me, and people are saying you can't help me! But you are my shield, and you will take away my shame. I shall sleep without worrying, because you will look after me.'

134 2 Samuel chapter 16, verse 15 to chapter 17, verse 23.

Ahithophel
Ahithophel was very wise and he was usually right. Both David and Absalom took his advice.

Hushai's plan
David had not gone far from Jerusalem. It was not possible for a large group of people to travel quickly; most of them were walking. When Hushai told Absalom to wait, he was giving David extra time to escape.

135 2 Samuel chapter 18.

Absalom's murder
Joab knew that David did not want Absalom killed. But he also knew that if Absalom lived, he would want to be king again. So Joab disobeyed his orders.

Messengers
Messengers were fast long-distance runners. They usually remembered their messages rather than writing them down.

David's grief
David loved his son and was sorry he had died, even though Absalom had rebelled against him. But David's grief made the army feel they had wasted their hard work, and that the victory wasn't worth having. So David went to thank his men for saving him, even though Absalom was killed in the process.

Long hair
Men and women had long hair at this time. Israel's law forbade men from cutting the hair at the side of their heads or from shaping their beards.

134 Hushai tricks Absalom

'Long live the king!' said Hushai, when he saw Absalom enter Jerusalem.

'What are you doing here?' asked Absalom suspiciously. 'Why didn't you go with David?'

'Because I want to serve you,' replied Hushai. Absalom believed him.

Then he asked Ahithophel, 'Tell me what you think we should do next.'

'Let me choose 12,000 men to attack David tonight,' said Ahithophel. 'I will kill David, and lead his troops back to Jerusalem.'

It was a good plan, but Absalom was undecided. 'What do you think?' he asked Hushai.

Hushai thought quickly. 'Ahithophel has not given you good advice,' he said. 'David will already be hiding. Wait a while, and then go after him. Make sure you lead the army yourself.'

Absalom liked Hushai's plan. Secretly, Hushai warned David.

When Ahithophel heard that Absalom had followed Hushai's advice, he went home and killed himself.

135 Joab disobeys orders

David prepared his men for the fight against Absalom. He put Joab and Abishai in charge. 'I want to fight with you,' he said.

But the soldiers did not think it wise. 'If you are killed, everything is lost,' they replied.

David reluctantly agreed. He shouted one last order, which everyone heard. 'Do not harm my son, Absalom!' he cried.

The two armies fought one another in the forest. David's soldiers were stronger. Absalom came riding through the forest, weaving his way through the trees, his hair flowing behind him. Suddenly, he was pulled from his mule as his thick hair caught in the branches.

'Absalom is hanging in a tree,' said one of the soldiers to Joab.

'Why didn't you kill him?' asked Joab. 'I would have rewarded you.' But the soldier had heard David's order.

Joab found Absalom and killed him.

'Don't tell the king that Absalom is dead,' said Joab to the messenger who ran off with the news of their victory.

'I will run to the king, as well,' said David's friend, Ahimaaz.

David was waiting for news of the battle.

'We have won!' cried Ahimaaz who got there first.

'Is Absalom alive?' asked David. Ahimaaz did not answer.

'Is Absalom alive?' David asked the other messenger.

'I wish all your enemies would end up like him,' the messenger replied.

Then David knew that Absalom was dead. 'Oh, my son, Absalom,' cried David. 'I wish I could have died instead of you!'

136 Adonijah takes control

When David was an old man, the affairs of the nation no longer interested him. He was more concerned with being comfortable and keeping warm. His fourth son, Adonijah, saw his chance to take control. 'I will be king now,' he said.

Joab gave Adonijah his support. Benaiah and Nathan, the prophet, remained loyal to David.

'Have you heard that Adonijah has made himself king, and King David knows nothing about it?' said Nathan to Bathsheba. 'I thought David had promised that your son, Solomon, would be the next king.'

Bathsheba listened to Nathan. She agreed to warn King David.

137 Bathsheba warns King David

Adonijah and his supporters were holding a feast. They did not invite Solomon. Meanwhile Bathsheba and Nathan waited to see King David.

'Adonijah has made himself king,' said Bathsheba. 'Joab has betrayed you and has joined him. You promised me that our son, Solomon, would be king.'

'It is true, your majesty,' confirmed Nathan.

'I will keep my promise,' David assured Bathsheba. 'Take Solomon, and let him ride on my mule to Gihon. Make sure that Benaiah goes too. Once you are there, anoint Solomon as my successor.'

Benaiah and Nathan did as David had asked. 'Long live King Solomon!' shouted the people.

138 Adonijah is deserted

Adonijah and his guests were just finishing their feast when they heard the sound of the trumpet.

'What's that noise?' asked Joab.

A messenger announced, 'David has made Solomon king!'

Immediately Adonijah's supporters ran away and left him. Adonijah was terrified. He panicked, and ran to the temple. He clung on to the horns of the altar. He was certain Solomon would kill him.

'I will not harm you,' said King Solomon. 'Go home,' he said, as Adonijah bowed low before him.

136 1 Kings chapter 1, verses 1-14.

Benaiah
Benaiah was one of David's top 30 soldiers.

137 1 Kings chapter 1, verses 15-40.

Power and kingship
There were no fixed rules about who should be king after David. There were plenty of people who wanted the job. Adonijah got a small army together and hoped he would get enough people to support him. But the people still loved David, and they accepted his choice of Solomon as next king.

138 1 Kings chapter 1, verses 41-53.

Solomon
David chose the right man to be king. But because David did not ask other people's advice, some were against Solomon.

Horned altar

Adonijah fled to a worship centre where he clung to the 'horns of the altar'. No one was allowed to kill someone who did this, because it was a sign they wanted God's mercy and help. Altars had raised corners which looked a bit like animal horns.

139 1 Kings chapter 2, verses 1-12.

David's tomb

Rich people and kings were buried in tombs cut into the rocks. Poor people were buried in caves. They were fully dressed and not put in coffins first. The site of David's tomb was still known in Jesus' time.

📖 See Feature pages 22-23.

David's life

David had helped Israel to defeat its enemies and to become a wealthy country. He had made a new capital city, Jerusalem, and had brought the ark of the covenant into it. Despite his mistakes and failures, he loved God and wanted others to love him too.

140 1 Kings chapter 2, verses 13-46.

Adonijah's plan

Adonijah wanted one of David's slaves as a wife because it would give him power over the palace staff. The person who controlled the staff could then claim the right to be king.

141 1 Kings chapter 3, verses 1-15.

Wisdom

'Wisdom' means knowing the right thing to do or say. There are two books of wise sayings in the Bible: Proverbs and Ecclesiastes.

Some of Solomon's proverbs

'Calm words soothe angry people, but bitter words make them worse.' 'Starting a quarrel is like making a hole in a dam – so don't do it.' 'People who live for pleasure will never get rich.'

139 David's last days

David knew that he had not long to live. He sent for Solomon, and spoke to him. 'I am going to die soon,' he said, 'and the throne of Israel will belong to you and your descendants. Remember to obey God and to follow him faithfully. If you do as God says, he will bless you.'

Solomon listened carefully. 'Watch Joab,' warned David. 'Remember what he did. He is a murderer. Make sure that he is punished.'

Not long after, David died. He had ruled for forty years, and under his leadership Israel had become a strong nation.

140 Solomon becomes king

Solomon was king of Israel, but Adonijah still wanted to be king.

He approached Bathsheba, Solomon's mother, and asked her to speak up for him. 'Please ask Solomon if I can have one of my father's slaves as my wife,' he said.

Bathsheba told Solomon of Adonijah's request. But Solomon did not trust him.

'Why do you speak for Adonijah?' Solomon asked his mother. 'He is playing games with us! He must die for his cunning.'

When Joab heard that Adonijah was dead, he ran away. He hid in the tent of the Lord. 'Nobody will dare harm me here,' he thought. But Benaiah found Joab. He had orders from King Solomon to kill him.

Solomon promoted Benaiah and made him commander of his army. He was a loyal friend and a brave fighter. Now Solomon was fully in control of Israel.

141 Solomon's strange dream

Solomon went to Gibeon to make some sacrifices to God. During the night he had a strange dream. As Solomon slept, he heard God saying, 'You may ask me for whatever you want.'

'You are so good to me,' replied Solomon. 'You have given me so many people to govern. Please help me by giving me the gift of wisdom.'

God was pleased. 'You could have chosen wealth, or power, or a long life,' said God. 'But instead, you chose wisdom. I will give you what you have asked for, and I will give you wealth, power and a long life as well. If you obey me, you will be the greatest of kings.'

Solomon woke up. But he clearly remembered his dream.

142 The two mothers

One day, two women came to see Solomon. They shared a house together. Both of them had given birth to baby boys.

'Your majesty,' cried one of the women. 'One night, this woman and I went to sleep with our babies. During the night, her baby died, and she swapped her dead baby for my living son. As soon as it was morning, and I saw the dead baby by my side, I knew that it was not my son.'

'That's not true!' argued the other woman. 'My son is alive; yours is dead!'

'Bring me a sword!' ordered Solomon. 'Cut the baby in half! Then each woman can have a share!'

But the first woman loved her son. 'Don't harm him!' she pleaded with the king. 'She can have him.'

'Do as the king says!' replied the other woman. 'It's fair!'

Immediately Solomon knew which woman was the baby's mother. He ordered that the baby be handed to the first woman.

Everyone in Israel was amazed at Solomon's wisdom.

143 Building God's temple

Under Solomon's leadership, the Israelites enjoyed peace. The time was right for Solomon to build a temple for God.

He sent a message to the king of Tyre. 'I want to build God a temple,' he said. 'The best cedar trees are in Lebanon. Fell some for me, so that I can use the wood. I will pay you whatever you want.'

The king of Tyre was happy to help Solomon. He supplied him with all the wood he needed.

Meanwhile God told Solomon the temple's design. King David had already bought a plot of land. Now Solomon could start to build. The stones were prepared in the quarry and brought to the site. He ordered the building of the porch, the Holy Place and the 'Holy of Holies'. He lined the internal walls with highly carved wood, and covered them with gold. Then he filled the temple with all the things that God required, taken from the tent of meeting.

Finally, in front of all Israel's elders, the ark of the covenant was brought to the temple, and put into the 'Holy of Holies', and the cloud of God's presence filled the temple.

'Praise God!' said Solomon in front of all the people.

142 1 Kings chapter 3, verses 16-28.

Solomon's idea
He wouldn't really have cut the baby in half. He knew that the threat would make the real mother plead for the baby's life even if she couldn't look after him.

143 1 Kings chapters 5 to 8.

Cedar trees
The cedar is a large fir tree with spreading branches. It used to be very common in Palestine, but few are left there now. Its wood is very strong and attractive, and was used for building.

The temple
Though not large by today's standards, this may have been the largest building the Israelites had at this time. It was about 27m/88ft long by 9m/30ft wide. It had the same shape as the tent of meeting with two rooms. But it also had big pillars at the entrance and store rooms around the sides.

Inside the temple
There were two rooms. The first, the Holy Place, had a gold-covered altar on which incense was burned; a table for the special 'Bread of the Presence' put there each week; and ten lampstands. The second room, the 'Holy of Holies', contained only the ark of the covenant. The walls of both rooms were lined with cedar wood panels, covered with gold and decorated with carved flowers, trees and cherubim.

📖 See Feature pages 82-83.

📖 WORSHIP

When Moses came down from Mount Sinai, he brought God's words to the Israelites: 'I am the Lord your God who brought you out of Egypt where you were slaves. Worship no God but me.'

The Israelites were called to be different from the other nations around them. Their whole lives and their worship were to be based on God's laws and on a special agreement or covenant: if they trusted God and kept his laws, then he would always look after them and protect them.

OTHER GODS

From the very beginning the Israelites' religion was different from the religions of other nations who lived near them.

For example, Canaanites, like the Egyptians, Greeks and Romans, had many gods and goddesses who had influence over different parts of life: war, weather, fertility, money and so on.

These gods were represented by statues, which the people bowed down to worship.

God's laws forbade the worship of statues or idols (gods made of wood, metal or stone). God is one god, invisible, the maker and ruler of the earth and everything in it.

The tent of meeting

While the Israelites were living in tents on the way to the Promised Land, they built a special tent. Outside it, they heard God's Law, said prayers, offered gifts and sacrifices and praised God in words and music. In an inner tent (the 'Holy of Holies') was the ark of the covenant, the special box covered in gold which held the stone slabs with the Ten Commandments written on them. Only the High Priest was allowed to enter the 'Holy of Holies'. This reminded the people that God was great and holy, and was to be treated with respect.

The tent of meeting reminded the people that God was always with them. It was the Israelites' centre of worship until the temple was built.

The tent of meeting was made of red, blue and purple cloth covered with two layers of waterproof leather and supported by a frame of wood covered in gold.

The 'Holy of Holies'

The ark of the covenant

The altar of burnt-offering

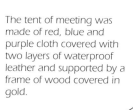

Solomon's temple

Priests All priests were descended from Aaron, Moses' brother. When the High Priest died, his son took over. Only the High Priest was allowed to enter the 'Holy of Holies' in the temple. Priests had to prepare and offer sacrifices, and teach the people God's Law.

The early church

Jesus and his followers often went to worship at the temple and in synagogues. After Jesus' death and resurrection, his Jewish followers continued to worship in the temple and went into synagogues all over the Roman Empire to tell people the good news of Jesus.

Gradually the 'church' (which means the followers, or 'body' of Christ) started to meet together in people's homes. It was a very informal way of meeting and the believers would share food, pass on the message of Jesus and pray and praise God together.

When David became king of Israel he brought the ark of the covenant to his new capital city of Jerusalem. Later, David's son, King Solomon, built a magnificent temple to replace the tent of meeting as the 'house of God'. It was lined with cedar wood from Lebanon, and the walls were covered with gold. It took thousands of craftsmen about seven years to build the temple, using the finest stone, wood, gold, silver, and precious jewels.

Ordinary people did not worship inside the temple, but gathered in the courtyard where the sacrifices took place. Every day priests burned incense (as a prayer) in the Holy Place inside the temple. Only once a year, the High Priest would go into the 'Holy of Holies' to offer a sacrifice.

From this time all Jews visited the temple in Jerusalem for the religious festivals. Solomon's temple was destroyed, and replaced. By New Testament times the temple had been rebuilt by King Herod. This is where people in Jesus' time went to worship God.

Synagogues

About 600 years before Jesus was born, Jerusalem and Solomon's temple were destroyed and the Jews were taken captive to Babylon. They started to meet for prayer and the study of God's Law in small groups. After they returned to Jerusalem and rebuilt the temple, each community met in special buildings called synagogues. No sacrifices took place there. The men and women sat separately, and the

writings of Moses and the prophets were read aloud.

MEETING TOGETHER

Worship is to be part of everyday life for God's people. The special day to join with other believers to worship God is the Sabbath (Saturday) for Jews, and Sunday (the day when Jesus rose from the dead) for Christians.

144 1 Kings chapter 9, verses 1-9.

145 1 Kings chapter 10, verses 1-13.

Sheba
This was a country in Arabia, probably in the same area as modern Yemen. Solomon had trading links with many Arabian countries.

Trade
Traders took wool, linen, clothes, olive oil, grain and live sheep and cattle from Israel to Egypt, Arabia and countries to the east. They brought back spices, gold, precious stones, horses and chariots, and exotic foods. They even brought apes and baboons which a few rich people kept as pets!

Solomon's food
King Solomon had to feed his many wives and children and his large number of servants. They ate 30 cattle and 1000 sheep every day!

146 1 Kings chapter 10, verse 14 to chapter 11, verse 3.

Solomon's throne
This was a large chair built at the top of six steps. Its armrests had carved lions standing beside them. There were also two carved lions on each step. It was made of wood with layers of ivory to decorate it.

144 God's warning to Solomon

'I have heard your prayers, and I will make the temple you have built into a special, holy place,' promised God.

'But,' God warned Solomon, 'if you disobey me, and neglect to follow my laws, your children will not be kings, and I will reject this magnificent temple which you have built.'

145 The visit of the queen of Sheba

The queen of Sheba heard of Solomon's greatness. She wanted to see him for herself.

She arrived in Jerusalem with many attendants and plenty of expensive and exotic gifts to give to the king. She saw the magnificent palace that Solomon had built. She tasted fine food and wine. She noticed how his servants were dressed, and she saw Solomon worship God in the temple. She talked to Solomon and asked him questions. He could answer everything. She was impressed with everything she saw.

'I heard all about you, in my country,' the queen said to Solomon, 'but I thought it was an exaggeration! Now I know the truth. You are far greater than I had been told. Let me praise your God for making you such a great and wise king!'

146 Solomon's power and wealth

As Solomon's reputation grew throughout the whole world, he became richer and richer. Every foreign visitor who came to hear Solomon's wisdom brought expensive gifts. And Israel traded with many different nations, making money for Solomon.

Soon Solomon had so much gold that every household item that was used in his palace was made from it. Nothing was made of silver; there was so much gold, silver was worthless. He kept fine horses and chariots, and grew cedar trees.

Solomon built himself a throne. It was made out of gold and ivory, and decorated with lions. No one had ever seen anything so spectacular before.

But Solomon was careless. He ignored God's warnings. He married foreign wives, who bowed down to idols and did not know the true God.

147 Solomon disobeys God

The years passed. Solomon grew older. He saw his wives worship their gods, and he began to do the same.

God saw Solomon's disobedience. He was angry with him. 'I warned you,' said God, 'and you have ignored me. I will take the kingdom of Israel away from your children because of your disobedience. Yet because of your father's constant love for me, I will allow you to be king for the rest of your life. But your son will not be king over all Israel. He will only rule over two tribes.'

148 Cracks in the kingdom

Old enemies, with long-held grievances against Israel, began to grow in strength and threaten the peace that Solomon had taken for granted.

A man called Hadad was determined to cause trouble for Solomon. Born in Edom, he had been forced to escape from his home to Egypt when he was a boy. Joab, the commander of King David's army, had invaded Edom, killing all the men who remained. Years later, when Hadad learned that David and Joab were dead, he returned to Edom, determined to get back at Solomon whenever he could.

Within the kingdom of Israel there was a man called Jeroboam. He was hardworking and able. Solomon gave him responsibilities. But what Solomon did not know was that God had already chosen Jeroboam for a very special purpose.

149 Jeroboam flees

One day Jeroboam left Jerusalem. As he went on his way he met the prophet Ahijah.

Suddenly, Ahijah took off the new cloak he was wearing and ripped it into twelve pieces. 'Take them!' he said, giving ten pieces to Jeroboam. 'This is a picture of what God will do for you. Once Solomon is dead, he will make you king over ten of the tribes of Israel.'

Jeroboam looked at the pieces of cloth in his hand. 'David's grandson will be allowed to be king over only two tribes,' continued Ahijah. 'Remember to follow God and to obey him, and he will be with you and your descendants.'

When Solomon heard what had happened he tried to kill Jeroboam. But Jeroboam escaped to Egypt.

147 1 Kings chapter 11, verses 4-13.

Solomon's wives
Kings in Solomon's day would marry into the royal family of another country to show they agreed with a trade or political deal. Solomon had about 700 such wives. They brought their countries' gods with them, and Solomon forgot he should only worship the one true God.

Gods
Most gods were pictured as animals. Bull calves were popular. Some statues of gods may also have been pillars (like obelisks or totem poles). They were carved from wood or stone, or made from metal cast in a mould.

See Feature pages 82-83.

148 1 Kings chapter 11, verses 14-28.

Edom
Edom was a desert country south of the Dead Sea. Its people were descended from Esau, Jacob's brother. Wars between Edom and Israel had begun in King Saul's time.

149 1 Kings chapter 11, verses 29-40.

Jeroboam
Jeroboam returned from Egypt when Solomon died and became the first king of the northern kingdom of Israel.

150 1 Kings chapter 12, verses 1-24.

Solomon's death
Solomon was a great king. He used the peace won by his father, David, to make the country very wealthy, by charging taxes on traders who passed through it and by getting the people to build big palaces and public buildings. He was famous for his wisdom, but in his later years he began to drift away from God.

Two kingdoms
This split happened in about 930BC. From now on, the ten northern tribes are called 'Israel' and the two southern tribes are called 'Judah'. Each had its own king.

151 1 Kings chapter 12, verse 25 to chapter 13, verse 34.

Golden calves
Bull calves were used by many tribes as symbols of gods. They stood for fertility and strength. It is possible that Jeroboam intended people to think of them as signs of the invisible God's presence, like the ark of the covenant in Jerusalem. But unfortunately, people began to worship the statues instead of God.

See Feature pages 82-83.

150 The kingdom is divided

Solomon died and his son, Rehoboam, succeeded him. He went to the ancient city of Shechem, hoping that the people would proclaim him king.

But Jeroboam acted quickly. He left Egypt and joined with the people from the northern tribes of Israel at Shechem. Instead of hailing Rehoboam king, they challenged him. 'Your father, King Solomon, made us work hard. If you want us to obey you, promise to make our work easier.'

Rehoboam was shocked. 'Come back in three days' time,' he replied.

Rehoboam turned to his father's old officials. 'Tell me what to do,' he said.

'Agree to it,' said the old men. 'Make their workload lighter.'

But Rehoboam was not happy with their reply. He sought advice from his friends, young men whom he had recently promoted.

'Don't give in!' said his friends. 'Tell them that you will make them work harder, and you'll whip them if they don't!'

Rehoboam liked that idea. Three days later he gave his reply.

'We don't have to be ruled by you!' shouted the people from the northern tribes. 'You are not one of us! We are going home.'

Rehoboam returned to Jerusalem. The northern tribes made Jeroboam their king. The kingdom of Israel was no longer united.

151 King Jeroboam's golden calves

Jeroboam was anxious. His people still needed to worship but the temple in Jerusalem was now in the southern kingdom of Judah, under Rehoboam's control.

'If the people return to Jerusalem, how can I trust them to remain loyal to me?' thought Jeroboam.

He sought advice, and quickly made two golden calves. 'These are your gods,' he said to the people. 'You don't have to go to Jerusalem to worship. You can worship them here!'

Jeroboam placed the statues in two strategic cities, and went to worship them himself.

One day, as Jeroboam went to worship the calves, a prophet who had come from Judah challenged him. 'Be warned!' he shouted. 'God has seen what you have done. One of King David's descendants, called Josiah, will overthrow all the bad things you have done! To prove this is from God, your altar will crack in two and the ashes will fall on the ground.'

'Seize him!' shouted Jeroboam, pointing at the prophet. Suddenly his hand was frozen into position. He could not move it.

Jeroboam heard a loud, deep crack, and he saw the altar split in two, and the ashes scatter across the ground.

'Help me!' he begged. 'Ask God to make my hand move again.'

The prophet prayed, and Jeroboam's hand was restored. The prophet left. But Jeroboam continued to disobey God.

152 The prophet Ahijah's warning

Jeroboam's son, Abijah, was very ill. 'Disguise yourself and go to Ahijah the prophet in Shiloh,' said Jeroboam to his wife. 'Ask him what will happen to our son.' Jeroboam's wife took some bread, cakes and honey to give to the prophet, and set off on her journey.

Ahijah was an old man, and could not see. But God told him, 'Jeroboam's wife is coming to see you. She is disguised but I will give you the words to say to her.'

Jeroboam's wife arrived. 'I know who you are,' said Ahijah. 'Prepare yourself, for God has given me some bad news. He has seen your husband's disobedience, and because of this his family will be punished. When you get home, your son will die, and his death will sadden everyone. But by dying he will be spared a worse fate, for God has seen that he is good.'

Jeroboam's wife returned home. Everything happened as the prophet had said.

153 The warring nations

Meanwhile Rehoboam established his kingdom of Judah. He strengthened and fortified his cities against attack. He gave each of his sons a city to rule over, and made sure they married well.

But then he grew careless, and stopped obeying God. He built shrines and altars to other gods. His people copied him.

God was angry with what he saw. He allowed the king of Egypt to attack Jerusalem and plunder the temple and the palace, taking all the treasures. Israel and Judah waged war against each other. Peace between the nations was over.

154 Ahab becomes king of Israel

King after king ruled the northern kingdom of Israel. They were all the same. They all failed to obey God.

At last Ahab became king. He was evil, and his behaviour made God more angry than any of the kings who went before him. Ahab married a woman called Jezebel. She was from a foreign country and bowed down to the god, Baal. When Ahab set up an altar to Baal in the temple, God was very angry. He was determined to stop the evil spreading.

---

152 1 Kings chapter 14, verses 1-20.

Shiloh
Halfway between Jerusalem, capital of Judah, and Shechem, capital of Israel, Shiloh had been the Israelites' main place for worship before David conquered Jerusalem (stories 103, 104).

153 1 Kings chapter 14, verses 21-31.

Egypt's king
The king of Egypt at this time was Shishak, who ruled from about 945BC to 924BC. After Solomon's death he invaded the southern kingdom of Judah and took treasures from the temple in Jerusalem.

154 1 Kings chapter 16, verses 29-33.

Ahab and Jezebel
Many years have passed. Ahab became king about 870BC. Jezebel, his wife, came from Tyre, in Canaan. She was a Phoenician, not an Israelite.

Baal
'Baal' was like a surname for many Canaanite gods.

Jezebel's Baal was probably Baal-melquart, which was supposed to control the weather. It was the god of Jezebel's home town, Tyre, which was on the coast.

See Feature pages 44-45.

155 1 Kings chapter 17, verses 1-6.

Elijah
Elijah's home town was Tishbe in Gilead, an Israelite area east of the River Jordan.

156 1 Kings chapter 17, verses 7-24.

The widow's oil
The woman was a widow. It was not easy for widows to find work, so they relied on the kindness of others. God showed how much he cared for her and Elijah by making sure she did not run out of the flour and oil she needed to make them food.

Bread making
Bread was usually made in the form of flat cakes rather like large crumpets or thick pittas.

📖 See Feature pages 54-55.

157 1 Kings chapter 18, verses 16-46.

Mount Carmel
This is a small mountain, covered in trees, about 530m/1740ft high, about 20km/12 miles inland from the coast of northern Israel.

Jezebel's prophets
As they prayed to Jezebel's god, Baal-melquart, the priests cut themselves with knives. They believed that Baal liked human sacrifice, so it would smell the blood and answer their prayers.

155 Elijah brings bad news

God chose a prophet called Elijah to deliver his warning. 'God has told me to tell you that for the next few years there won't be any rain, not even any dew, until I say so,' Elijah told King Ahab.

Elijah left the king, and waited to hear what God wanted him to do next. 'Cross over the River Jordan and hide,' said God. 'Go to the Cherith brook. There you will have water, and I will send some ravens to bring you food.'

Elijah obeyed God. The ravens brought him food. But Elijah's words came true. It did not rain. The sun beat down and the ground was dry and parched. Soon the water in the brook dried up.

156 God looks after Elijah

The famine grew worse. 'Go to Zarephath,' said God to Elijah. 'A woman who lives there will provide you with food.'

When Elijah reached the gates of the town he saw a woman gathering sticks for firewood. 'Please will you give me some bread and water?' he asked.

'I don't have enough for my own family,' she replied. 'This wood is to cook one last meal for me and my son before we die.'

'Don't be afraid,' said Elijah. 'Make your meal, only give me some bread as well. God promises that if you do this you will have flour and oil for as long as the famine lasts.'

The woman did as Elijah asked. Her flour and oil never ran out. And Elijah stayed there for many days.

Some time later the woman's son grew ill and died. The woman turned on Elijah. 'Did you come here to make my son die?' she sobbed.

Elijah took the dead boy and laid him on the bed. 'Lord God,' he cried. 'Why have you allowed this? Please give the boy back his life!'

Suddenly, the boy started to breathe again. Elijah carried him to his mother. The woman looked at Elijah. 'Now I know you are God's friend,' she said.

157 Contest on the mountain

The famine continued. 'Speak to King Ahab,' God told Elijah. 'Then I will let it rain.'

Ahab was angry. 'You troublemaker!' he cried.

'I'm not the troublemaker!' said Elijah defiantly. 'You have brought trouble by refusing to obey God. Now tell the people to go to Mount Carmel. Bring all the prophets of Baal with you.'

The people gathered on Mount Carmel. Elijah issued his challenge. 'I am the only prophet of the living God,' he said, 'and there are 450 prophets of Baal. Let us each prepare a sacrifice. Call upon Baal to send down fire to burn it, and I will ask the same of my God. The true God will be the one who sends down fire.'

The prophets agreed. All day they prayed to Baal to send down fire. Nothing happened. 'Is your god asleep?' Elijah asked.

Then Elijah made his altar and prepared his sacrifice. In addition he dug a trench round it, and soaked the altar with water.

'Lord God,' cried Elijah. 'Show everyone here today that you are the one true God.' Immediately the sacrifice burst into flames. Everything was consumed by fire.

The people fell to the ground. 'The Lord is the true God,' they cried.

'Seize the prophets of Baal and put them to death!' commanded Elijah. Then he turned to Ahab. 'You may celebrate!' he said. 'The rain is coming.'

So Ahab got into his chariot and set off for home.

158 Death threats for Elijah

When Queen Jezebel heard what Elijah had done, she threatened to kill him. Elijah was terrified. He ran to the desert. 'Let me die,' he said to God. He was exhausted and fell asleep.

An angel touched him. 'Get up and eat,' said the angel. Elijah looked up, and saw some water and freshly baked bread. He ate and drank, and then fell asleep again.

The angel touched him for a second time. 'Eat some more and refresh yourself for the journey ahead.'

Elijah ate and set out for Mount Horeb. He found a cave, and settled down for the night.

'What are you doing here?' asked God.

'I have done my best to serve you,' said Elijah. 'But they are trying to kill me!'

'Stand on the mountain,' said God, 'and see me pass by.'

A powerful wind suddenly sprang up. It ripped through the mountains, shattering and splintering the rocks in its path. But God was not in the wind. The earth shivered and shook. But God was not in the earthquake. Then came fire. But God was not in the fire.

Finally, there was a gentle whisper. Elijah left the cave, and stood on the mountain. He knew it was God. He heard a voice.

'Go back the way you have come,' said the still, small voice of God. 'Anoint Jehu to be king of Israel, and Elisha to succeed you as prophet.'

159 Elijah's new helper

Elijah found Elisha ploughing a field. Immediately, Elijah took off his cloak and flung it around Elisha's shoulders.

The young man left his oxen and ran after Elijah. 'Let me say goodbye to my parents before I go with you,' he said.

Elijah looked at his successor. 'Go back home and say goodbye,' he said.

Elisha went home before leaving to follow Elijah.

Elijah's altar
The Bible says that Elijah repaired an existing altar. It is possible that God had been worshipped on Mount Carmel in the past, but the altar had not been used for a long time. He made it with twelve stones, one for each of the tribes of Israel.

Fire
The people had stopped trusting God. They were given a very clear sign that there is only one true God, and that idols are useless.

158 1 Kings chapter 19, verses 1-18.

Mount Horeb
Also called Mount Sinai, this is a long way to the south between Israel and Egypt. Moses was given the Ten Commandments there (story 52).

Elijah's feelings
Elijah was very tired. He couldn't think straight, so he ran away. He felt frightened by Jezebel's threat, because he had forgotten that God could protect him. When God didn't speak in the wind, quake and fire, he felt God had left him. He hadn't, of course, as Elijah soon found out.

159 1 Kings chapter 19, verses 19-21.

Elijah's cloak
Elijah gave Elisha his cloak as a sign that Elisha would one day take over his work. It was like handing over the baton in a relay race. But for a while, Elisha would learn by working with Elijah.

160 1 Kings chapter 21.

Naboth's land

Israelite kings were not allowed to take away someone's land just because they wanted it. But Canaanite kings didn't care about their people – and Jezebel was the daughter of a Canaanite king.

Vineyards

Grapes were an important part of people's diets, as fresh fruit, raisins and wine. Naboth would have worked hard in his vineyard, and it was probably the main way he and his family could earn money.

Seals

Ahab's seal was probably a pattern engraved on clay, ivory or metal. It would make a special mark when pressed into hot wax, which would harden when cool. Anything with the seal on carried the king's authority.

161 2 Kings chapter 2, verses 1-14.

Prophets

Often they lived or worked together in groups to help each other. Sometimes a well-known prophet like Elijah would be their leader.

Elijah's death

The chariot and horses would remind Elisha that God was fighting for Israel. Elijah's cloak falling to the ground told him that God would work through him as powerfully as he had worked through Elijah.

160 Naboth's vineyard

There was a man called Naboth who lived in Jezreel. He owned a vineyard near King Ahab's palace. One day, Ahab spoke to Naboth.

'Your vineyard would make me an ideal garden. Sell it to me, and I will give you a good price. Or, if you prefer, I will give you a better vineyard in exchange.'

But Naboth did not want to lose his vineyard. It had belonged to his father and his grandfather, so he declined King Ahab's offer. Ahab was angry. He lay on his bed and sulked.

'Pull yourself together,' said Queen Jezebel. 'You're the king! I'll get Naboth's vineyard for you.'

She wrote some letters. She put Ahab's name on them and used his seal. 'Organize a day of fasting and invite Naboth,' she wrote to the elders of Jezreel. 'Arrange for two people to publicly accuse him of cursing God and the king. Then stone him to death.'

The plan worked. Naboth was killed and Ahab got the vineyard.

'Find Ahab,' said God to Elijah. 'Tell him that he will die for what he has done to Naboth. Everyone in his family will be punished.'

Elijah told the king. Ahab tore his clothes. He was sorry and afraid. God saw Ahab. He gave him another chance.

161 Elijah is taken to heaven

The prophets Elijah and Elisha knew that it was their last day together. Elijah set off for Bethel. 'Stay here!' he said to his young friend.

But Elisha refused. 'I will not leave you,' he said.

As they walked they met some other prophets. 'Do you realize that God is going to take Elijah away?' they asked Elisha.

'Yes,' he replied.

When they reached the Jordan Elijah took off his cloak, rolled it up, and struck the water with it. Immediately a pathway appeared through the river and the two men crossed to the other side.

'Ask me for whatever you want before I leave you,' said Elijah.

'Give me twice as much of your faith and power,' said Elisha.

'If you see me leave this earth, you will have what you have asked for,' said Elijah.

Suddenly a chariot and horses made of fire appeared in the sky. They descended and came between Elijah and Elisha. A whirlwind swirled up, and Elijah was taken into heaven.

Elijah's cloak fell to the ground. Elisha picked it up. He rolled it up and struck the river as Elijah had done. A pathway appeared.

'You have the faith and power of Elijah,' said the group of prophets as they watched him.

162 The widow's oil

One day a poor widow came to
see Elisha. She was very upset.

'My husband died owing a
man some money,' she said.
'Now he wants to take my
two sons to be slaves.'

'What do you have at
home?' Elisha asked
kindly.

'Nothing,' replied the
woman desperately,
'only a little bit of oil.'

'Ask your neighbours to
give you as many empty
jars as they have,' ordered
Elisha. 'Go home with your sons. Then shut the door, and pour oil
into all of the jars!'

The woman did as Elisha told her. She filled each jar full of oil.
When the last jar was full, the oil ran out.

'Now sell the oil and pay off your debts. Then you and your sons
can live on the money you have left,' said Elisha happily.

163 Elisha's gift to the rich woman

A rich woman at Shunem offered Elisha a meal whenever he was
passing, for she knew that he was a man who loved God. She also
asked her husband to make a small room for him to stay in. The
room had a bed, a table, a chair and a lamp.

One day, when Elisha was staying at their house he asked, 'You
have been so kind to me. Is there anything I can do for you?'

The woman could not think of anything, but Elisha's servant had
noticed that the woman did not have any children.

'This time next year you will hold your baby son in your arms,'
promised Elisha.

Everything happened just as Elisha had said and a year later the
woman gave birth to a baby boy.

164 The death of the rich woman's son

The rich woman loved her son dearly. One day when he was older,
the boy became ill and died. So his mother carried him up to
Elisha's room and laid him on the bed. Then she saddled a donkey
and set out to find Elisha at Mount Carmel.

'Why did you allow me to have the happiness of a son, only to
take him away from me?' she cried.

Elisha returned home with her. He went in to his room, shut the
door and prayed to God. He put his mouth over the mouth of the
dead boy. Slowly the boy's body grew warm. Elisha waited. The boy
sneezed and opened his eyes. He was alive!

'Here is your son,' said Elisha to the woman.

162 2 Kings chapter 4,
verses 1-7.

Miracles
This miracle is like Jesus
feeding over 5,000 people
with five loaves and two fish
(story 256). Sometimes God
does something which
seems impossible. Other
miracles might have natural
explanations but are
amazing because of God's
control over the timing of
the events.

163 2 Kings chapter 4,
verses 8-17.

Shunem
This was in the north of
Israel, about 32km/20 miles
south-east of the Sea of
Galilee.

Room for a prophet
Prophets often moved from
place to place. As travel was
slow, they needed
somewhere to stay. The
woman offered Elisha a
room whenever he was in
her district.

164 2 Kings chapter 4,
verses 18-37.

Illness
In Elijah's day there were no
hospitals. Doctors used
ointments made from the
resin of trees and mixed with
herbs. Olive oil and wine
were also mixed with herbs
to make medicine. Many
people died quite young.

See Feature pages 54-55.

165 2 Kings chapter 5, verses 1-18.

Aram
This was a large country north of Israel. Some Bible versions call it 'Syria'. Its capital was Damascus. Arameans spoke the Aramaic language. It had become the chief language everywhere for traders and rulers.

Naaman's cure
Having to do something ordinary made Naaman feel small and humble. It reminded him that God is great and must be obeyed.

166 2 Kings chapter 9, verses 1-13.

Jezebel
She was King Ahab's wife. She came from Phoenicia, and brought false gods and bad ways of living to Israel (stories 154 and 157).

📖 See Feature pages 44-45.

Jehu is king!
Jehu was commander of part of Israel's army. His friends spread their cloaks on the ground for him to walk over, like a 'red carpet' for a special person.

167 2 Kings chapter 9, verse 14 to chapter 10, verse 36.

The killings
These rulers were bad people and had led Israel away from God and his laws. Elijah had prophesied that 'the dogs will lick Jezebel's blood'; they did, when she fell to the ground, dead.

165 Naaman is healed

The two nations of Israel and Aram fought frequently. The commander of Aram's army was a man called Naaman. He was a brave soldier but he suffered from leprosy.

Naaman's wife had an Israelite slave girl. 'I know a prophet in Israel who could cure my master,' she said.

Naaman went to the king of Aram and got permission to go to Israel. The king agreed, and wrote a letter to the Israelite king: 'I have sent Naaman to you so that he can be cured of leprosy.'

When the king of Israel read the letter he was horrified. He did not want to upset the king of Aram, but he knew there was no cure for leprosy. Elisha heard about Naaman. 'Send him to me,' he said.

Naaman and his attendants went to Elisha's house. But Elisha did not come out. Instead he gave Naaman a message, 'Go and wash seven times in the Jordan.'

Naaman was furious. He expected to be treated with some respect. He turned to go.

One of his servants spoke up. 'Sir,' he said, 'you would have obeyed the prophet if he had asked you to do something difficult or brave. Don't be too proud to do something simple.'

Naaman knew he had been given wise advice. When he came out of the river, his leprosy had vanished. He had been cured.

166 Jehu is anointed king

After King Ahab's death, his son Joram became king. Queen Jezebel still influenced Israel. No one in Ahab's family remembered or obeyed God.

Elisha took a young prophet to one side. 'Take this bottle of oil, and find a man called Jehu,' he said. 'Speak to him on his own, and then anoint him. Declare him king of Israel. Then run away immediately!'

The prophet did as Elisha had told him. He saw some soldiers sitting together. He knew that Jehu was among them. 'I have a message for you,' he said.

Once they were on their own, the prophet poured the oil on Jehu's head. 'God has chosen you to be the king of Israel. You must kill all who remain in Ahab's family, as punishment for their disobedience.' Then the prophet ran.

'What did he want?' asked one of the soldiers when Jehu returned.

'He told me that God has anointed me king,' said Jehu slowly.

The men took off their cloaks and blew the trumpet. 'Jehu is king!' they cried.

167 Punishment for Ahab's family

Quickly Jehu gathered his troops and set out towards Jezreel to find King Joram. Ahaziah, king of Judah, was with him.

Jehu galloped towards Jezreel. The lookout saw him approach. 'The man leading the troops is driving his chariot like a lunatic!' he reported. 'Jehu drives like that!'

The two kings went out to meet Jehu. 'Have you come in peace?' asked King Joram.

'There can be no peace while you and your mother rule us!' cried Jehu. As Joram fled Jehu shot an arrow into his heart.

Ahaziah fled. 'Kill him too,' cried Jehu.

Queen Jezebel heard what had happened. She painted her eyes and did her hair. She watched for Jehu from her window.

'Have you come in peace, you murderer?' she asked.

'Who will help me?' cried Jehu. Her servants nervously looked down. 'Throw her out!' he cried.

The men took hold of Jezebel and threw her out of the window. She died instantly, leaving Jehu free to rule Israel.

168 A wicked grandmother

As Queen Mother, Athaliah had power and influence in Judah. When she knew that her son, Ahaziah, was dead, she systematically killed the entire royal family, until no challengers remained. Then she ruled Judah for six years.

But her grandson, Joash, had escaped. He was taken to the temple where Athaliah would never find him. A priest called Jehoiada looked after him and taught him about God.

When Joash was seven years old, Jehoiada secretly sent for the palace and temple guard and asked for their loyalty. Then he put the crown on Joash's head and a copy of God's Law in his hands. 'Stay close to your king,' he ordered the guards, as they led Joash out to face the people. 'Behold the king of Judah!'

'Long live the king!' shouted the people when they saw him.

Athaliah heard the commotion. When she saw that Joash was king, she tore her clothes in fury. 'Treason!' she cried.

'She must die!' said Jehoiada. Joash was king. Everyone rejoiced.

169 Joash repairs the temple

Joash had listened to everything Jehoiada had taught him about God. The temple had been neglected and had fallen into disrepair.

'Use the money that the people give to you to repair the temple,' said Joash to the priests. But the temple was not repaired. Joash called Jehoiada and the other priests to account for the lack of progress. 'You have been spending the money on yourselves,' said Joash. 'Now everything must be spent on repairing the temple.'

Jehoiada found a large chest. He made a hole in the top of it, and put it by the side of the altar for the people to put money in.

So the temple was repaired, and Joash tried to lead his people back to God.

168 2 Kings chapter 11.

Back to Judah
The stories about Elijah, Elisha and Jehu were set in Israel, the ten northern tribes. This story and the next are set in Judah, the two southern tribes. Ahaziah, king of Judah, had been killed while visiting Israel.

God's Law
Kings in Judah were supposed to rule according to God's Law, so Joash is given a copy of it to remind him. It was probably written on a scroll, and may have been a copy of the Ten Commandments or a summary of them.

📖 See Feature pages 6-7.

169 2 Kings chapter 12.

The temple
Built by Solomon over 100 years before (story 143), the temple had not been looked after. People had followed other gods, and no longer gave money to the priests.

Chest
This was probably a large wooden box, the sort of thing people would store clothes or other items in.

170 2 Kings chapters 13 to 16.

A long time
This story covers about 80 years, from about 814BC to about 732BC.

171 2 Kings chapter 17, verses 1-23.

The Assyrians
Assyria was a large country to the north and east of Israel, covering parts of modern Syria and Iran. The people built large libraries and studied science and maths. They organized their society carefully with chosen leaders in each place, and many civil servants to help them. They built large temples and palaces which were richly decorated with animals, birds, and scenes from daily life. This final defeat of Samaria (Israel's capital) took place in 722BC. Israel was a country no more.

Captives
It was usual for conquering kings to take hostages away. They replaced them with refugees from other countries. It cut down the risk of a rebellion.

172 2 Kings chapters 18 and 19; Isaiah chapters 36 and 37.

Shalmaneser's obelisk
This monument was built by the Assyrian king to record his many victories over other nations. One picture on it shows 13 Israelites bringing him silver, gold, vases and other containers as a tribute.

170 Israel's evil kings

While Joash reigned over Judah, Jehu's family ruled the nation of Israel. His son, Jehoahaz, did not obey God. But when the Arameans made Israel suffer, Jehoahaz remembered God. He cried out to God for help. God listened and came to Israel's rescue.

But when Jehoahaz's son, Jehoash, became king, the people went back to their old ways. Elisha died, and the king of Aram continued to attack.

King after king of Israel failed to obey God. They let evil men have power, and let the people worship other gods.

Things could not have been worse. But God had not forgotten Israel. Neither had he forgotten the promises he had made.

171 The Assyrians capture Israel

When Hoshea became king of Israel, King Shalmaneser of Assyria attacked Israel and defeated Hoshea's army. Hoshea was allowed to remain as king, but Israel had to pay heavy taxes to Assyria.

Desperate to be free from Assyrian control, Hoshea plotted with the king of Egypt, asking him to be his ally, so that together they could overthrow the Assyrians.

When the plot was discovered, the Assyrian army poured into Israel. Shalmaneser threw Hoshea into prison, and marched on towards Samaria. The people defended themselves, but after a three-year siege were defeated.

Shalmaneser captured the people, and had them taken away to Assyria. Then he filled the land that God had given to the Israelites with people from other tribes, who bowed down to other gods.

172 Hezekiah's trust is rewarded

At last Judah had a good king! Hezekiah followed God and God was pleased with him. He defeated the Philistines, and refused to give the Assyrians the tribute they demanded. He was defiant.

As the Assyrian army swept through Israel, Judah waited. Then the enemy struck, conquering some of Judah's key towns.

Hezekiah acted swiftly, and sent the Assyrian king a message. 'We want peace! Name your price!'

The king did so. To raise the money Hezekiah stripped the temple of its treasures. But the king was not satisfied. He sent his army to Jerusalem.

'Give in to Assyria!' shouted the Assyrian general so that everyone could hear. 'You can't win! Your God cannot save you!'

Hezekiah prayed. He sent messengers to the prophet Isaiah. He needed good advice.

'God says, "Don't be afraid. The Assyrians will return home,"' Isaiah replied.

Suddenly, the Assyrian general received news of another attack and left Jerusalem. Before he went he gave Hezekiah a letter.

'You fool! Don't rely on your God to save you!' he wrote.

Hezekiah read the letter and prayed again. 'Show everyone that you are the only true God. Save us from our enemies.'

'God has heard your prayer,' said Isaiah. 'The Assyrians will not enter the city, nor will they shoot an arrow.'

The Assyrians made camp. By morning thousands of the soldiers were dead. The king returned home to Nineveh.

173 The shadow on the sundial

Hezekiah became very ill. The prophet Isaiah visited him. 'God has decided that the time has come for you to die,' he said. 'Make sure you have done whatever you need to.'

Hezekiah turned to face the wall. With tears rolling down his cheeks he prayed, 'Lord God, please remember how I have tried to serve you.'

As Isaiah left the palace, he heard God speaking to him. 'Go back and give Hezekiah a message from me. I have seen his tears and heard his prayer. In three days' time, he will worship me in the temple. I will give him another fifteen years of life.'

Isaiah rushed back to tell the king. 'How can I be sure?' he asked Isaiah. 'I need a sign.'

'Do you want the shadow on the sundial to move ten steps backwards or forwards?' asked Isaiah.

'Backwards!' exclaimed Hezekiah. 'It always moves forwards.'

So Isaiah prayed and the shadow on the sundial moved ten steps backwards. God had given Hezekiah more time.

174 Wicked King Manasseh

Manasseh became king when he was twelve years old. At first he reigned with his father, but when Hezekiah died, he took full control. He started to worship idols and foreign gods. He prayed to the sun, the moon and the stars. He sacrificed his children. Then he brought idols into God's temple.

God was angry with Manasseh. He sent prophets to warn him. 'Remember what happened to Israel,' they said. 'God says that he will destroy us, and wipe us out, like a person who wipes out a dish and then turns it upside-down.'

Manasseh did not care. He did not listen.

The Assyrians attacked. They took Manasseh prisoner. They humiliated him and put a hook in his nose, bound him in bronze chains, and took him to Babylon.

Then Manasseh remembered God. 'I am so sorry for all the things I have done,' he cried. God heard Manasseh. He forgave him and let him return to Jerusalem.

Manasseh destroyed the altars and the idols he had made. He told the people to obey God. Some listened, but others carried on in their old ways.

Isaiah
The Old Testament contains a large book of Isaiah's teachings (see stories 181, 182). He may have been a member of the royal household. He helped to keep people in Judah faithful to God during a very difficult time.

See Feature pages 12-13.

Mystery deaths
It is possible that many soldiers died of dysentery, a disease which spreads quickly in unhygienic places.

173 2 Kings chapter 20, verses 1-11 and Isaiah chapter 38, verses 1-8.

Moving shadow
It does not say that the sun itself moved backwards or that the earth stopped spinning. But Hezekiah saw an unexpected change in the shadow on the steps (used as a sundial for telling the time). It convinced him that Isaiah was telling God's truth.

174 2 Kings chapter 21, verses 1-18 and 2 Chronicles chapter 33, verses 1-20.

Manasseh
The king was involved with 'the occult' but he turned back to God and destroyed all the objects he had used for pagan worship.

See Feature pages 44-45.

175 2 Kings chapters 22 and 23.

The old scroll
Many people believe this was the book of Deuteronomy, now the fifth book in the Old Testament. It contains many of the social and religious laws which God gave to Moses.

See Feature pages 6-7.

176 2 Kings chapter 23, verse 31 to chapter 24, verse 20.

Babylon
Babylon is south of Assyria. The Babylonians had beaten the Assyrians and were now the world's super-power. Nebuchadnezzar, the king of Babylon, built large palaces and impressive gates. One palace had a series of terraced gardens on its roofs; they were called 'the hanging gardens' and became one of the wonders of the world.

177 2 Kings chapter 25.

Judah destroyed
Judah suffered like Israel. But Jeremiah, the prophet, said that within 70 years, some of Judah's people (or their children) would return, and the country would start again. His words came true (stories 183-190).

175 King Josiah's sorrow

When Manasseh's son, Amon, was assassinated, the people made Josiah king of Judah. He loved God and led his people to follow him.

The temple needed repairing. One day Josiah spoke to his secretary. 'Go and find Hilkiah, the High Priest. Tell him to use the temple money to restore it.' When the work was under way, Hilkiah discovered an old scroll. It had not been read for years. It had God's laws written on it.

When Josiah heard what was written on the scroll, he wept and tore his clothes. 'Find someone who can tell me what God wants us to do. We have broken all of his laws. He must be so angry with us.'

Hilkiah hurried to find the prophetess, Huldah. 'God is angry,' she said. 'But he has seen the king's sorrow. Judah will be destroyed, but not in Josiah's lifetime.'

Josiah summoned the people to the temple. The Law was read out. Everyone heard it. 'I promise to serve God with all my heart,' declared Josiah. 'We promise too,' declared the people.

176 The growing power of Babylon

After Josiah died, Judah's kings returned to their wicked ways. Meanwhile, a new nation, Babylon, grew in strength and power. King Nebuchadnezzar conquered countries and took captives.

It was not long before Babylonian troops surrounded Jerusalem. King Jehoiachin surrendered and Nebuchadnezzar took him and his family to Babylon. He stripped the palace and the temple of their treasures, and took anyone who had a talent or a special gift captive.

Then Nebuchadnezzar made Jehoiachin's uncle, Zedekiah, the puppet king of Judah.

177 The destruction of Jerusalem

King Zedekiah of Judah tried to rebel against Nebuchadnezzar. He did not listen to the prophets who warned him against such stupidity.

Once more, Nebuchadnezzar and the Babylonian army invaded Judah and marched to Jerusalem. They camped around the city, laying siege to it.

There was no escape. The Babylonian army took Zedekiah prisoner and brought him before Nebuchadnezzar who sentenced him, tortured him and took him to Babylon.

Then Nebuchadnezzar ordered the destruction of Jerusalem. His men broke down the walls and burned the temple.

Jerusalem was destroyed. Judah had been conquered and the people taken into captivity. God's people were no longer living in the land God had promised them.

THE PROPHETS

This section tells the stories of some of the prophets
especially chosen to communicate God's message to his people.
The word 'prophet' in the Old Testament means 'called by God'.

For years the prophets pleaded: 'Turn back to God and keep his laws'. The people had strayed away from God, and as a result, they had become selfish and greedy, forgetting to look after people who were sick or poor, widowed or fatherless or from another country. The prophets' message was hard: if God's people did not do as he asked, their country would be destroyed. The prophets were unpopular, but they also promised that God would give people a fresh start in the future.

The stories here are about prophets who lived at different times and came from different backgrounds. Their stories sometimes overlap with the events described in the Kings of Israel section, and all of them lead up to the terrible time when their prophecies came true and Jerusalem and Samaria were destroyed.

The story of the prophet Jonah is also here. His message was to the people beyond the boundaries of Israel and Judah: God loves all people, and wants them to turn away from their bad ways and to know his love and mercy.

178 Be warned!

God's people in Israel had everything they could want, but they had stopped following God's laws. So God chose Amos to warn them. Amos was a shepherd in Judah. He also looked after the fig trees.

'Amos,' God said, 'I want you to go to Israel to give my people a message.'

So Amos went to Bethel.

'Be warned!' he said to the nations who surrounded Judah. 'God has seen your sins. He has seen how violent and cruel you are.'

'Be warned!' he said to his own people in Judah. 'God has seen what you do. You are no different from other nations. Although you know God's laws, you don't keep them.'

Then he spoke to the people of Israel. 'Be warned! You ignore God's Law and you worship idols. You have plenty of money and possessions but you cheat poor people. You make a show when you worship God, but it means nothing to you. Don't think you will escape God's punishment.'

178 Amos chapters 1 to 9.

Judah and Israel
The time is about 750BC, shortly before Israel, the ten northern tribes, was conquered by Assyria. Amos came from Judah, the southern tribe, so his message was not popular in Israel.

Fig trees

They grew up to 12m/40ft high. The fruit was sometimes pressed into slabs or 'cakes'. The wood of the tree was used to make coffins.

Bethel
An important city 19km/12 miles north of Jerusalem, close to Israel's border with Judah (see story 24).

179 Amos chapter 7, verses 1-9.

Visions
Sometimes God spoke to prophets through dreams. At other times God used the things they saw around them to give them a message.

Plumb line
This was a piece of string with a heavy weight on the end. Builders hung it as a guide to make sure a wall was upright.

180 Hosea chapters 1 to 14.

Hosea
He lived at the same time as Amos, about 750BC, and spoke to the northern kingdom of Israel.

Slave price
A slave could become free if someone paid the slave's owner some money. This was sometimes called 'redeeming' the slave.

God's love
Hosea's life is meant to be a picture of God's endless love for the people he has made.

181 Isaiah chapter 6.

Isaiah
This vision began Isaiah's work for God in about 740BC when King Uzziah died. Isaiah spoke mostly to the southern kingdom of Judah, and lived in Jerusalem with his family.

179 Amos, the trouble-maker

God gave Amos a vision: 'I saw God himself standing beside a well-built wall. He was holding a plumb line in his hand to show how straight it was. God was holding his plumb line against his people. He knows how crooked they are and how they have disobeyed him. He will punish them.'

Amaziah the priest was angry when he heard what Amos was saying. He wrote to the king: 'Amos is stirring up trouble. He says that you will be killed, that Israel will be conquered, and the people taken into exile.'

He went to Amos. 'Get out!' he said. 'Go back home! Go and give God's messages to your own people!'

180 The loving husband

Then God chose another man, Hosea, to be his messenger. 'Your whole life will be a picture for my people in Israel,' said God. 'I want you to marry a woman who will hurt you, and make you sad. She will leave you and forget all about you. But you will keep on loving her.'

So Hosea married Gomer, and they had some children. But she left him for another man. Eventually she became a slave.

'Now go and get your wife back,' said God. 'Buy her out of slavery. Live together and keep on loving her.'

Hosea paid the price to get his wife back, and he loved her.

'I love the people of Israel just like you love Gomer,' explained God. 'They have hurt me and made me sad. They have ignored me and left me for other things. They will be punished, but I will keep on loving them.'

181 Isaiah's vision

One day, a man called Isaiah was in the temple. He had a vision of God.

High above Isaiah was a magnificent throne. On it sat God himself, great and majestic, and wonderful beyond imagining. He was wearing the robe of a king, which was so long that it filled the whole temple.

Isaiah looked up. He saw some strange creatures with six wings. The seraphs darted and flew about the temple, calling to one another, 'Holy! Holy!

God, the Lord Almighty, is holy!'

As soon as they spoke, everything shook, and the room filled with smoke. Then Isaiah realized that he was standing in the presence of the most holy God. 'Help me!' he cried. 'What can I do? I am a sinner and I live among sinful people!'

One of the seraphs flew down to the altar and picked up a burning coal with a pair of tongs and flew towards Isaiah. It touched his lips with the coal and said, 'Your guilt has been taken away. God has forgiven your sins!'

Then Isaiah heard the voice of God. 'Who will be my messenger?' Isaiah did not hesitate. 'I will!' he said. 'I am here. Send me!'

182 The future king

God sent Isaiah to his people with a message: 'God has seen all the wrong things you have done. No one will escape God's punishment. Time is running out.'

Most people ignored him. The kings did not want to hear what the prophet had to say. 'Turn away from your wrongdoing,' Isaiah told the people of Judah, 'and say sorry to God before it is too late.'

No one wanted to hear bad news. But Isaiah also had good news: 'God will remember us. Something wonderful will happen. A child will be born and his coming will be like a great light for all people everywhere. He will be called the Prince of Peace. He will be born into the family of King David, and God's own Spirit will be with him.'

Some time later Isaiah told the people, 'This child will be rejected by his people. He will suffer and die, but when he dies he will take the punishment for our sins, so that we can be forgiven. Wait and see.'

Isaiah was certain that God would send a Saviour for his people.

183 God's messenger

Jeremiah was another prophet. He was only a teenager when he first heard God speaking to him. As his father was a priest, he was destined to become a priest too. But God had other plans for him.

'I have known you since before you were born,' said God. 'It was then that I chose you to be my messenger.'

Jeremiah was surprised. 'But I'm only a child,' he answered. 'I don't know how to be a prophet!'

'I will be with you,' God replied. 'I will rescue you from your enemies.'

Suddenly Jeremiah felt a hand touch his lips. 'I have just put my words in your mouth,' said God.

A picture started to form before Jeremiah's eyes. In his vision he saw a pot, full of a scalding, boiling liquid. It was tilting towards the south and the burning liquid was ready to gush out.

'The people of Judah have been disobedient. They worship idols, they do not obey my laws. They will be destroyed by an enemy from the north,' explained God. 'Now Jeremiah, get ready to tell them my message. They will not like it, and they will be angry with you. But remember, I am with you.'

Seraphs
Their name means 'burning ones'. They might be the same as the 'living creatures' Jesus' friend, John, saw (see story 362).

182 Isaiah chapters 1, 9, and 53.

The child
Isaiah's prophecy about the child to be born into King David's family looks forward to the birth of Jesus over 700 years later.

📖 See Feature pages 12-13.

The suffering Messiah
Isaiah's later prophecy refers to Jesus' suffering and death on the cross. There was a growing belief that a Messiah or Saviour would come to rescue the Israelites. He was usually thought of as a king like David, who was a great fighter. But Jesus came to save his people from sin and death, not from their political enemies.

183 Jeremiah chapter 1.

Jeremiah
Preaching between about 620 and 585BC, before and after the time when Jerusalem was destroyed by the Babylonians, Jeremiah came from a priestly family.

Jeremiah's vision
The pot of boiling liquid represented the Babylonians who would sweep down on Judah from the countries to the north (the Assyrian Empire) which they had conquered.

184 Jeremiah chapters 18 to 19.

The potter
As Jeremiah watched the potter at work God showed him that the people he had made needed to be shaped to be perfect. When they made mistakes, God had to reshape them to be useful again.

185 Jeremiah chapter 36, verses 1-7.

Scrolls
Scrolls were long rolls of parchment made from the cleaned and flattened skin of animals such as calves, goats or sheep. The skin was stretched, scraped, dried and scraped again to take away the shiny surface, then rolled up until needed.

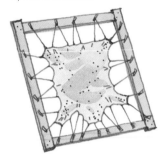

An important date
Jeremiah dictated his message in 605BC. King Nebuchadnezzar had just beaten the Egyptians who had protected Judah. Now Judah was open to attack.

Baruch
Coming from a family of scribes, Baruch was a well-educated man.

Banned
Jeremiah had already been beaten and put in the stocks. The people did not like his message so they banned him from going near the temple.

184 The clay on the wheel

The years passed. Jeremiah kept warning the people of Judah about the disaster that would certainly come unless they turned back to God. But nobody wanted to listen.

One day, Jeremiah heard God's voice. 'Go down to the potter's house. Watch what he is doing, because I want to give you a message.'

Jeremiah stood in the potter's house and watched as the potter threw a lump of clay onto the spinning wheel. The clay spun on the wheel, and the potter carefully cupped his wet hands around it, pulling the clay up and out into the shape of a pot. But suddenly the wheel stopped spinning. The pot was misshapen and useless. The potter picked up the clay, made a new shape and threw it back on the wheel once more.

'Learn from the potter,' said God. 'I have as much power over the people of Judah as that potter has over the clay. I will let the people of Judah suffer, so that in the end they will become something useful and perfect.'

185 The words on the scroll

For many years Jeremiah had warned the people of coming disaster. But still they did not turn back to God. Even when the Babylonians attacked Judah from the north, no one took Jeremiah's message seriously.

'Buy a scroll,' said God to Jeremiah, 'and write down everything I have ever told you. Perhaps when the people hear it, they will see how wicked they have been, and I will be able to forgive them.'

Jeremiah dictated everything to Baruch, who wrote Jeremiah's words down on the scroll.

'Take this scroll to the temple,' said Jeremiah. 'I have been banned from going there. Go on a special day, when there will be lots of people there. Read to them everything that you have written. Maybe they will understand what they have done, and ask God to forgive them.'

186 King Jehoiakim burns the scroll

Baruch went to the temple and read from the scroll. The people listened to all the things God had told Jeremiah about what would happen. Eventually one of King Jehoiakim's secretaries, Jehudi, heard about it. 'Come and read the scroll to me and my colleagues,' he said.

So Baruch went to the secretaries' room in the royal palace. He read Jeremiah's words. The men listened. They heard God's warning. They were terrified. 'We must tell the king,' they said. 'And you and Jeremiah must hide.'

Jehudi, the king's secretary, took the scroll to King Jehoiakim. It was winter and he was sitting by an open fire. Jehudi unrolled the scroll and read. He had only read a few columns before Jehoiakim told him to stop. The king took a knife, cut the words from the scroll and threw them carelessly into the fire. The more Jehudi read, the more Jehoiakim cut from the scroll and threw into the flames, until the whole scroll was burned. The king and his attendants were not the slightest bit worried.

The king sent his men to find Jeremiah and Baruch but they were well hidden.

'Start again,' said God to Jeremiah. 'Write on another scroll. I will punish Jehoiakim because he has refused to listen to me.'

187 Two baskets of figs

Nothing could stop the Babylonians attacking Judah. They captured officials, builders and craftsmen and took them away to Babylon. King Nebuchadnezzar of Babylon asked Zedekiah to be king of Judah.

The people who remained in Jerusalem thought they had escaped God's punishment. They were pleased with themselves. But the people in captivity remembered the words of warning the prophets had given them. They wished they had listened. They were sorry they had disobeyed God.

Jeremiah also remained in Jerusalem. One day he was near the temple. 'Look at those two baskets of figs,' said God. 'What can you see?'

'One basket is full of good, ripe figs,' replied Jeremiah. 'The other figs are rotten. They're useless!'

'Think about the figs,' said God. 'The people who are in captivity in Babylon are like the good figs. I will watch them and look after them, until the time is right for them to return. But the rotten figs are like King Zedekiah and all those who are left in Jerusalem. They are so bad that they are not fit to be saved.'

186 Jeremiah chapter 36, verses 8-32.

Secretaries

Only a few people could read and write. People like Baruch wrote letters and business papers for others. In later times these writers were called scribes and they became experts in Jewish law.

📖 See Feature pages 178-79.

187 Jeremiah chapter 24.

Judah attacked

The Babylonians attacked in 597BC. The leaders and skilled people were taken away to stop Judah rebelling or growing strong again.

Good figs

The children of people who were taken away would return about 70 years later. They were like the good figs in the basket, and would make a fresh start for God's people. But they would be opposed by those who had stayed behind (stories 207-214).

Zedekiah

He was the uncle of Jehoiachin, who had been taken away. His real name was Mattaniah, but Nebuchadnezzar forced him to change it to show he would do everything the Babylonians said.

188 Jeremiah chapter 32.

Siege
Often armies camped around the city they were attacking to frighten the people and stop them going out for food and water. Then they would grow weak and be beaten easily.

Jeremiah's field
People thought Jeremiah was mad to buy a field when the Babylonians were about to come and take over all the land. But it was a sign of hope, that one day the land would belong to the people of Judah again.

There were no coins in Jeremiah's time. He paid for the field with lumps of silver to an agreed weight measured in shekels: a shekel was just under 12g/0.5oz. He paid 17 shekels, about 200g/7oz.

189 Jeremiah chapter 37.

Egypt attacks
Judah had an agreement that Egypt would protect it if it was attacked. Jeremiah had always said this was not God's plan and that it wouldn't work.

Prison
People who committed crimes usually had to pay fines or were punished by being beaten, not put in prison. Jeremiah's prison was probably a room inside the palace guardroom where the soldiers lived. Soldiers dealt with any trouble or law-breaking.

188 Under siege

Now the city of Jerusalem was under siege from the Babylonians. King Zedekiah imprisoned Jeremiah in the courtyard of the palace. 'Why do you keep telling me that God wants us to give in to the Babylonians?' he asked.

Jeremiah explained that God had shown him what was to happen, but Zedekiah would not believe him.

In the midst of all the confusion, God spoke to Jeremiah, 'Your cousin Hanamel will come to see you. He will want you to buy a field from him. Do so.'

So when Jeremiah received a visit from Hanamel, he bought the field, and had the papers signed, sealed and witnessed. But Jeremiah had doubts. Why buy land when God had already said that everything was going to be destroyed?

'Lord God,' said Jeremiah. 'I know that nothing is impossible with you, but why did you want me to buy that field?'

'That field is a sign of what will happen,' said God. 'Jerusalem will be destroyed, because my people have refused to listen to me. But I promise that they will come back to live here, and fields will once more be bought and sold. I will look after my people. I will give them good things, and I will be their God.'

189 Jeremiah thrown in prison

King Zedekiah still refused to listen to Jeremiah, but he sent him a message. 'Pray to God for us.'

Then the Egyptians attacked the Babylonians and the Babylonians gave up their siege of Jerusalem.

'Don't think our troubles are over,' said Jeremiah. 'This is what God has said will happen. The Egyptians will stop their attack, and the Babylonians will return to Jerusalem and they will destroy us.'

Now the siege was over, Jeremiah was free to leave the city. He decided to go to see the field he had bought.

'Why are you leaving the city?' demanded the captain of the guard. 'You traitor! You are going to join the Babylonians!'

'That's not true!' cried Jeremiah. But the soldier would not listen. Jeremiah was beaten and locked up in prison.

Day after day, Jeremiah stayed in the prison. So much time passed that Jeremiah thought the king had forgotten him. Then Zedekiah sent for Jeremiah.

'Have you any message from God for me?' asked King Zedekiah.

'Yes!' replied Jeremiah. 'You will be destroyed by the Babylonians. Now let me out. I have done nothing wrong!'

King Zedekiah released Jeremiah.

190 At the bottom of the well

Jeremiah continued to warn people about the disaster which was to come. 'God has told us to surrender to the Babylonians,' he said. 'If we do, we will live.'

Some of the soldiers listened. They did not want to fight.

'Jeremiah is discouraging the soldiers,' some officials told the king. 'He should be put to death!'

'Do what you want,' said Zedekiah weakly.

So the officials took Jeremiah and threw him into a deep well. It was empty. Jeremiah sank into the mud at the bottom. As he sat in the darkness, he thought he was going to die.

'Your majesty,' said Ebed-Melech, one of the king's officials, when he heard what had happened. 'Jeremiah will die if he is left in the well. These men have acted wickedly against him.'

Zedekiah was weary. 'Bring him out before he dies,' he said.

Ebed-Melech found some rope and hauled Jeremiah up out of the well and into the light.

191 The Babylonians attack

'I want to know the truth!' said King Zedekiah. 'What will happen to me?'

'I have told you many, many times,' said Jeremiah, 'but you do not listen. Unless you surrender to the Babylonians, you and your family will die.'

'But I'm afraid!' wailed Zedekiah. 'What will they do to me if I surrender?'

'If you obey God, you will live,' Jeremiah reassured him.

But Zedekiah did not listen. The Babylonians laid siege to Jerusalem once more and Zedekiah tried to escape. The Babylonians took him captive. They raided the temple, set fire to the buildings and broke down the walls. They put the people in chains and took them off to Babylon. Only a few poor people were left behind to work in the fields.

A captain in the Babylonian guard saw Jeremiah, who was in chains. 'All this happened just as you said it would, because your people ignored your God,' said the captain. 'I will let you go. You can come with me to Babylon, or you can stay here. You are free to make your own decision.'

Then Jeremiah knew that God had kept his promise. He had rescued him. Jeremiah turned away. He wanted to stay in his own land of Judah, living with the poor.

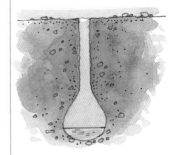

190 Jeremiah chapter 38.

The well
This was used to store rainwater underground and was very deep. It would be impossible to climb out without a ladder or rope. Wells or cisterns like this were usually shaped like an onion at the bottom, with a long narrow shaft leading up to the surface. It took 30 men to pull Jeremiah out of the sticky mud.

Joseph was thrown into a similar well by his brothers (story 33).

191 Jeremiah chapter 38, verse 14 to chapter 40, verse 6.

More captives
This second attack happened in 586BC, 11 years after the first (story 187). The captives taken away from Jerusalem had to walk to Babylon, about 1450km/900 miles away.

Jeremiah's last days
Sadly Jeremiah would not stay for long in Jerusalem. Some people killed the governor of the city and fled to Egypt, forcing Jeremiah and Baruch to go with them. Jeremiah continued to speak God's word even in Egypt.

192 Jonah chapter 1, verses 1-3.

Jonah

He probably lived around 750BC, about the same time as Amos and Isaiah.

Nineveh

This was the capital of Assyria, Israel's enemy. It housed about 120,000 people and had beautiful palaces and government buildings. Water was brought to it along a 48km/30 mile canal.

Tarshish

This was probably in Spain, the opposite direction to Nineveh.

193 Jonah chapter 1, verses 4-16.

Ships and storms

The ship was quite small, powered by sails and oars. Heavy storms often happen in the Mediterranean Sea; the apostle Paul was shipwrecked by one (stories 331-33).

Drawing lots

They probably put some pebbles in a bag, with one pebble specially marked. Each person drew out a pebble. The one who got the marked pebble was chosen.

Sailors' gods

The sailors prayed to the gods their families had chosen as their special gods. They may have prayed to small images of the gods.

192 God sends Jonah

Jonah was a prophet, one of God's special messengers. One day he heard God speaking to him.

'I want you to go to Nineveh, the capital of the Assyrian Empire,' said God. 'I have seen the wicked things that go on there. I know how disobedient the people are. I want you to go there and preach my message.'

But Jonah did not want to go to Nineveh. Instead, he ran in the opposite direction, towards the port of Joppa. He found a ship that was sailing to Tarshish, paid his fare, went aboard and hid himself.

193 Jonah at sea

Jonah went below deck, and fell into a deep sleep.

Outside the sky turned black and the wind suddenly changed direction. The sea grew rough and the wind and the waves battered against the ship. The sailors were petrified. They thought they were going to drown. They threw their cargo into the sea to lighten the ship. They clung on to one another and cried out to their own gods.

'Help us! Save us!' they shouted. But the storm kept raging.

The captain noticed Jonah was missing. He went below deck to find him.

'Wake up!' he cried, shaking Jonah. 'How can you sleep when we are all going to die? Pray to your god to save us!'

'This storm is someone's fault!' cried the sailors to one another. 'Let's find out who.' They began to draw lots. Jonah was chosen.

'What have you done?' they asked Jonah, through the howling wind.

'I have run away from the living God,' he replied. 'The God who made the land and the sea.'

'How can we make the storm go away?' they asked.

'Throw me into the sea!' said Jonah. 'This is all my fault. Nothing else will save you and the ship.'

The sailors were horrified. They did not want Jonah to drown. They tried to row back to shore, but the wind and waves grew more and more wild.

The sailors prayed to the living God. 'Forgive us for killing this man!' they cried, and picked up Jonah and threw him into the sea.

Immediately the storm stopped. The sailors sank to their knees. They had seen the power of the living God.

194 Inside a big fish

As soon as Jonah hit the water, a huge fish rose up from the sea, and swallowed him whole.

It was dark inside the fish. Jonah began to think. He thought about the way he had behaved, how he had tried to run away from God. He was frightened and he did not know what was happening. He felt as though he had been buried alive.

'Help me,' he said to God. 'You have hurled me into the very heart of the sea. I can feel the currents swirling about me. I can hear the waves crashing over my head. But I know that you are able to save me.'

Suddenly Jonah felt himself being thrown forward out of the fish's mouth as it vomited him on to dry land. Jonah was alone. He had been inside the fish for three days and three nights.

195 God's love for his people

Jonah went to Nineveh. 'Be warned,' he cried. 'God has seen your wickedness! In forty days he will destroy Nineveh.'

The people heard what Jonah said. They believed his message. 'Everyone must fast and pray!' declared the king. 'Perhaps God will see how sorry we are and will not destroy us.'

God watched the people of Nineveh.

'I will not destroy them,' he said.

Jonah was furious. 'I knew you'd forgive them!' he said angrily. 'That's why I didn't want to come to Nineveh in the first place! These people don't deserve to be forgiven. You might as well kill me instead!'

Jonah made a shelter outside the city and sulked. God let a vine grow, to give Jonah some shade. Jonah was pleased. But the next day, God allowed a worm to eat the vine. The vine died and Jonah sat in the heat of the sun.

'Let me die!' he cried to God.

Then God spoke to Jonah. 'Why are you so angry? Listen! I let the vine grow, and I let the vine die. It is only a vine, but you are angry. Try to understand how I feel about the thousands of people who live in Nineveh. They hardly know right from wrong, but I know them and love them because I made them. I do not want them to die. Jonah, do not be angry because I chose to save them.'

194 Jonah chapter 1, verse 17 to chapter 2, verse 10.

The fish
The story does not tell us what fish this was. The word used here simply means 'something huge', and when Jesus refers to it later, the word he uses means 'big fish' or 'sea monster'. The point of the story is that God rescued Jonah from certain death, even though Jonah had done something wrong.

A sperm whale has a throat large enough to swallow a man whole, and pictures of this story usually show a whale.

195 Jonah chapters 3 and 4.

Jonah's anger
Instead of being pleased that the people believed his message and were sorry for all they had done wrong, Jonah was angry. He did not understand that God could love Israel's enemies. It was an important lesson for God's people; through Jonah they learned that God loves everyone.

Jonah's vine
This was probably a castor-oil plant. It grows very quickly and has large overhanging branches and wide leaves which can provide shade.

THE STORY OF JOB

There is no other book in the Bible quite like the Book of Job.
It is mostly written as a long poem. But no one knows for sure who wrote it, or
when. Even the place in which the story is set – Uz – is unknown.

It is nonetheless a very important book. The story is simple. Job is a good man who loves God and has always kept God's laws. He is rich, and has a large, happy family. He has everything he could want. One day, in a series of dreadful disasters, he loses everything. Then he is ill. His sufferings have begun.

Job is a man who knows and loves God. Even though his life is in ruins, it does not stop him from coming to God to worship him. Job refuses to blame God for his troubles, but Job's friends blame him for bringing it all on himself. At that time people thought that God rewarded people for being good by giving them wealth and happiness. They thought the opposite was also true: if God was angry with someone, then he would punish them and make them suffer. But Job knew that his wrongdoings did not deserve so great a punishment.

The story of Job looks at a common question: why do good people suffer bad things? Job and his friends do not get a direct answer to that question but, by the end of the book, they begin to understand that God is more mysterious and far greater than Job's troubles and all his questions. In the end, God gives Job back his health and he starts a new life.

196 Job chapter 1, verse 1 to chapter 2, verse 10.

God's enemy
Satan is the name given to the devil. It means 'someone who accuses others'. He is an evil spirit who is opposed to God and God's people. He is pictured as a snake or serpent in the story of the Garden of Eden (story 3).

Satan's power
The writer of Job shows us that Satan cannot do anything he likes. He is like a dog on a long lead; God holds him back from doing more damage.

196 Job's troubles

Job was a wealthy man. He owned thousands of sheep and camels, and hundreds of donkeys and oxen. He had a large and happy family. He was also a good man. He was honest and he obeyed God.

One day God's enemy, Satan, came to God. 'Where have you been?' asked God.

'Roaming the earth,' replied Satan.

'Have you seen Job?' asked God. 'He is a truly good man. There is no one else like him.'

'It's easy for him to be good,' sneered Satan, 'when you have given him so much. If everything were to be taken from him, I bet he wouldn't follow you or be obedient to you. He'd be just like everyone else.'

'Take away everything he has,' said God. 'But do not harm him.'

Satan left God's presence and went to work. He caused freak lightning to fall from the sky and burn up the sheep and servants. Raiders carried off the camels, and a whirlwind killed Job's children.

Job was devastated. But he still came to God to worship him.

'He would not worship you if he became ill and was in pain!' challenged Satan angrily.

'We'll see,' said God. 'But do not take his life.'

Then Job was covered all over in painful sores.

'Curse God and die!' urged his wife.

'No,' replied Job. 'We enjoyed the good things that God gave us and now we must accept trouble and suffering.'

197 Job's friends

Job had three friends. When they heard about his troubles they came to see him. At first they were shocked. He looked so different. They tore their clothes and wept, they felt so sorry for him. No one knew what to say, so they sat with him, in silence, for seven days.

At last Job spoke. 'Why was I born?' he cried. 'What I dreaded most has happened to me.'

'Well,' said Eliphaz. 'As far as I know, no one suffers in the way you are suffering without having done something terribly wrong. You must have sinned. Go and tell God what you have done, and then you will be well again.'

'But I have not done anything wrong,' said Job.

'Well, if you won't admit you've done something terrible, no wonder you are still suffering!' said Bildad. 'Think back to how God has worked in the past. Surely he doesn't let good people suffer?'

'As far as I know, I haven't done anything!' replied Job. 'I will ask God to tell me what, if anything, I have done, and why I am suffering.'

'Maybe you have done something so terrible you will have to suffer even more!' responded Zophar.

'You three are of no comfort to me!' cried Job. 'I know what I have and have not done. One day the truth will be known.'

But although Job prayed earnestly to God, there was no answer.

198 God speaks to Job

Suddenly God spoke. 'You have asked me why you are suffering. Now let me ask you something.'

'Where were you when I laid the foundations of the world? Have you ever been to the place where I store snow and hail? Can you send a bolt of lightning through the sky? Have you ever given strength to a horse or taught a hawk to fly?'

'I don't know what to say,' replied Job. He had no answer.

'But you must answer me,' continued God, 'because you have questioned what has happened to you. I made the hippopotamus and the crocodile. They are wild and dangerous and everyone is afraid of them. Yet still you think you can speak to me as an equal, you think you can understand everything I do!'

Job felt very small. He realized how great God was. He did not need to know why he was suffering. He knew that God would not let him down.

'I said things I did not understand,' said Job. 'There are things which are too wonderful for me to know.'

'Your friends were wrong,' said God. 'You did not suffer because of your sin. They must ask you to forgive them.'

Job forgave his friends. Then God blessed Job. He gave him far more than he had had before, and he enjoyed a long and prosperous life.

197 Job chapter 2, verse 11 to chapter 31, verse 40.

The problem
The friends believe Job is suffering because he has sinned. But the Bible doesn't say that suffering is a direct punishment for our wrongdoing. It happens to all sorts of people because the world is imperfect.

The friends
They kept quiet for a while. But when they did speak they brought clever arguments instead of the comfort, love and support Job needed.

A fourth speaker
Job had another friend called Elihu. He told Job that suffering had a purpose. It was like the painful training an athlete does, and makes people ready to serve God.

198 Job chapters 38 to 42.

God is great
God has made all things, including the crocodile and the hippopotamus, and only he understands everything.

Job encourages God's people to trust God even when things go wrong.

INTO EXILE AND BACK

Starting at the court of King Nebuchadnezzar in Babylon, this section begins
with the story of Daniel. Everything the prophets had said had come true.
In about 587BC, Jerusalem and its temple were destroyed and most of the
people were taken away to Babylon. This time is known as 'the exile'.

Babylon was about 1450km/900 miles from Judah, and most of the people had to walk there. The people started a new life in a foreign land with different customs. Some of them, like Daniel and his friends, were chosen to work in the royal palace. Others, like Ezekiel the prophet, encouraged the people by reminding them that God had not left them.

After about fifty years the Babylonians were conquered by the Persians. (The book of Esther gives us a picture of life in Persia.) The new king, Cyrus, allowed many of the captives in Babylon to return home if they wanted to go. Some of the children and the grandchildren of those who had left Jerusalem decided to make the long journey back. When they arrived, they began to rebuild the ruined temple and mend the city walls.

Life was hard. Jerusalem was in ruins. Some people who had been living there a long time didn't like the newcomers at all and tried to stop them rebuilding the city. But with the encouragement of Ezra and Nehemiah, the temple was finished, and the city walls repaired.

After Ezra read God's Law to the people, they dedicated their lives to God afresh, and looked forward to the new king, foretold by the prophets, who would be sent by God. It was 400 years later that the birth of this king, Jesus, was recorded in the New Testament.

199 Daniel chapter 1, verses 1-21.

Forbidden foods
In Babylon, the first portion of all foods was offered to pagan gods. The Babylonians also ate pigs and horses which the Jews were not allowed, and all other meat was butchered in ways which broke Jewish food laws. So Daniel chose to eat things which were the least 'unclean'.

📖 See Feature pages 54-55.

The king's diet
To eat the food someone had prepared for you was a sign that you were loyal friends. Daniel wanted to show he was loyal to God first, so he wouldn't eat the food chosen by the king.

199 A special diet

When King Nebuchadnezzar conquered Jerusalem, he took Jewish captives back to Babylon. He asked Ashpenaz, his chief officer, to select some young men to be educated and trained as his advisors.

'I want the best,' he ordered. 'Choose those who are healthy, intelligent and quick to learn.'

Four of the young men chosen were from the royal palace in Judah. One of them was called Daniel. Now Daniel and his friends were well looked after. They were given food and wine from the king's own table. But Daniel was unhappy. He did not want to eat any of the foods which were forbidden by God.

'If you don't stay strong and healthy, the king will have me executed!' said Ashpenaz. 'He has chosen your diet himself.'

Daniel had an idea. He spoke to the guard. 'Just give me and my friends vegetables and water,' he said. 'Do it for ten days. If we look weak and ill after that time, we will eat whatever you like.'

Ten days later, Daniel and his friends were healthier than the other young men. God blessed them and gave them special abilities, and Daniel was able to understand visions and dreams.

After three years' training, the four young men were presented to Nebuchadnezzar. He was amazed at their wisdom and understanding. He put them to work.

200 Nebuchadnezzar's dream

King Nebuchadnezzar was worried. His mind was full of strange thoughts and vivid dreams. He wanted to know the meaning of them.

'Tell us what you dreamed, and we will explain it to you,' his wise men replied.

The king shook his head. 'No, you tell me what I dreamed and what it means, or I will have you all killed!'

'It's impossible!' they cried. 'No one on earth could do that!'

Nebuchadnezzar was angry and ordered their execution.

Arioch, the king's official, set off to carry out the order.

'Why is the king doing this?' asked Daniel.

When Arioch explained, Daniel asked to see the king and begged for time to be able to tell him the meaning of the dream.

'Pray to God,' he urged his friends.

During the night, God showed Daniel the meaning of the dream. The next day he went to the king.

'Your majesty, only God can tell you the meaning of your dream,' began Daniel. 'You saw a huge statue, with a golden head, chest and arms of silver, bronze thighs, legs of iron and feet of iron and clay. A strange rock came and shattered the statue. Then the pieces blew away, and the rock became a mountain as big as the earth.'

'This is what it means,' continued Daniel. 'Everything you have has been given to you by God. You are the golden head. Other powerful kingdoms will come after you, but God will set up a kingdom that will be greater than any of them.'

King Nebuchadnezzar fell at Daniel's feet. 'Your God is the true God!' he cried.

201 The golden statue

It did not take long for Nebuchadnezzar to forget Daniel's God.

Instead, he made an enormous statue. It was made of gold, and he set it on a plain for everyone to see. Then Nebuchadnezzar called everyone of any importance to stand before the statue.

Suddenly a herald appeared. 'This is a royal command,' declared the herald. 'As soon as you hear the sound of music, you must bow down and worship the statue King Nebuchadnezzar has made. Anyone who fails to do this will be thrown into a furnace of fire!'

The music sounded. Everyone fell down to worship the statue.

200 Daniel chapter 2, verses 1-49.

Dreams
God does sometimes speak through dreams in the Bible (stories 24, 34, 35, 227).

The dream statue
Nebuchadnezzar's dream seems to foresee kingdoms which would replace Babylon as world leaders in the future: the chest, the Persian Empire; the thighs, the Greek Empire; and the legs and feet, the Roman Empire.

God's kingdom
Daniel reminds Nebuchadnezzar that God is king over all nations. God's new heaven and earth would replace all other kingdoms one day.

Daniel's God
The king made Daniel ruler over the province of Babylon because his God was able to tell him the meaning of his dream.

201 Daniel chapter 3, verses 1-7.

The golden statue
This was 27m/90ft high and only 2.7m/9ft wide. The king wanted to unite his empire with just one religion.

The furnace
This may have been a kiln for firing pottery, or an oven for melting metal, with an open top and an open door at the side.

202 Daniel chapter 3, verses 8-30.

Astrologers
Astrologers believe the stars control people's lives and show what will happen in the future.

The highest temperature
The heat was controlled by bellows forcing air into the fire chamber. Seven bellows were pumped at the same time to make the furnace as hot as possible. It was so hot that the soldiers who took the three men to the furnace were killed by the heat.

The fourth man
God protected the three men. The fourth person was probably an angel.

203 Daniel chapter 5, verses 1-30.

Many years
The date of this story is probably about 539BC, shortly before the Persians conquered Babylon.

Belshazzar
A new Babylonian king, Nabonidus, had taken over from Nebuchadnezzar. Nabonidus was always away fighting wars, so he left his son, Belshazzar, in charge of things at home.

The hand writing
The words were for everyday weights and measures, so the meaning was not obvious.

202 Into the furnace

'Your majesty,' said some of King Nebuchadnezzar's astrologers. 'Not everyone is obeying your decree. There are three Jews, Shadrach, Meshach and Abednego, who refuse to worship the statue.'

The king was furious. He sent for the three men. They were Daniel's friends, and they had been given positions of great responsibility.

'Is it true that you refuse to obey me?' he demanded.

The three men replied, 'If you throw us into the fire, our God is able to rescue us. And even if he does not, we will not worship anyone but him.'

In a rage, the king ordered that the furnace be heated to the highest temperature, and that the three men be tied up and thrown into the fire.

Nebuchadnezzar watched as they were thrown in. Suddenly he shouted, 'I can see four men walking around in the fire! Get them out!'

The three men stepped out of the fire, completely unharmed.

'Praise the living God!' exclaimed Nebuchadnezzar in amazement. 'He sent an angel to rescue you, because you were prepared to die rather than worship the statue I had made.'

Then Nebuchadnezzar issued another decree. 'No one must say anything against the living God!'

203 The writing on the wall

The years passed. A new king ruled in Babylon. His name was Belshazzar. One day he gave a magnificent feast. He invited all his nobles, and ordered that the wine be served in the gold and silver goblets that Nebuchadnezzar had taken from the temple in Jerusalem. The guests ate and drank. They raised their goblets and shouted, 'Praise be to the gods of silver and bronze!'

Suddenly the fingers of a human hand appeared and the fingers moved against the wall. The feasting stopped. Belshazzar shivered and shook as the fingers began to write. He was terrified and collapsed on the floor.

The fingers wrote: 'MENE, MENE, TEKEL, PARSIN.'

'Whoever can tell me the meaning of this will be the most powerful person in the land after me,' promised the king.

All the magicians and wise men examined the writing. No one could tell him the meaning. Then the Queen Mother remembered Daniel, so he was sent for.

'Tell me what it means, and I will reward you,' said the king. 'I don't want a reward,' said Daniel. 'God sent this hand to write on the wall because he has seen your wickedness. Your kingdom will be taken by the Medes and the Persians.'

Belshazzar knew he had heard the truth. That night the Persian army attacked and Belshazzar was killed.

204 A plot against Daniel

When Darius the Persian became king, he made Daniel one of his top three administrators. Daniel worked hard and Darius was so impressed he wanted to put Daniel in charge of the whole kingdom. The other officials were jealous of Daniel. They wanted to bring him down. But however hard they tried, they could not find fault with anything Daniel did.

'It's useless!' they whispered to one another. 'The only way we will ever find fault with Daniel is if it has something to do with his God.'

Slowly an idea began to take shape. They went to see King Darius. 'Your majesty, may you live for ever!' they said. 'We all think that you should issue a decree. No one must pray to anyone but you for the next thirty days. If they do, they should be thrown into a den of lions!'

Darius was flattered. He liked the idea. He even put it in writing. Now it was law. Not even the king could alter it.

205 Daniel and the lions

Daniel heard about the decree, but as usual he went to his room upstairs three times a day to kneel before God and pray.

The men who were jealous of Daniel watched as he prayed and then they went to see the king.

'Your majesty,' they said, 'are we right in thinking that anyone who disobeys your decree will be thrown into a den of lions?'

Darius nodded. 'This decree cannot be altered,' he said.

'But Daniel pays no attention to it,' they said.

Darius was horrified. He knew he had been trapped. He desperately tried to think of a way to rescue Daniel. He knew he was a good man.

'But the law cannot be altered,' repeated the men.

Darius had no choice. He ordered Daniel to be thrown into the lions' den. 'May your God save you,' he said to Daniel.

That night Darius could not sleep. As soon as it was morning, he returned to the lions' den.

'Daniel!' he cried. 'Has your God saved you from the lions?'

'Yes, he has!' shouted Daniel from the den. 'He sent an angel to stop them from hurting me.'

'Release Daniel from the den!' cried Darius, overjoyed to find Daniel alive. 'And punish those men who have tried to hurt him.'

And so Daniel continued faithful to God for the rest of his life.

204 Daniel chapter 6, verses 1-9.

Darius
He may have been the governor of Babylon city, rather than king of the whole country. Such a person would be like a king in local affairs.

Praying to the king
Sometimes kings said they were sons of the gods, so Darius' decree or law would not have surprised the people.

205 Daniel chapter 6, verses 10-28.

The law
The Persians had a rule that said no rule could be changed! 'The law of the Medes and Persians' still means that something can never be changed.

Lions
Lion hunting was a favourite sport of kings in this part of the world. The lions were kept in pits and released so that the king could chase them in his chariot.

Daniel's life
Daniel lived for some while after this. The Bible contains several visions which God gave him about the future, including one of a great 'Son of man' which seems to be a glimpse of Jesus in heaven before he came to earth.

206 Ezekiel chapters 1 to 3.

Ezekiel
Ezekiel, like Daniel, was probably quite young when he was taken to Babylon.

Vision of God
God cannot be seen because he doesn't have a body. People who have visions of him often see lights, clouds or fire, which stand for what God is like: purity and power. Ezekiel fell down because he became aware of that power.

The creatures
These sound like those John saw in his vision of God (story 362). They also teach something about God and heaven. The wheels and wings are pictures of how God and his messengers can be anywhere at any time.

207 Ezekiel chapters 4 and 5.

Ezekiel's picture
Ezekiel drew his picture on a moist clay tablet.

God's message
Ezekiel probably stood his picture in the sand, built a model of ramps beside it and put down lumps of clay for soldiers. He had to lie down beside it and act it out for over a year. But people watched and understood the message.

206 A vision of God

Ezekiel was a priest. When Nebuchadnezzar attacked Jerusalem he had been taken captive and then had settled with other Jewish exiles on the banks of the Kebar River in Babylon.

One day Ezekiel had a great vision of God. First he saw a storm cloud moving towards him. Lightning flashed around the cloud, surrounding it with brilliant light. In the centre was a fire which glowed with intense heat, and within the fire, Ezekiel saw four strange winged creatures which zipped through the sky with lightning speed. Then Ezekiel saw the four creatures moving on the ground, and each had two crystal wheels, trailing fire. The sound of their wings was like a marching army or the roar of a waterfall.

Then Ezekiel heard a voice. The creatures lowered their wings. Above a sapphire throne Ezekiel saw something like a man. He glowed with a brilliant fiery light, and shone with all the colours of the rainbow.

Ezekiel fell to the ground. He knew he was in God's presence.

'Stand up!' said the voice. 'I have chosen you to be my messenger to the Israelites. You must give them my message, even though they will not want to hear it.'

207 Ezekiel's obedience

From the time that Ezekiel had his first vision of God, his job was to take God's message to his people. 'You must warn them,' said God.

The people watched as Ezekiel drew a picture of Jerusalem on a clay brick. Then he made armies, battering rams and ramps, and acted out an attack.

'Ration your food,' said God. Ezekiel ate only a little each day. The people guessed that Jerusalem was being besieged.

'Cut off your hair,' said God, 'and divide it into three piles. This will be a picture of what will happen to my people. Burn one pile in the model city, and chop up another pile with your sword.'

Ezekiel did as he was told, then he took the third pile of hair and threw it in the air. It disappeared on a gust of wind. He found a few strands on the ground and tucked them carefully in his cloak, as if they were very precious.

God would not let all of his people be destroyed. He would look after a few of them, and bring them home again.

208 Ezekiel and the dry bones

Ezekiel understood God's message: his people would suffer and die, but God would keep some of them safe, and take them home to Jerusalem.

Ten years after Jerusalem had been completely destroyed, and God's people in Babylon were ready to give up hope, Ezekiel had another vision. He was standing in the middle of a dry and lifeless valley. The ground was scattered with human bones.

'Do you think these bones can live again?' asked God.

'Only you know that,' replied Ezekiel.

'Speak to them!' said God. 'Tell them that I can make them live!'

Ezekiel spoke. 'God can make you live!' he said. 'He will put you together again. He will give you breath.'

A rattling sound echoed through the valley, and one by one the bones moved and locked together, to form skeletons. Slowly the bones were held together with muscles and tendons, and were wrapped in new skin. Then there was quiet.

'Tell the wind to give these bodies breath!' said God.

Ezekiel spoke to the wind, and the bodies began to breathe. They stood up, and formed a large army.

'I will breathe new life into my people,' said God. 'I will do all that I have promised. Then everyone will know that I am God.'

209 Back to Jerusalem

For years the Jewish captives had lived in Babylon. But now the Babylonian Empire was finished. Cyrus, king of Persia, was in control.

One day, Cyrus issued a surprising decree to the Jewish people. 'I know that God has put me in charge of many people and many nations. He has told me to rebuild the temple in Jerusalem. And so any of you who wishes may return to Jerusalem to help with the work. Those who want to help in other ways can make donations of gold or silver or livestock.'

Everyone was excited. God's promises were coming true! And so a group of excited people, led by Zerubbabel, prepared to leave.

'I will give you all the things Nebuchadnezzar took from the temple,' said Cyrus. 'They don't belong here. They belong with you.'

Laden with all the things they had been given, God's people began their long walk home.

208 Ezekiel chapter 37, verses 1-14.

Dry bones
These are a picture of how the people felt in Babylon. They had no hope of ever being close to God again or of living in their own land. They felt as if they had died.

The wind
In the Bible the same word is used for wind, breath and spirit. Here it is a picture of how God's Spirit brings new spiritual life to people. He changes them and helps them to know and love him.

209 Ezra chapters 1 and 2.

Cyrus
He was the Persian king who defeated Babylon and took over the empire. This event took place in about 538BC.

The return
Cyrus told many different peoples, not just the Jews, to go home. He respected people's faith. The prophet Isaiah calls him 'God's servant'.

Ezra's silver and sheep
The silver and gold were gifts of money from the Persian king. The Jews also took back the treasures which Nebuchadnezzar had looted from the temple. The livestock were partly gifts and partly their own property which they had accumulated over more than 50 years.

Zerubbabel
Zerubbabel was the grandson of King Jehoiachin (story 176). He was a natural choice as leader because he belonged to the old royal family, but he was never called 'king'.

210 Ezra chapters 3 to 6.

Jeshua
Jeshua was the High Priest.

Rebuilding
Cedar wood was brought in ships down the coast from Lebanon and carried over land to Jerusalem on carts. Carpenters sawed and planed it to line the inside of the temple. Stonemasons used chisels and saws to cut blocks of limestone for the walls.

Opposition
The opponents were mostly people who had not been taken into exile and didn't want the Jews to take over control of Judah.

Haggai and Zechariah
Haggai may have been quite old and could remember the previous temple. Zechariah was a priest born in Babylon.

The temple
Over 20 years after the exiles returned to Jerusalem, the temple was finished. It was not as large or beautiful as Solomon's temple had been.

📖 See Feature pages 82-83.

211 Esther chapter 2, verses 1-18.

Xerxes
Xerxes ruled the Persian Empire about 486-465BC. His palace would have been beautiful, with tall pillars, highly decorated walls and grand flights of steps.

210 Rebuilding the temple

When God's people returned home from Babylon, they went first to their home towns. A few months later they all met up in Jerusalem to help rebuild the temple. Jeshua and Zerubbabel rebuilt the altar first. Although the temple was still in ruins, they wanted to show God that they were putting him first by making a sacrifice.

Then they started work on the temple. They hired stonemasons and carpenters. The people gave their gold and silver; they bought cedar wood from Tyre and Sidon in exchange for food, wine and oil.

When the foundations were restored, the people met together to thank God.

'God is good!' they sang. 'His love and goodness last forever!'

But some of the people who were already living in Judah when the exiles returned were not happy. In the years that followed they made up stories about them, and wrote letters full of lies to the kings who were ruling at the time.

'Do not give up!' encouraged the prophets, Haggai and Zechariah. 'Keep on building!'

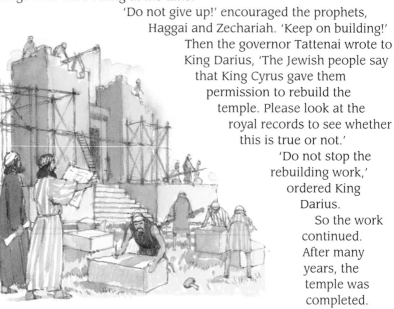

Then the governor Tattenai wrote to King Darius, 'The Jewish people say that King Cyrus gave them permission to rebuild the temple. Please look at the royal records to see whether this is true or not.'

'Do not stop the rebuilding work,' ordered King Darius.

So the work continued. After many years, the temple was completed.

211 Esther is made queen

In the land of Persia lived King Xerxes. He was fabulously wealthy and had everything money could buy. One day he sent to every province in his kingdom to find the most beautiful women so that he could choose one of them to be his queen.

One of the women was called Esther. She was very beautiful and was descended from the Jewish captives who had been taken from Jerusalem by the Babylonians. She had been brought up by her uncle Mordecai because both her parents were dead, and when she was taken to live in the palace with the other girls, her uncle warned her, 'Don't tell them that you are Jewish.' And neither did Esther tell them that Mordecai was her uncle.

After a year of beauty treatments, the young women were taken to the king. When Xerxes saw Esther he gave her a crown.

'You shall be my queen!' he told her.

212 Plots in the palace

Esther's uncle, Mordecai, worked as a palace official. One day he overheard two of King Xerxes' officers planning to kill the king.

When Mordecai told Esther what he had heard, and Esther told the king, the officers were executed. But although the incident was written down in Xerxes' palace records, Mordecai was not rewarded.

At that time the king gave great powers to a man called Haman. Everyone bowed at Haman's feet – except Mordecai.

Haman was angry. He hated Mordecai. He wanted revenge, not just on him, but on his people, for he knew that Mordecai loved the living God.

'Your majesty,' said Haman to Xerxes. 'Did you realize that the Jewish people, who live throughout your kingdom, do not obey your laws? I think you should issue a decree ordering that every one of them be killed on a certain day in eleven months' time.'

The king agreed and ordered his secretaries to write out the decree. He gave Haman his signet ring. 'Do what you like,' he said.

213 Esther risks her life

Mordecai tore his clothes when he heard about the decree. He gave Esther's servant a message, 'Tell Esther to beg the king for mercy. Even she will not escape. Maybe God planned for her to be queen, so she could save her people.'

'Pray and fast for me,' replied Esther. 'I will do whatever I can, even if I have to die.'

The next day, Esther went to see the king. He would have given her half his kingdom if she had asked for it.

'I have prepared a banquet for you and Haman. Please come,' she said.

The king agreed. When Haman received his invitation, he was delighted. He walked past Mordecai, who did not bow. Haman was angry.

'Build a gallows and ask the king to hang Mordecai on it!' laughed his friends.

212 Esther chapter 2, verse 19 to chapter 3, verse 15.

Bowing to Haman
Usually the Jews did not mind bowing to kings and officials as a sign of respect. But Haman was descended from the Amalekites, who had been enemies of the Jews for centuries. Amalek had bullied the Israelites and rebelled against God. Haman seems to have had the same attitude.

Signet ring
This made a special mark in clay or wax. It was the sign of the king's authority. It gave Haman as much power as the king himself.

213 Esther chapter 4, verse 1 to chapter 5, verse 14.

Esther and the king
Although Esther was queen, it was the custom for her to live separately from the king. As a woman, she could only see the king and talk to him when he invited her. If she spoke first when he was in a bad mood, she could be executed! But he was feeling generous, so he let her speak.

The queen's request
Esther was beautiful and it seems that Xerxes loved her. Men and women in Persia used oils to protect their skin from sunburn and perfumes to keep flies and smells away. Some women painted their nails, dyed their hair and wore lipstick and eye shadow.

214 Esther chapter 6.

God's timing
The king's discovery is just in time. It forces Haman to postpone his request to kill the Jews, giving Esther time to reveal the plot first.

215 Esther chapters 7 to 10.

Gallows

In Persia, criminals were sometimes executed by being rammed onto a sharp stake. People were also sometimes killed by a sword and their bodies hung on a stake for all to see.

Changing law
The Persians' rule which said no previous rule could be changed (story 205) meant that the king had to make a new law to let the Jews kill anyone who tried to kill them. It meant that nobody tried.

Annual celebration
Each year Esther's achievement is still celebrated in the feast of Purim. The name 'Purim' comes from a word meaning 'lots', because Haman drew the date of his intended murder out of a hat.

214 Mordecai is rewarded

That night, King Xerxes could not sleep. 'Read me the history of my reign,' he said to one of his servants.

The servant read. He came to the time when Mordecai had overheard the plot against the king.

'How was he rewarded?' asked the king.

'He wasn't,' said the servant.

Just then Haman arrived at the palace. He wanted to ask the king to agree to Mordecai's hanging. But Xerxes wanted his advice.

'What do you think is a suitable reward for someone with whom the king is pleased?' he asked.

Haman smiled to himself. He felt sure that the king was talking about him. 'Dress him in a royal robe,' said Haman. 'Let him ride one of your own horses through the streets. Proclaim in a loud voice so that everyone can hear, "This is how the king rewards the man he is pleased with!"'

'Excellent!' said the king. 'Please do this for Mordecai.'

Haman felt ill. He obeyed the king, but as soon as he could, he rushed home.

'You are in terrible trouble!' cried his friends. 'The king is pleased with Mordecai. You will be punished!'

Haman had no time to think. The king's servants arrived to take him to Esther's banquet.

215 The enemy is discovered

The banquet began.

'What would you like me to give you, Queen Esther?' asked Xerxes.

'Your majesty,' said Esther. 'Please save my people. Someone wants to destroy them, and they will all be killed.'

'Who wants to destroy your people?' demanded the king.

'Haman!' said Esther, pointing at him.

Haman was terrified. The king looked angrily at him.

'Have mercy, Queen Esther!' begged Haman. But he knew that there was no escape.

'Haman has built a gallows on which to hang Mordecai,' said a servant.

'Let him hang on it instead!' said the king. 'Take him away!'

Esther told the king everything. 'Please do not let my people be killed,' she begged.

'I cannot undo Haman's decree, but I can help the Jews fight their enemies and defend themselves,' replied the king.

Then Xerxes gave Mordecai all the power that he had once given to Haman. The Jews were safe. Every year after that they met to remember how Queen Esther had saved them.

216 Ezra returns to Jerusalem

More than sixty years after the first group of exiles returned to Jerusalem, another group followed. Ezra, their leader, was a priest and a good teacher. He had studied God's Law and knew it well.

King Artaxerxes of Persia had given Ezra permission to return. He wrote, 'I decree that you may return with anyone who wants to go. Take a copy of God's Law, and my treasurers will give you what you need. You must teach the people God's laws and report back to me.'

Ezra was amazed. He called the people to get ready. 'I have not asked the king to protect us on our journey,' he said, 'because I had already told him that God would look after us. So let's fast and pray before we go.'

When they arrived in Jerusalem, they met with the others who had returned. Some of the leaders came to Ezra, embarrassed. 'Since we have returned, some of our people have married people who do not believe in the living God.'

'What?' cried Ezra, tearing his clothes. He fell on his knees. 'I am so sorry,' he prayed. 'We never learn. We make the same mistakes again and again. Please forgive us.'

Some of the people heard what Ezra said. They knew he was right. A large group of men, women and children joined him. They cried to God with him.

'We have sinned,' they said. 'Forgive us and show us how we can obey you.'

217 Nehemiah asks for help

In Babylon there lived a faithful servant of God called Nehemiah. He was the cupbearer to King Artaxerxes.

One day Hanani, his brother, brought news from Jerusalem. 'The city walls are still in ruins,' he reported.

Nehemiah wept when he heard this. He refused to eat and he prayed. 'Lord God, please listen to my prayer. I know that we, your people, have disobeyed you. I am sorry for all the wrong things we have done. I know that we were taken into exile because of our disobedience. But you also promised to return to Jerusalem those people who were obedient. Please let me go back to Jerusalem.'

Nehemiah went to see King Artaxerxes.

'Why do you look so sad, Nehemiah?' asked Artaxerxes.

Nehemiah knew that God was with him, so he told the king what he had heard. 'Please let me go to Jerusalem,' he said. 'And if you agree to let me go, please provide me with protection for my journey and the materials to rebuild the city gates and walls.'

God answered his prayer. Artaxerxes agreed to everything.

216 Ezra chapters 7 to 10.

Exiles
The Jews became exiles when they were forced to live in Babylon.

Ezra
Ezra was a scribe and a priest.

Artaxerxes
He was king of Persia and ruled from 464 to 424BC.

Sixty years
Ezra went to Jerusalem in about 458BC, after the time of Esther.

The journey
They took a long route from Babylon to Jerusalem, 1450km/900 miles, to avoid the dry and hilly desert. Usually a group carrying gold and silver would have had an armed guard to protect them from robbers.

Wrong marriage
The Jews were forbidden to marry people who were not Jews, because this would weaken the nation's faith in God (see stories 154, 157).

See Feature pages 22-23.

217 Nehemiah chapter 1, verse 1 to chapter 2, verse 8.

Nehemiah
As cupbearer to the Persian king, Nehemiah had to taste the wine before the king in case it had been poisoned.

218 Nehemiah chapter 2, verse 11 to chapter 4, verse 23.

Broken walls
The people who had returned to Jerusalem about 60 years before had built the temple (story 210). But Jerusalem itself could easily be attacked as it had no walls or gates.

Opponents
The people who tried to stop the building this time were Samaritans, Ammonites and Arabs. None of them wanted to see a strong Jewish city, because it would threaten their control over the region.

Nehemiah's prayers
As soon as a problem came, Nehemiah prayed quietly to God in his heart. He also knew that God expected him to be sensible, so as he prayed he also did practical things to protect his workers.

219 Nehemiah chapter 5.

People in debt
The law of Moses said that Jews should not charge interest to other Jews when they lent them money. People had been breaking this law, so some had grown rich at others' expense. People who owed a lot of money had to sell their homes and fields to pay it back.

218 Repairing the city walls

Nehemiah did not tell anyone else the plan that he had for rebuilding the city walls. Three days after he arrived in Jerusalem, he crept out during the night to examine them. All that remained were piles of rubble; and the gates were burned.

The next day he went to the city officials and told them his plans, and how King Artaxerxes had given him permission.

The people started work straight away. They organized themselves into groups, each working on different sections of the wall.

But there was opposition. Two Samaritans, Sanballat and Tobiah, did not want God's people to succeed. At first they laughed and made fun of them.

'It's pathetic!' they cried. 'If a fox were to walk along the top of that wall, the whole thing would collapse!'

Then they made plans to raise an army to come and attack them.

But Nehemiah kept on praying. He told the workers to arm themselves and to keep on working. Even when Sanballat and Tobiah plotted to kill him, Nehemiah went on praying.

When the walls were completed, the new gates were hung. All the people met together. The walls of Jerusalem had been rebuilt in fifty-two days.

219 Nehemiah and the poor

While the building work was going on, a fierce argument broke out between the people. Some of the returned exiles were very wealthy. Others were poor. The wealthy lent large sums of money to the poor, but when the poor could not repay their debts, they took away their fields.

'Once our fields have gone we have no way of making any money,' cried the people to Nehemiah. 'Then we are forced to sell our children into slavery.'

When Nehemiah heard this he was very angry. He called the people together. 'What you are doing is against God's Law,' he cried. 'We are all members of the same family. We shouldn't be hurting one another. Give back everything which does not belong to you.'

The people listened to Nehemiah. He was right. He was their leader, and they respected him. He worked as hard as any of them, and always used his position for the good of the people.

220 Ezra reads God's Law to the people

Once the walls were finished, Nehemiah called everyone together.

Ezra climbed a high wooden platform in the square before the water gate. He carried the scrolls which contained God's Law, and he read them out loud. Everyone listened and understood. They began to cry when they realized how disobedient they had been.

'Do not cry,' said Nehemiah. 'Today is a special day. Today we must be happy because we have heard and understood God's Law. Go and have something good to eat and drink, and share what you have with each other.'

Day after day the people listened to Ezra as he read God's Law. They remembered how God had looked after his people since they first left Egypt. They remembered their disobedience.

'We are sorry for all the things our ancestors did to make you angry,' they said to God. 'We are sorry for all our sins.'

221 Festival time

It was time to dedicate Jerusalem's new walls to God. The people came together. The Levite singers met, some bringing harps.

Nehemiah gave instructions and the singers formed two choirs. Each choir processed around the top of the wall in opposite directions, while the people followed.

They met together in God's temple. Every man, woman and child sang to God. Everyone was happy and filled with joy. They knew that God had kept his promises.

222 God promises a special king

The people settled down to life in Judah. They forgot about the exile and how thankful they had been to return. The new life wasn't all they thought it would be, and sometimes it was a struggle.

'It's boring to worship God,' they moaned. 'People who don't bother with God do just as well as us. It's not fair.'

God gave Malachi a message for them. 'I love you, just as I have always loved you from the beginning. Remember how a child obeys his father. Think about how a servant respects his master! Well, I am your father and your master.

'But watch out! God himself is coming to live with you! Look for his messenger who will prepare the way. The one who comes will come to judge, and he will come to save. He will be like a furnace fire which makes gold and silver pure, removing all the rubbish that spoils it. The people who serve him and do what is right will be full of joy on that day!'

After the prophet Malachi had spoken God's words, there were no more prophets in the land for 400 years.

220 Nehemiah chapters 8 and 9.

Remember the exodus
The Jews looked back to the exodus (stories 47, 48) when Moses led the Israelites out of Egypt, as a special time of God's help. When things went wrong later, they remembered that God hadn't changed; he could help them again if they asked him.

See Feature pages 44-45.

221 Nehemiah chapter 12, verses 27-47.

Levites
These were temple ministers who organized the worship and singing, and looked after the furnishings.

See Feature pages 82-83.

Round the wall
The people walked around the walls before going to the temple as a sign that God was in charge of the whole city. They believed that walls were not enough to protect them; they needed God, too.

222 Malachi chapters 1 to 4.

Malachi
He probably worked about the same time as Nehemiah, around 430BC. His name means 'God's messenger'.

See Feature pages 12-13.

Another prophecy
Malachi said that in the future a prophet would come who would be like Elijah. His job would be to tell people to get ready for Jesus, by turning back to God. He was speaking of John the Baptist (story 235).

📖 THE NEW TESTAMENT

The New Testament is made up of the final twenty-seven books of the Bible. It includes the four Gospels, which are about Jesus' life and teaching, and the Acts of the Apostles, which tells the story of how the Christian church started and grew. There is also a collection of letters to Christians in the early church, and a vision called the Revelation to John. Some of the New Testament was written by people who had known Jesus during his life, or by people who had talked to them, and the rest by close followers of Jesus who understood his message.

Acts of the Apostles

This book records the activities of Jesus' followers for the first thirty years of the early church after the coming of the Holy Spirit. Written by Luke, it tells how the apostles, and especially Paul, took Jesus' message to other countries in the Roman Empire. The good news of Jesus was for all people everywhere (see stories 293-333 The Early Church).

The four Gospels

The first four books of the New Testament were written by Matthew, Mark, Luke and John some years after Jesus' death and resurrection. The first followers of Jesus passed on what they had heard and seen by word of mouth, but these written accounts of Jesus' life and teaching were an important next stage in passing on the gospel, which means 'good news' (see stories 223-292 The Good News).

Ancient traditions say that Matthew and John were two of Jesus' twelve apostles, people he chose to work with him; Mark was a close friend of Peter, also an apostle; and Luke was an educated Gentile (non-Jewish) doctor, a friend of the apostle Paul. He was also the author of the Acts of the Apostles (see above right).

The first three Gospels are very similar and in parts use almost the

same words. It is thought that Mark's Gospel was written first and that Matthew and Luke used his Gospel or the same source. But each Gospel is different, for each one sees Jesus from a particular angle.

Where Jesus lived Jesus lived in Nazareth, in the region of Galilee. It was in the north of the country, some distance from Jerusalem, the capital city. Here, for the most part, ordinary people lived ordinary lives. Jesus learned to be a carpenter there. Many of them were farmers and fishermen. No one expected that the Messiah would come from such an out-of-the-way place.

MESSIAH

This is the Hebrew word meaning 'chosen one', and many Jews in Old Testament times believed that God had promised to send a king, descended from King David, who would bring freedom for God's people. The followers of Jesus believed that he was this 'chosen one'. The Greek word for Messiah is 'Christ'.

Language Although Jesus himself spoke in Aramaic, the Gospel writers chose Greek, a language spoken throughout their country and the Mediterranean lands where the first Gentile churches were started. This meant the message could be read by everyone.

The Letters

Most of the letters in the New Testament were written by Paul, a man who had been violently opposed to the message of Jesus, until his life (and his name) was completely changed (story 302). After that he fearlessly took the Christian message to Jews and Gentiles alike. Even in prison he wrote letters to Christians to help them understand more about Jesus, and how to live good lives. He wrote to guide the leaders of the churches and to encourage them, especially in times of persecution, when people were hurt or even killed for believing in Jesus. Other letters were written by Peter, John, and Jude. The Letter to the Hebrews is not signed (see stories 334-359 Letters to Churches).

The Book of Revelation

This book is difficult to understand. It is a vision, written down by John, and full of symbols and hidden meanings. Written at a time when Christians throughout the Roman Empire were being persecuted and killed, it tells of a great struggle between good and evil, and how the power of God will finally triumph, when there will be 'a new heaven and a new earth' (see stories 360-365 A Vision of Things to Come).

Herod's Temple In Jesus' time all Jews came to worship God in the temple at Jerusalem, especially at the time of the great religious festivals. The temple was called 'the house of God'.

COVENANT

'Covenant' is another word for 'testament'. The Old Testament is about God's covenant with his special people, the Jews. Paul says that the 'new covenant' with God through Jesus means that anyone can come to know God, who will forgive their sins, and promises them life after death, if they put their faith in Jesus.

THE GOOD NEWS

For hundreds of years the people of the Old Testament had been waiting
for the 'chosen one' or Messiah to be sent by God to save his people.
The followers of Jesus came to believe he was this special person.
The stories in this section are all about him.

Jesus' birth was marked by special events. People knew that God had chosen this baby for an unusual job. When he was about thirty years old, Jesus began to teach people that God loved them. To please God they needed to trust him and to love and care for each other. Crowds followed Jesus everywhere he went because he told them simple stories rather than giving them many rules to follow. He also showed God's loving care by healing people from all sorts of illnesses; and he showed God's power by performing miracles.

But Jesus had enemies. Some of the religious leaders put him on trial and had him executed for religious 'crimes'. Then the most amazing thing happened: Jesus rose from the dead. Now his followers had no doubt that Jesus was God himself in human form. He had come to rescue people from the results of their wrongdoing and to help them to know God in a new way. These stories come from the four Gospels: Matthew, Mark, Luke and John.

223 Luke chapter 1, verses 5-25.

Drawing lots
Priests in Judea did other jobs to earn a living. There were so many priests that they only served in the temple occasionally and drew lots to decide who should burn incense.

Incense
Frankincense was burned in the temple's 'Holy Place' (the first of its two inner rooms). It was a sign of the people's prayers to God.

Gabriel
This is the name of one of the chief angels close to God in heaven.

223 Zechariah and the angel

Zechariah and his wife Elizabeth lived in the hill country in Judea. They were an elderly couple who loved and obeyed God. But they were sometimes sad because they did not have any children.

One day Zechariah left home to go to Jerusalem. He was a priest, and it was his turn to serve in the temple. He met the other priests and they drew lots to see which one of them would have the special once-in-a-lifetime job of burning the incense. This time Zechariah was chosen.

, Zechariah went into the temple and lit the incense. It began to burn. The people waited outside, praying.

Suddenly, out of the darkness, a figure appeared beside Zechariah. It was an angel. Zechariah was terrified.

'Don't be afraid,' said the angel. 'God has heard your prayers. You will have a son called John, and God's Spirit will be with him in a special way. He will bring great joy to many people. He will point them to God, so that they will be ready for him.'

'Can this be true?' asked Zechariah.

'My name is Gabriel,' said the angel, 'and I stand in God's presence. Because you have not believed my message, you will not be able to speak until everything I have told you has happened.'

Outside the temple, the people were beginning to wonder why Zechariah was taking so long. And when he came out, Zechariah tried to tell them about the angel. He waved his arms and mouthed the words, but he could not speak.

Then he went back home. Before long, Elizabeth found she was expecting a baby.

224 Gabriel's message

In the town of Nazareth in Galilee there lived a young woman called Mary. She had promised to marry Joseph, the local carpenter.

One day, when Mary was busy at home, she was startled by a surprising visitor. It was the angel Gabriel.

'Mary,' said Gabriel. 'God is with you!'

Mary was worried and confused. What did the angel mean?

'Don't be afraid!' said Gabriel. 'God is pleased with you and he has chosen you to have a son called Jesus. He will be a king – a king who will reign for ever!'

'How will this happen?' asked Mary. 'I'm not even married.'

'God's own Spirit will come to you, so that your child will be called the Son of God. God is able to do anything. Even your relative Elizabeth is expecting a baby! With God, nothing is impossible!'

'I want to serve God,' said Mary. 'Let everything that you have told me happen.'

And the angel left her.

225 Mary visits Elizabeth

So Mary left Nazareth to visit Elizabeth. It was a long journey to the hills of Judea.

When Elizabeth heard Mary's voice, she felt her own baby move inside her. He was jumping for joy. She was so excited. 'God has specially blessed you!' she told Mary. 'And he will do the same for your baby. You have believed God, and he will bless you because of it.'

'God is great!' said Mary. 'I am just an ordinary woman. It is God who has done great things.'

After three months, Mary went home to Nazareth.

226 John is born

Eight days after Elizabeth's baby was born, he was circumcised and named according to the tradition.

'You must call him Zechariah, after his father!' said their relations.

'No!' said Elizabeth. 'His name is John.'

'John?' said their friends. 'You don't know anyone called John. No one in your family has that name. What do you think, Zechariah?'

Zechariah made signs with his hands. He asked for a writing board and stylus. He wrote, 'His name is John.'

As soon as he had written the words, Zechariah spoke for the first time since he had met Gabriel. 'Praise God!' he shouted. 'God will do what he promised long ago, he will send a Saviour into the world! And my child has been chosen to prepare for his arrival!'

Everyone was astonished. What could it all mean?

224 Luke chapter 1, verses 26-38.

Promised to a carpenter
Mary and Joseph were not yet married, but an engagement could not be broken except by death or by divorce.

📖 See Feature pages 178-79.

225 Luke chapter 1, verses 39-56.

Long journey
Mary lived in Nazareth, near Lake Galilee in the north. The Judean hills were near Jerusalem, in the south. Mary probably walked around 112km/70 miles.

Three months
Mary may have stayed with Elizabeth until John was born.

226 Luke chapter 1, verses 57-59.

Naming and circumcision
Boys were circumcised at eight days old as a sign that they were members of the Jewish community. The name their parents had chosen would be formally confirmed then.

📖 See Feature pages 22-23.

Writing board
This was a flat piece of wood in a wooden frame covered with wax. A sharpened feather or reed was used to scratch letters on the wax. The wax was then softened and smoothed over, and the board used again.

227 Matthew chapter 1, verses 18-25.

God's Son
The angel told Joseph that Mary's baby was God's Son, made without the need of a human father. Jesus was therefore God and human at the same time.

Saviour
'Jesus' means 'God saves'. The people hoped for someone to rescue them from the Romans. Instead Jesus came to rescue people from the effects of their wrongdoing.

228 Luke chapter 2, verses 1-5.

Caesar Augustus
As first emperor of the Roman Empire, 31BC - AD14, he raised money for his conquests and government by charging everyone a poll tax and a land tax.

Bethlehem
This little village near Jerusalem is about 120km/75 miles from Nazareth. King David had grown up here (story 111).

229 Luke chapter 2, verses 6-7.

New-born babies
Strips of linen were wound tightly around them as people believed it helped the baby's limbs grow straight and strong.

See Feature pages 22-23.

227 Joseph's dream

Joseph did not know what to do when he found out that Mary was expecting a baby. He did not want everyone to gossip about her or be unkind to her. But he was not sure he should still marry her.

'Perhaps I'd better call off our engagement without much fuss,' he thought to himself sadly.

But one night, as he lay asleep, Joseph had a strange dream. An angel appeared to him and said, 'Joseph, do not worry about marrying Mary. She is expecting a very special baby, God's own Son, who will be the Saviour of the world. You must call the baby "Jesus".'

When Joseph woke up he remembered what the angel had said and so he went ahead and married Mary.

228 The journey to Bethlehem

Caesar Augustus, the Roman emperor, held censuses to raise more taxes. He ordered that everyone in his empire should go to the town of their ancestors to be counted. Because Joseph belonged to the family of King David, he had to go with Mary to Bethlehem.

Mary and Joseph left their home in Nazareth and made their way, through Galilee and Samaria, to the Judean village of Bethlehem. It was a very long journey.

229 Mary's baby

By the time Mary and Joseph had arrived in Bethlehem, so many people had come to register their names that the whole village was crowded.

Mary felt tired and weary from the journey. Joseph tried to find a place for them to stay. He went from house to house looking for a room where they could sleep. Everywhere was full. There was no room even at the inn. Eventually they found shelter in a place where animals were kept.

But while they were in Bethlehem, Mary's baby was born. She carefully wrapped him in strips of cloth and placed him gently on the hay in a manger, because there was no room anywhere else.

230 The shepherds' king

That night on the hills which surrounded Bethlehem, a group of shepherds were looking after their flocks of sheep.

Suddenly a brilliant light burst through the night sky. An angel appeared from within the light. The shepherds fell to the ground, and huddled together. They were terrified.

'Don't be afraid!' said the angel. 'I have come to bring you some good news, the most wonderful news for the whole world. Tonight, in Bethlehem, a baby has been born. He is the Saviour of the world. See him for yourselves! You will find him wrapped in strips of cloth, lying in a manger.'

As the shepherds heard the angel's words, the sky suddenly exploded with light and the sound of hundreds of angels, singing and praising God.

'Glory to God in the highest heaven!' they sang. 'And peace on earth.'

When the angels had gone, the shepherds looked at each other. 'Let's go to Bethlehem and find the baby,' they said as they ran down the hillside.

They found the place where Mary and Joseph were staying. They saw the little baby, lying in a manger, and they knew that what the angels had told them was true.

'Praise God!' they said to everyone they met. 'We have seen and heard the most amazing things tonight!'

231 The wise men

At the time that Jesus was born, some wise men living far away to the east saw a strange star in the sky.

The wise men studied their charts to find out what the star might mean. They concluded that a king had been born, so they decided to follow the star. They did not know where it would take them.

Eventually the wise men reached Jerusalem. They went to King Herod's palace. 'Where is the new king?' they asked. 'We have come to pay our respects, to welcome and worship him.'

Now when Herod heard that the wise men were looking for a new king, he was very worried. He ordered a meeting with all his advisers. 'Years ago the prophets said that God would send a new king,' he said. 'Did they say where he would be born?'

'In Bethlehem,' replied the advisers.

Herod thought quickly. 'Go to Bethlehem,' he told the wise men. 'If you find the king, let me know. Then I will be able to worship him as well.'

230 Luke chapter 2, verses 8-20.

Manger
A manger holds hay for animals to eat. Poor families often used a manger as a bed for their babies. It was a safe place to be in a small, dark house.

📖 See Feature pages 140-41.

Wonderful news
When Jesus was six weeks old, he was taken to the temple where his mother made the usual sacrifice. Here she was told by Anna and by Simeon that Jesus was God's promised Messiah and had a special place in God's plans.

231 Matthew chapter 2, verses 1-8.

The wise men
'Magi', priests from Persia or Arabia, believed that the movements of the stars showed what would happen in the future. Their visit was a sign that Jesus was the Saviour of all people.

Herod
Herod the Great had been made 'king' by the Romans, who ruled Judea, but he did not have much power. He built many great places, including the temple in Jerusalem, palaces, castles, and a harbour at Caesarea.

📖 See Feature pages 82-83.

Bethlehem foretold
About 700 years before, the prophet Micah had said that Bethlehem would be the birthplace of the Messiah.

232 Matthew chapter 2, verses 9-12.

Where Jesus was
By the time the Magi reached Jesus, Mary and Joseph would have found a better place to stay.

The gifts
Gold was given as a gift fit for a king. Frankincense, a sign of a priest, perhaps showed that Jesus would bring people to God. Myrrh, used to anoint dead bodies, pointed forward to Jesus' death for people's sins.

233 Matthew chapter 2, verses 13-18.

Herod's order
Herod was known to be very cruel. He even killed three of his own sons.

234 Luke chapter 2, verses 41-52.

Passover festival
This event celebrates the day the angel of death 'passed over' the Israelites (story 46). Quite often people travelled in large groups with the women and younger children near the front and the men and older children at the back. Mary and Joseph probably each thought that Jesus was with their partner's group.

My Father's house
Jesus is referring to the temple. Even at this age he knew that he had a special relationship with God, his real 'Father'.

See Feature pages 82-83.

232 Gifts for the king

So the wise men went to Bethlehem. They followed the star until they reached a house. They went inside, and found Mary with her young child. The wise men bowed down to worship Jesus, the new king. They presented him with special gifts – gold, frankincense and myrrh.

But during the night, the wise men had a strange dream. When they woke they knew they had been warned not to return to Herod. They went home, avoiding Jerusalem.

233 Escape to Egypt

Then Joseph also had a strange dream. He saw an angel.
'Wake up!' said the angel urgently. 'Herod intends to kill Jesus! Take your family and escape to Egypt!'
Joseph did not waste time. He woke up Mary and Jesus. They left in the middle of the night, and set off for Egypt.
It did not take long for Herod to realize that he had been tricked by the wise men. He was furious.
'Every boy less than two years old must die!' he ordered. Nothing and nobody could stand up to King Herod.

234 Lost in Jerusalem

When King Herod died, Mary and Joseph returned to Nazareth. Like all Jewish people, they went to celebrate the special Passover festival in Jerusalem each year.
When Jesus was twelve years old he went with Mary and Joseph and a group of other people from Nazareth to the festival in Jerusalem. At the end of the festival they set off for home.
After Mary and Joseph had been walking for a day, they found that Jesus was missing. They looked for him among their friends and relatives, but nobody knew where he was. They all thought he was with someone else.
Mary and Joseph went back to Jerusalem and searched for three days. Eventually they went to the temple. There was Jesus, surrounded by experts and teachers. He was listening to them, and asking questions. Sometimes he spoke, and everyone was surprised by his answers. He understood so much.
'Where have you been?' asked Mary. 'Your father and I have been very worried about you.'
'Didn't you know I would be in my Father's house?' Jesus replied. But they did not understand what he meant.
He went back home with them. He was a good son. As he grew up, Mary remembered all the special things that had happened to him.

235 John the Baptist

When Elizabeth and Zechariah's son, John, grew up, he went to live in the desert. One day, John knew that it was time to start doing the job that God had given him.

John started to talk to people about God. Crowds came to listen to him. 'Stop doing things that are wrong, and obey God,' John told them. 'Come and be baptized, as a sign that you are sorry, and that God has forgiven you.'

The people came to John to be baptized. 'It is not enough to have been born in the same family as Abraham,' he said. 'It is not enough to be one of God's chosen people!'

The people were shocked. 'What can we do then?' they asked.

'If you have two tunics, or plenty of food, share what you have with someone who has nothing. If you are a tax collector, don't cheat people. If you are a soldier, treat people fairly.'

'Is John God's Saviour?' the people whispered to each other.

John heard them. 'I baptize you with water. But someone is coming who is much more powerful than I am. He will baptize you with God's own Spirit!'

One day Jesus came to see John. He wanted to be baptized. As Jesus came out of the water, God's Spirit came down from heaven like a dove, and rested on Jesus.

Then a voice from heaven said, 'You are my Son. I love you very much. I am pleased with you.'

236 Jesus in the desert

God's Spirit led Jesus into the desert and stayed with him. For many days Jesus ate nothing and he was hungry.

Then God's enemy, the devil, said to him, 'Prove that you are God's Son! Tell a stone to become bread.'

'Life is more than bread,' replied Jesus, quoting God's Law.

Then the devil led Jesus to a very high place. They saw every kingdom and country spread before them. 'I am in charge of the world,' whispered the devil. 'I will give it to you, if you worship me.'

'God has said that we must worship only him,' replied Jesus.

Then the devil took Jesus to Jerusalem. They stood on the highest part of the temple. 'I know what God has said,' continued the devil. 'He has said that he will send his angels to swoop down from heaven to protect you. Let's see God's power at work. Throw yourself off the temple!'

Jesus refused to listen. 'God's Law also says that we must not test him!' he replied.

Eventually the devil left Jesus alone. He had tried to tempt Jesus to do something wrong, but Jesus had not given in.

235 Luke chapter 3, verses 1-20.

Desert
It is likely that John's elderly parents died while he was young and that others looked after him. Luke's Gospel implies that he grew up in the desert, south of Jerusalem, probably near the Dead Sea.

Baptism
John immersed his followers in water as a sign that God had washed away their sins. The Jews baptized non-Jews who wanted to become members of their community, and they had other washing ceremonies too. John's method was not new, but his message was.

Jesus is baptized
Jesus did not have any sins to confess. He was baptized as a sign that he was willing to obey God fully.

God's Spirit
God's Spirit, or the Holy Spirit, is the name used for God when he is seen and felt at work in people's lives. The dove is a symbol of peace.

236 Luke chapter 4, verses 1-13.

The devil
The devil is probably an angel who rebelled against God. He now tries to oppose everything God does. It was the devil who tempted Adam and Eve (story 3).

Temptation
The temptations Jesus faced were to use his powers in the wrong way. Jesus resisted each one.

237 Mark chapter 1, verses 14-20.

Simon (Peter)
Simon was also called Peter. Both names mean 'rock'.

Fishermen

The men either waded into the water and threw nets, or dragged them behind a boat. Fish were sold fresh, or salted to make them keep longer.

Disciples
Meaning 'student', this is the name given to Jesus' twelve closest followers. They were also called 'apostles', meaning 'sent out'.

Capernaum
This was a town on the north shore of Lake Galilee.

Synagogue
The Jews met to worship God in this building which was also used as a school.

📖 See Feature pages 82-83.

238 John chapter 2, verses 1-11.

Weddings
These were times of great celebration with much feasting.

📖 See Feature pages 22-23.

Water pots
These tall stone jars held between 75 and 115 litres/ 16 and 25 gallons.

237 The four fishermen

Jesus went back to Galilee. As he journeyed throughout the region, he preached to the people. 'I have come to bring you good news from God,' he said. 'Stop doing bad things and do what pleases God!'

One day Jesus walked beside Lake Galilee and watched the fishermen as they cast their nets into the water. He watched two fishermen in particular. They were brothers called Simon and Andrew.

'Come and follow me!' Jesus shouted to them across the water. 'You will still be fishermen, but you will be catching people, not fish!'

Immediately Simon and Andrew left their nets and followed Jesus. Then Jesus saw James and John sitting in a boat with their father Zebedee, checking their fishing nets.

'Come and follow me!' called Jesus.

James and John got out of the boat and followed him.

These four were the first disciples of Jesus. He went with them to their homes in Capernaum. While they were there Jesus taught in the synagogue. Crowds of people came to him and he healed all of them who were ill.

238 The best wine of all

One day, Jesus and some of his disciples were invited to a wedding in the village of Cana in Galilee. Jesus' mother, Mary, had also been invited. It was a great party but before the celebrations were finished, the wine ran out.

Mary went to Jesus and told him what had happened.

'I can only do what my Father God wants me to,' Jesus replied.

Mary did not understand what Jesus was saying, but she knew that her son would help. 'Do whatever he asks you,' she whispered to the servants.

Jesus noticed six large water pots. They were empty. 'Fill them with water,' he said.

The servants did as Jesus asked.

'Now pour some out, and give it to the guest of honour.'

As the servants poured the water, they saw that it had changed into wine. They gave it to the guest of honour.

When the man tasted it he was surprised. 'How extraordinary!' he exclaimed to the bridegroom. 'People usually serve the cheap wine last – when their guests have had too much to eat and drink to notice. But this wine is superb, and you have saved it to the end.'

Jesus' disciples saw what Jesus had done and they began to realize that Jesus was very special.

239 The good news

Many people throughout Galilee had seen the way Jesus healed people and had heard him talk about the way God loved and cared for his people.

Then Jesus returned to his home town of Nazareth. On the Sabbath he went to the synagogue, as he always did when he was at home. He stood up, ready to read from the Scriptures. Someone handed him the scroll, containing the words of the prophet Isaiah.

'God's Spirit is on me,' read Jesus. 'He has chosen me to bring good news to the poor, to free those who are in chains, give sight to the blind, help those who are suffering and tell everyone that God's blessing has come.'

Jesus rolled up the scroll and sat down. 'That was written hundreds of years ago. Today it has come true!'

The people whispered among themselves, 'But he's no one special. He's only Joseph's boy!'

'Because that's what you think,' replied Jesus, 'you will not see anything special here.'

The people of Nazareth were angry. They felt insulted. They pushed Jesus out of town, towards the hills. They planned to throw him off a cliff. But Jesus just walked through the crowd, and went away.

240 The man on the mat

When Jesus visited Capernaum, crowds of people crammed into a house to hear him speaking about God. More people gathered around the open door to try to hear what he was saying.

Then four men came to find Jesus, carrying their friend, who was lying on a sleeping mat. He could not move because he was paralyzed. The four men wanted Jesus to help him but they could not get near the house because of the crowds.

They were so desperate that they went up the stairs outside the house which led to the roof. Then they started to dig through the roof. When they had made a large hole, they lowered the man on the mat through it, and watched as their friend lay before Jesus.

Jesus looked at the four men. He saw how certain they were that he could help them. He spoke to the paralyzed man. 'My son,' he said, 'your sins are forgiven.'

The religious experts who had been listening to Jesus were shocked. 'How dare he say he can forgive sins?' they muttered. 'Only God can do that!'

Jesus knew what they were thinking. He looked at the paralyzed man. 'Stand up, pick up your mat, and go home!' he said.

Immediately the man stood up. Everyone saw what had happened and they were all amazed. 'Praise God!' they said. 'We have never seen anything like this before!'

239 Luke chapter 4, verses 14-30.

Sabbath
The seventh day of every week was a day on which no work was to be done. People rested and worshipped God.

📖 See Feature pages 82-83.

Isaiah
Over 700 years before, Isaiah prophesied about the coming of Jesus (story 182).

Scroll
This was made from flattened papyrus.

📖 See Feature pages 6-7.

240 Mark chapter 2, verses 1-12.

Hole in the roof
The flat roof was made from wooden beams covered with thin branches and a layer of dried mud. It would be easy to dig a hole in it.

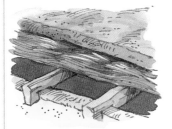

📖 See Feature pages 140-41.

The paralyzed man
Here Jesus teaches that even if God heals people who are ill, they need even more to have their sins forgiven.

Forgiveness
When Jesus forgave the man, he was doing what only God could do. The experts did not understand that Jesus was God in human form.

241 Mark chapter 2, verses 13-17.

Tax collectors
Matthew, also called Levi, probably collected money paid on goods bought and sold in the city.

📖 See Feature pages 178-79.

242 Mark chapter 6, verses 7-13.

The disciples' job
The disciples were sent out to tell people about Jesus, and sometimes to prepare villages he planned to visit.

243 Matthew chapter 5.

Hillside
The teaching in stories 243-246 comes from the 'Sermon on the Mount', which probably took place on a hillside by Lake Galilee.

Salt
Salt helped make food tasty, and stopped it going bad. Jesus is saying that his followers can stop the world being bad by showing his love and care to those around them.

Pharisees

This small group of Jews believed God's Law had to be kept very strictly. They had a list of 613 extra rules that said exactly what they should do about things like keeping the Sabbath.

241 Matthew, the tax collector

Jesus was walking beside Lake Galilee. Crowds of people followed him to listen to him speak.

By the side of the lake a tax collector called Matthew had set up his booth. He was collecting money for the Romans, telling people how much money they owed. People did not trust tax collectors.

Jesus walked past Matthew's booth. He stopped and beckoned to him. 'Follow me,' he said.

Matthew stopped what he was doing and followed Jesus. That evening he invited Jesus back to his house for dinner. He asked some of his friends, who were also tax collectors, to join them.

When the Pharisees saw that Jesus was Matthew's guest, they were disgusted. 'Why does Jesus mix with such terrible people?' they asked the disciples.

242 The twelve disciples

Although crowds of people gathered everywhere Jesus went, he had twelve special followers, who were his disciples – or 'students'.

One day Jesus spoke to them. 'Now it is your job to go to the villages and tell other people about God,' he said. 'I am going to give you my power and authority.' Then he gave them some instructions. 'Don't travel alone, but go in twos. You need not take anything with you. If you go somewhere where the people don't want to listen to you, leave quickly.'

The disciples went from village to village. They told people to live in God's new way and they healed those who were ill.

243 Living God's way

One day, there were so many people following Jesus that he went up on a hillside. He sat down and began to talk to the people about God's way of living.

'People who have true happiness are not proud, but know how much they need God's help and forgiveness,' Jesus said. 'If you follow God's ways, you will be like salt, sprinkled throughout the earth, or a light shining brightly for the whole world to see.'

The people listened. Then Jesus began to talk about God's Law, the Law the Pharisees knew so well. But Jesus spoke about God's Law in a new way.

'If someone hurts you, don't try to get your own back,' said Jesus. 'Go out of your way to help everyone. God's Law says that we must love those around us. Let us love those close to us, but also love our enemies as well! It's easy to love people who already love us. God wants us to be different. God is perfect. We must try to be like him!'

244 How to pray

'Be careful,' said Jesus, 'that you don't make a big show about praying, so that everyone will notice you, and think how good you are. God sees everything. So just talk to him simply and quietly and without a fuss.'

Jesus gave his disciples a pattern to use when they prayed to God. 'Begin by speaking to God,' explained Jesus. 'Say, "Our Father".'

'God is holy,' continued Jesus, 'so ask that God's name be treated as holy, and that God's kingdom will arrive quickly. Ask God for the things that you need for today, like bread. Then ask for God's forgiveness, and at the same time forgive anyone who may have hurt you. Ask him to help you not to do anything wrong that is against his Law.'

Jesus finished with a warning. 'Remember – if you don't forgive other people, God will not be able to forgive you.'

245 Don't worry

Jesus talked about the things that matter to everybody.

'Don't worry about anything!' he said. 'Don't worry about food, or drink, or what you're going to wear. Just look at the wild birds. They don't have huge stores of food. They simply rely on God to feed them. Don't you think he will take care of you as well as he takes care of the birds? You're not going to live longer by worrying about it! As for worrying about clothes, look at the beautiful lilies that grow in the fields. They do not work or dress themselves! God has made them beautiful. If you put God first, he will make sure that you have everything you need.'

246 The two houses

Some of the people who listened to Jesus wanted to live in a way that pleased God. But others did not like what they heard. So Jesus told a story.

'If you listen to me, and do what I say, you will be like a wise man who built his house on a rock. Before he started work, he made sure that his house had firm foundations on the rock. Then when the rain battered against the house, and the wind blew around it, it did not collapse.

'But if you take no notice of what I have said, you will be like a foolish man who built his house on sand. When the wind blew and the rain beat against his house, it had no foundations and so it fell down.'

244 Matthew chapter 6, verses 1-18.

Prayer
Prayer is talking and listening to God at any time and in ordinary words.

Father
Jesus told his followers to call God 'Daddy'. God, he said, was like an ideal father who loves and cares for his children and does not need to be feared. He gives them rules for their own good.

245 Matthew chapter 6, verses 19-34.

Lilies
The word Jesus uses means wild flowers such as the poppies, anemones and large white daisies that grew on the hillsides.

All you need
God promises to give what his children need (not necessarily everything they want) so that they can share what they have been given with others in need.

246 Matthew chapter 7, verses 24-29.

Jesus' stories
Jesus told many parables which take something ordinary and use it as a picture to teach something about God. This story means that lives built according to God's ways are more likely to stand firm in tough times.

247 Matthew chapter 8, verses 5-13.

The Roman centurion
A centurion was an officer in charge of 100 soldiers. The Romans had captured Judea and were thought of as enemies. By healing the servant of a Roman, Jesus showed that he cared for all people.

See Feature pages 158-59.

The healing word
Jesus only had to say something would happen, and it did. Jesus had God's authority and power.

248 Luke chapter 7, verses 11-17.

Nain
This was a small town south of Nazareth.

The woman's sadness
The woman had lost her husband and her son. Now she had no one to look after her as she grew old, in a society where women could not easily get paid work.

Funerals
The crowd in the procession would be wailing loudly. The body was carried on a stretcher on its way to be buried, probably in a cave rather than a hole dug in the ground.

See Feature pages 22-23.

249 Mark chapter 4, verses 1-20.

247 Jesus and the Roman officer

Jesus walked back to Capernaum and the crowd stayed with him. Suddenly a Roman centurion ran towards him. He was upset, and he rushed up to Jesus.

'Please will you help me?' he begged. 'One of my servants is very ill. He cannot move at all, and he is in terrible pain.'

'I'll come and heal him,' said Jesus.

But the centurion immediately said, 'Lord, I don't deserve to have you in my house. I know that if you just say that my servant is healed, he will be healed. I'm a centurion, and I know what it is to have power and authority. I tell people to come and go as I please, and they obey me. You have power and authority of a different kind, which comes from God.'

Jesus was amazed at the things the centurion said. 'I have not found anyone else who has as much faith as you do. Go home! Everything that you believed would happen, has already happened.'

The centurion went home. His servant was better. He had recovered at exactly the time the centurion had spoken to Jesus.

248 The widow's only son

Jesus and his disciples left Capernaum and walked to the town of Nain, followed by a large crowd. As they approached the town gates, another group of people was leaving the town. It was a funeral procession.

The body of a young man was being carried on a stretcher. The young man's mother walked sadly behind it. She was crying. He was her only son. She had no one else; her husband was already dead.

When Jesus saw the woman, he felt very sad. 'Don't cry,' he said.

The procession stopped. Jesus went up to the stretcher on which the body was laid. He touched it. 'Young man,' he said, 'get up!'

Immediately the young man sat up. He started to talk. Jesus took him by the hand, and helped him to his mother.

Everyone was amazed. 'Praise God!' they said. 'God has sent someone great to help us!'

More and more people heard about Jesus.

249 The story of the farmer and the seed

Jesus returned to Lake Galilee. He sat in a boat and talked to the crowds of people sitting on the beach.

'A farmer decided to sow some seed,' began Jesus. 'He took handfuls of seed, and cast it from side to side. Some fell on the path. It was quickly gobbled up by the birds. Some fell on soil that was full of stones. The seed grew quickly, but it did not last long. When the sun beat down upon it, it died, because it did not have good roots. Some seed landed near the thorns and could not grow properly. But some seed fell on good soil. It began to grow. It was strong and healthy. Eventually it produced a good harvest.'

Later on, when the disciples were alone with Jesus, they asked, 'What does that story mean?'

'The farmer is like a person who tells other people about God. The seed is the message that he brings. Some people who hear the message are like the soil on the path. They hear about God, but quickly forget about him. The stony soil is like the people who try to obey God, but give up when things get difficult. People who follow God, but get distracted by money or worries, are like the soil which grew near the thorns. Their faith is choked. But people who are like the good soil where the seed can grow up strong and healthy are the ones who will have fruitful lives that God can use.'

250 Secrets of God's kingdom

Jesus told many stories to explain what God's kingdom is like.

'God's kingdom is like this,' he said. 'Imagine that there is some treasure which has been hidden in a field. One day, a man accidentally finds the treasure. He buries it again quickly, then goes back home and sells everything he has so that he can buy the field.'

The people listened. Some of them understood. God's kingdom was more valuable than anything else.

'Or,' continued Jesus, 'God's kingdom is like a man who buys and sells pearls. One day he finds an extremely valuable pearl. So he goes home and sells all his possessions so that he can buy it.'

251 The storm on the lake

One evening, Jesus asked his friends to take him to the other side of the lake, so they set sail.

Jesus was tired. The crowds had followed him all day. He went to the stern of the boat, lay down, and rested his head on a cushion. He was soon fast asleep.

Suddenly the wind changed direction and the sea grew rough. Great waves crashed onto the boat, filling it with water. Jesus' friends felt sure that they were going to drown. But Jesus was still fast asleep.

'Don't you care if we die?' they shouted, waking him.

Jesus stood up. He spoke to the wind. It died down. He spoke to the sea, 'Be calm!' The sea was still.

Jesus looked at his frightened disciples. 'Why are you afraid? Don't you believe in me?'

Jesus' friends looked at him. They had no idea he had so much power. 'Who is he?' they asked one another. 'Even the wind and the waves do what he says!'

Sowing seed
Farmers broke up the soil with a plough pulled by oxen and then threw the seed corn over the soil. Some seed would fall in places where it could not grow well. Jesus' story encouraged the hearers to try to be like the good soil.

250 Matthew chapter 13, verses 44-46.

God's kingdom
This exists wherever a person or group of people tries to live God's way. It means 'where God is in charge and where his rules are kept'. Jesus said that God's way of living is so valuable that it's worth losing everything else for.

251 Mark chapter 4, verses 35-41.

Fishing boats
These were small, with oars and sails. With Jesus and his twelve friends, a boat would have been crowded.

Storms
Lake Galilee is an area of inland water surrounded by hills. At certain times cold air rushes between the hills and whips up the water into large waves.

Stilling the storm
The disciples believed that God controlled the world. Anyone who could tell the wind and waves what to do must be God.

252 Luke chapter 8, verses 40-42 and 49-56.

Ruler of the synagogue
This was not a priest, but a respected person in the town who looked after the synagogue building and organized the services.

Mourners

The people wailing would be close family, friends and people from the town.

See Feature pages 22-23.

Inside the house
Jairus kept on trusting Jesus even when he thought it was too late. Peter, James and John were Jesus' closest friends.

253 John chapter 3, verses 1-21.

Sanhedrin
The High Priest was usually the President of this, the Jews' most important group of rulers. It made up religious rules, but was also allowed by the Romans to judge legal cases and to order people to be arrested.

Nicodemus
He later helped Joseph of Arimathea put the body of Jesus in the tomb (story 285).

Born again
Jesus says the Holy Spirit helps people to understand who he is and begins to change them into the people he wants them to be.

252 Jairus' daughter

When Jesus returned to Capernaum, the crowds came out to greet him.

Jairus, the ruler of the synagogue, hurried to Jesus. Everybody knew him. He knelt at Jesus' feet.

'Please help,' he cried. 'My daughter is dying. She is only twelve. Please come and help her.'

Jesus followed Jairus as they made their way through the crowds.

One of Jairus' servants ran up to them. 'Sir,' he said. 'It's too late. Your daughter has just died. Don't bother Jesus any more.'

Jesus looked at Jairus. 'Don't be afraid by what you've just been told. Keep on believing, and your daughter will be well.'

By the time they arrived at Jairus' house, mourners were already crying and wailing outside. 'Stop crying!' said Jesus firmly. 'The little girl isn't dead, she's only asleep.'

Jesus went inside with the girl's father and mother, and Peter, James and John. Then Jesus held the little girl's hand. 'Little girl, get up,' he said. Immediately, she began to breathe again. She got up.

'Give her something to eat,' said Jesus.

Jairus and his wife were astonished by what they had seen, but Jesus told them not to tell anyone what had happened.

253 An important visitor

Many people heard about Jesus and the amazing things he did and the incredible things he said.

One of them was a man called Nicodemus. He was a Pharisee and a member of an important religious council, the Sanhedrin. He wanted to talk to Jesus but because he did not want anyone else to know what he was doing, he visited Jesus at night.

'Teacher,' said Nicodemus respectfully, 'God is obviously with you, or else you would not be able to do so many amazing things.'

Jesus looked at Nicodemus. He could see Nicodemus' longing to know more about God. 'To see God's kingdom, you must be born all over again,' said Jesus.

'But that's impossible!' said Nicodemus.

'Your mother cannot give birth to you again,' said Jesus. 'But God can give you a completely new life, by the power of his Holy Spirit.'

'How?' asked Nicodemus.

'By believing in the Saviour God has sent to the world. You see, God loves everybody. He wants to save people from doing wrong, and to give them life that will go on for ever. So God has sent his one and only Son into the world to show people how to be friends with God. Anyone who believes in God's Son will not die, but live for ever!'

254 The woman by the well

In the three years Jesus spent telling people about God he walked many miles. One time he went through Samaria, but when he reached the village of Sychar he had to rest. He felt tired and thirsty, so he sat by the well. The sun beat down on him. It was midday.

A Samaritan woman, carrying a water pot, walked towards him. 'Please will you give me a drink?' asked Jesus.

The woman looked at him. 'You're a Jew, aren't you?' she said. 'And I'm a Samaritan. Don't you know our people are enemies? How can you ask me for a drink?'

'If you knew who I am, you would be asking me for a drink!' said Jesus. 'I would not give you well-water, but God's living water, so that you will never be thirsty again!'

'That sounds good to me!' replied the woman. 'It would save me having to come here every day.'

'Go and tell your husband what I have said, and come back.'

'I haven't got one,' the woman replied.

'That's true,' said Jesus. 'But you have been married five times, and now you live with someone, but you aren't married to him.'

The woman was amazed. She forgot about her water pot, and ran to the town.

'Quickly!' she said to as many people as possible. 'Come and meet a very special man. He knows all about me! Could he be the Saviour God has promised?'

255 The death of John

The ordinary people thought that John the Baptist was one of God's special messengers, but some important people did not like what he said. They didn't want to hear about saying sorry to God for doing wrong things.

When John told Herod, the ruler of Galilee, that he should not be living with Herodias, his half-brother's wife, Herod was furious. He wanted to kill John, but was afraid of causing a riot. So Herod arrested John and put him in prison.

Some time later, on his birthday, Herod held a party. Herodias' beautiful daughter got up and danced. Herod was entranced and said, 'You can have whatever you want.'

The young girl did not know what to ask. So she went to her mother who said, 'Ask for John the Baptist's head on a plate.'

Herod was horrified. Deep down, he knew John was a good man. But all his guests had heard his rash promise. He could not refuse. So he ordered John's immediate execution.

254 John chapter 4, verses 1-42.

Samaria
This was a region in the middle of Judea. Orthodox Jews would take a longer route rather than travel through it because they did not like the Samaritans.

A woman at the well
This woman came at midday when she expected no one else to be there. Jews would not usually speak to women, so she was surprised when Jesus asked her for a drink. Like God, Jesus knew all about her.

See Feature pages 22-23.

God's living water
Jesus is using water as a picture of what God is like. People need to know God in order to live for ever just as they need water to live.

255 Mark chapter 6, verses 14-29.

John the Baptist
See stories 223, 226 and 235.

Herod Antipas
He was one of the sons of the Herod who tried to kill Jesus (story 233). He had persuaded his living brother's wife to divorce her husband in order to marry him, which was against Jewish law.

The young girl's dance
Herod's careless words lost John his head.

256 John chapter 6, verses 1-15.

Meals
Jesus had been teaching all day, so everyone was getting hungry. People at this time had their main meal in the evening.

📖 *See Feature pages 54-55.*

Philip and Andrew
They were two of Jesus' twelve disciples. Andrew, a fisherman, was the brother of Simon Peter. Philip came from another town on the shore of Lake Galilee.

The boy's lunch
The rolls were probably small loaves, round and flat. The two fish were probably the size of a pilchard or a sardine.

Jesus' miracle
This miracle showed Jesus' disciples that God cares about people and the details of their daily lives.

257 John chapter 6, verses 16-24.

Walking on water
This is another of Jesus' 'signs', a strange action that taught the disciples something important. Jesus was showing them that he was God and man (see also story 251).

Peter's faith
Simon Peter was able to do what Jesus told him for as long as he trusted Jesus. He sank when he panicked and began to think he had to do this incredible thing alone. In the Bible 'faith' means trusting or believing Jesus.

256 Food for all

One day Jesus went across Lake Galilee and up into the hills with his friends. A huge crowd followed him there, so he taught them about God's kingdom.

Jesus looked at all the people. There were more than 5,000 men, women and children. They were hungry and they had not eaten because they had been listening to him.

'Do you know where we could buy some bread?' Jesus asked his friend Philip.

'It would cost a fortune to buy enough bread for all of these people,' answered Philip.

Then Andrew, another disciple, noticed a boy in the crowd who was clutching five small barley rolls and two fish. He brought the boy to Jesus. 'This lad has some food,' he said, 'but it won't go very far!'

'Ask the people to sit down,' said Jesus.

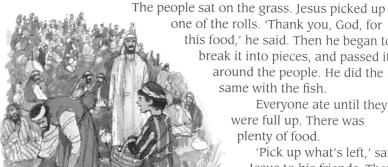

The people sat on the grass. Jesus picked up one of the rolls. 'Thank you, God, for this food,' he said. Then he began to break it into pieces, and passed it around the people. He did the same with the fish.

Everyone ate until they were full up. There was plenty of food.

'Pick up what's left,' said Jesus to his friends. They collected twelve baskets full of leftover pieces.

257 Walking on water

In the evening Jesus said goodbye to the crowd, and told his disciples to go back across the lake without him. He needed to be alone. He wanted to spend time talking to God, his Father.

It was night and the disciples were in the boat. It was hard work sailing against the wind, being rocked by the waves.

Suddenly, they saw a figure walking on the water.

'It's a ghost!' they cried. They were terrified.

'Don't be afraid!' said the figure as it walked towards them. 'It's me, Jesus!'

Peter heard Jesus' voice. 'If it's really you,' he shouted, 'tell me to come to you on the water.'

'Come on,' said Jesus.

Peter stepped out of the boat, onto the rocking waves. Cautiously he walked towards Jesus. But then a gust of wind blew around him. He panicked and began to sink. 'Help!' he cried.

Immediately Jesus took Peter's hand, and stopped him from sinking. 'Why didn't you believe?' he asked, as he led Peter back into the boat.

The wind stopped. The other disciples who had seen it all knelt before Jesus. 'You really must be God's Son,' they said.

258 The man who could not hear

When Jesus was travelling through the Decapolis, the region of the ten towns, a group of people came out to meet him. They brought with them a deaf man who could hardly talk.

'Please touch him,' they said.

Jesus took the man away from the crowds. When they were alone, Jesus reached out and put his fingers in the man's ears. Then he took some saliva from his own mouth and touched the man's tongue.

Making sure that the man understood what he was doing, Jesus looked up to heaven. He sighed. He knew how much the man had suffered.

'Open up!' Jesus ordered.

Suddenly the man could hear. His tongue moved in his mouth. He could talk!

The people were amazed. They began to talk to each other about what had happened.

'Don't tell anyone,' Jesus said. But he could not stop them talking. They could not keep quiet.

'Jesus does everything well!' they said. 'Because of him, deaf people can hear and dumb people can speak.'

259 On the mountain

One day Jesus went with his closest friends, Peter, James and John, to a high mountain, so that they could be alone together.

While they were there something strange happened. The friends saw Jesus' face shining like the sun. His clothes glowed a brilliant white.

Suddenly two men appeared. They stood beside Jesus and they talked to him.

Jesus' friends knew who the two men were.

'Let us build a shelter for you all,' said Peter enthusiastically. 'One for you, and one for Moses and Elijah!'

But before Peter could finish speaking, a bright cloud came over them and a voice spoke from heaven.

'This is my Son,' said the voice. 'I love him. I am pleased with him. Listen to him.'

At the sound of God's voice, Jesus' friends fell to the ground. They were terrified.

While they were lying there, they felt someone touch them. They looked up to see Jesus. He was on his own.

'Don't be frightened,' he said. 'And don't tell anyone what has just happened. Wait, until God's Son has come back from the dead.'

258 Mark chapter 7, verses 31-37.

The Decapolis
This was a group of towns south of Lake Galilee and east of the River Jordan. Many people living here were non-Jews (Gentiles).

The secret
Jesus wanted people to trust God because of his teaching, not because of the amazing things he did. His miracles were done out of compassion for the people he helped.

259 Matthew chapter 17, verses 1-9.

Jesus changes
This event is called his 'transfiguration'. It means that Jesus shone with the purity and light of heaven. Just before this Peter had said he believed Jesus was the Son of God. This was proof that Jesus was.

Moses and Elijah
Moses (stories 39-71) and Elijah (stories 155-161) talked about why Jesus needed to die and rise from the dead.

Shelters
Peter may have been thinking of the annual festival of 'Booths' in which the Jews lived in shelters to remember the 40 years the Israelites camped in the desert.

Back from the dead
Jesus often warned his disciples that he would have to die and rise from the dead. They never really understood what he meant until it happened (see stories 286-92).

260 Luke chapter 10, verses 25-37.

God's Law
The man's answer was a well-known summary of the teaching about how to live and worship God.

📖 See Feature pages 22-23.

Jericho road
Jericho was 24km/15 miles north-east of Jerusalem. The road went through lonely countryside where people were open to attack from robbers.

Priest and Levite
A priest offered sacrifices at the temple. A Levite helped with other aspects of worship.

Samaritan
Samaritans (story 254) and Jews hated each other, so this was the last person you would expect to offer help. Jesus was saying that anyone who needs help is our 'neighbour'.

261 Luke chapter 10, verses 38-42.

Mary and Martha
Jesus had come with his twelve disciples for a meal so Martha had a lot of cooking to do. But Jesus wanted Martha to think about what was most important in life. For her it was getting the meal ready. For Mary it was learning about God. Jesus said Mary was right: he would not always be there to teach them.

260 The story of the good Samaritan

Many people came to hear what Jesus had to say. One day an expert in God's Law asked him a difficult question, hoping to trap him.

'Teacher,' he said. 'How can I live with God for ever?'

'What does it say in God's Law?' Jesus asked.

'Love God with everything you have, and love your neighbour as you love yourself,' replied the man.

'Then you know the answer,' said Jesus.

'But who is my neighbour?' asked the man.

'Let me tell you a story,' said Jesus. 'There was once a man who was walking from Jerusalem to Jericho. He was attacked by some robbers, who beat him up and left him half dead by the side of the road. A priest came along. He saw the injured man, but ignored him. He walked past on the other side. A Levite followed the priest. He stopped and looked at the injured man, but kept on with his journey. At last a Samaritan came by. He saw the poor man, and stopped. He felt so sorry for him that he bandaged his wounds, put the man on his donkey, and took him to an inn. He gave the innkeeper two silver coins, and asked him to look after the injured man. "I will give you some more money when I return," he said.'

Then Jesus looked at the man who had asked him the question. 'Who was a good neighbour?' he asked.

'The Samaritan,' said the man. 'He loved the injured man.'

'Do the same as him,' said Jesus.

261 Mary and Martha

In the little village of Bethany, not far from Jerusalem, lived two sisters, Mary and Martha, who were friends of Jesus. He was always welcome at their house.

One day Jesus and some of his friends arrived. Mary sat by Jesus' feet and listened to everything he had to say.

But Martha was very busy. She had many things to do. She wanted everything to be just right for Jesus. She saw Mary, sitting at Jesus' feet, and she felt cross.

'It's not fair,' she said to Jesus. 'Mary is just sitting there, doing nothing, while I am having to do all the work. Tell her to help me!'

Jesus looked at Martha. 'Martha!' he said. 'Don't get so worried! There are always many things to do, but what Mary has chosen to do now is important. Don't tell her to stop.'

262 The good shepherd

One day, when Jesus was talking to a crowd of people, he began to talk about himself.

'I'm like a good shepherd,' he said, 'because I am willing to die for my sheep. When someone who is not a real shepherd looks after sheep, he leaves them at the first sign of trouble. If a wolf comes and attacks the flock, he runs away because he doesn't really care about them. But I am the good shepherd and I know my sheep and my sheep know me. I love them.'

'Jesus is mad!' whispered some of the people in the crowd. 'What is he talking about?'

But others listened. They heard what Jesus was saying. They wanted to understand.

263 'Come out, Lazarus!'

One day Jesus received a message from his friends Mary and Martha.

'Come quickly!' they said. 'Our brother Lazarus is dangerously ill.'

Jesus heard the message. But he did not come straight away. He waited two days before he set out for Bethany.

By the time Jesus arrived, Lazarus was dead. He had been buried for four days.

Martha came out to meet Jesus. 'If you had been here earlier, Lazarus wouldn't have died,' she said. 'But even now I know that God will give you whatever you ask for.'

'Lazarus will live again,' said Jesus. 'I am the resurrection and the life. If you believe in me you will live for ever. Do you believe, Martha?'

'Yes, I do!' said Martha, and she ran to fetch her sister.

When Mary saw Jesus she fell at his feet. She was crying. She was so unhappy. Jesus knew how sad she was, and he cried with her.

They took Jesus to Lazarus' tomb. 'Open it up!' he ordered.

'But he's been dead for days!' cried Martha.

Once the tomb was open, Jesus prayed. 'Father God, thank you that you have heard my prayer. May everyone now believe that you have sent me into the world.'

Then Jesus called out, in a loud voice, 'Come out, Lazarus!'

Slowly Lazarus shuffled out. He was still dressed in his grave-clothes, but he was alive!

262 John chapter 10, verses 1-21.

Shepherds

The shepherd had to guard his flocks against wolves and people who might steal the sheep. He also had to lead the flock to find grass and water. Jesus was saying that he would look after people who trusted him, and give them what they needed.

263 John chapter 11, verses 1-44.

Two days

Jesus didn't hurry to his friend as he had hurried to other people who were ill because he knew that he needed to raise Lazarus from the dead to teach his disciples an important truth about himself.

Resurrection

Many Jews at this time believed that the dead would rise and have a new life in heaven.

Life for ever

Jesus told Martha that he came into the world so that anybody who trusted him could live for ever. He said that death was not the end of life, but the start of a new life with God in heaven.

In the tomb

Lazarus was buried in a tomb – probably a cave – not a hole in the ground. Martha didn't want the tomb opened because there would be a nasty smell from the decaying body. The graveclothes were bandages wound tightly round the body, with spices in between the layers (see also stories 248 and 285).

📖 See Feature pages 22-23.

HOMES

In Bible times a home was where the family lived, ate, slept and worked. The family often included many children, as well as grandparents and other relatives. Aunts and uncles and their children probably lived nearby. Sons would learn the family trade from their fathers; and daughters would learn how to run the household from their mothers.

The home was a place where strangers were welcomed and given food and rest. Animals often shared the family home; and in early times, everything the family needed was made or produced at home.

MUD BRICKS AND BRUSHWOOD

Houses were built of mud bricks, hardened in the sun, and the floors were of hardened earth. There were steps or a ladder up to the flat roof which was made by laying wooden beams across the tops of the walls and then covering them with branches and brushwood. On top was a layer of clay which was made smooth with a stone roller.

The roof was strong enough to walk on but could be broken into (see story 240). After heavy rainfall, the roof would usually leak and need mending. Sometimes grass would grow on the roof!

Living in tents

About 4,000 years ago, in the time of Abraham, Isaac and Jacob (stories 10-38 The Patriarchs), the people in the Bible were nomads. They lived in family groups in tents and moved from place to place, taking their flocks and herds wherever they could find water and good pasture. Their tents were similar to those still used by nomads like the Bedouin people today.

The tents were made from animal skin or woven goat's hair. They were waterproof and kept out the heat. Each tent was divided into two rooms by a curtain, with the entrance room used for the men, and the inner tent used by the women and children. Some rich families had a separate tent for the women (Abraham's wife, Sarah, had her own tent).

Everything in the tent was light and easy to carry. When it was time to move on, people folded up their tents and belongings and carried them on the backs of donkeys to the next stopping place.

The nomads always camped near water. Sometimes they found an oasis or a spring, or they dug a well. Water was stored in animal skins.

They often stayed in one place long enough to plant crops and dig wells. In later times, villages grew up in the best camping places.

Houses

In later times, people lived in towns or villages. They built simple houses close together. Most houses had one room and a flat roof. The whole family lived in the one room.

Many household tasks were done outside. Inside there was often a raised platform for sleeping and eating, and the rest of the building was used for sheltering the animals at night. The windows were small to keep out the heat in summer, and the cold in winter.

The flat roof could be used for drying fruit or flax, weaving, praying, or talking to your neighbours. In summer, it could be used for sleeping, or to keep cool, when a temporary shelter of branches would protect people from the sun. By law, the flat roof had to have a wall around it to stop people falling off.

Some richer people liked to build on an extra room on the roof. It was probably a room like this (an 'upper room') where Jesus and his friends met to share the Passover feast (story 278).

Cooking This woman is cooking a lentil and vegetable stew on the fire. On the flat stone by the fire is some bread. The stone was first made hot in the fire, and then used to cook bread.

Oil lamps At night, light came from a simple clay lamp, burning olive oil. The wick was made of fibres of the flax plant, from which linen was also made.

Bedding There were no beds. At night the family lay down together on padded mats on the floor. They kept their clothes on and wrapped themselves in their cloaks. In the morning, the bedding was rolled up for the day.

Bigger houses

By the time of Jesus, some wealthy people lived in large houses built around a courtyard, and protected by a large, heavy door. Their houses were more like Roman houses, and some of the richest people had glass in their windows.

264 Matthew chapter 25, verses 1-12.

Weddings

📖 See Feature pages 22-23.

Jesus' return

Jesus said that he would come back to earth one day. Everyone who had loved Jesus would be with him in heaven; the rest would be shut out of God's presence. Being 'ready' meant living as he taught, all the time.

265 Luke chapter 15, verses 11-24.

Inheritance

A father's wealth would be divided between his sons, usually after his death.

Famine

Famine occurs when stormy or very dry weather destroys the crops. Joseph helped the Egyptians during a long famine (stories 35-37).

Pigs

The Jews were not allowed to keep or eat pigs; they were classed as 'unclean' animals.

Father's reaction

God is like the father in the story: he waits, sadly and patiently, when people turn from him, but is overjoyed when they are sorry and come back to him.

Ring and sandals

The ring and the sandals were signs that he was part of the family again.

264 The story of the ten bridesmaids

Some time later, Jesus was talking to his disciples about the future.

'Once there were ten bridesmaids,' said Jesus. 'Each bridesmaid had a little oil lamp. She needed it to welcome the bridegroom to the house that night. Five of the bridesmaids had brought some spare oil. But the other five were foolish. Hours passed and the bridegroom was nowhere to be seen. Everybody was tired. The bridesmaids fell asleep.

'Suddenly,' said Jesus, 'in the middle of the night, they heard a noise. "The bridegroom is coming! Wake up!" someone shouted.

'The bridesmaids stumbled to their feet and picked up their lamps.

'"Give us some oil!" pleaded the five foolish bridesmaids. "We've been waiting so long, we've run out of oil!"

'"Go and buy some!" said the others, so the foolish bridesmaids hurried off. But while they were away, the bridegroom arrived. The wise bridesmaids were ready. They held up their lamps and walked with him into the wedding feast. The door was shut.

'"Let us in!" shouted the foolish bridesmaids, outside the door.

'"I don't know who you are," said the bridegroom, and he turned them away.'

The disciples were thoughtful. 'Make sure that you are ready for my return,' said Jesus, 'because nobody knows when it will be.'

265 The lost son

Jesus told another story.

'A man had two sons. One day, the youngest son said to his father, "Dad, please can I have now my share of everything that I will inherit when you die?" So the father divided everything that he had between his two sons.

'Before long, the youngest son left home. He took all his money, and went far away. He had a great time enjoying himself. But after a while his money ran out.

'Then a terrible famine swept across the country. There was nothing to eat. The young son took the only job he could find, looking after some pigs. He was so hungry, he wanted to eat the pigs' food. And no one gave him anything to eat.

'The young man thought back over everything he had done. "The people who work for my father have far more than I have now. I'll go home. I will tell Dad how sorry I am for what I have done. I will ask if I can work for him."

'But before the son reached home, his father saw him in the distance. He ran to meet him and hugged and kissed him.

'"I have done some terrible things," cried the

son. "I'm so sorry. I don't deserve to be treated as your child. Just let me be a servant."

'But the father called to one of his servants. "Fetch the best clothes for my son. Give him some sandals and put a ring on his finger. Prepare a feast. We're going to celebrate! I thought my son was dead. He was lost, but now I've found him again!"'

266 Ten sick men

As Jesus was approaching Jerusalem he passed through a village on the border of Samaria and Galilee. Ten men came out to meet him. They called from a distance. 'Jesus! Help us!'

Jesus could see that the men had leprosy. He knew how much they suffered. He wanted to help them.

'Go to the priest,' Jesus told them. 'Show him your skin.'

The ten men obeyed Jesus. They walked down the road. But as they went, they looked at one another. Their skin was healthy. The leprosy had gone!

Nine of them kept on walking, but one of the men turned round. 'Praise God!' he shouted. He walked up to Jesus and knelt at his feet.

Jesus looked at the man. He was a Samaritan. 'There were ten of you,' said Jesus. 'Where are the others?' The man did not reply. 'You are the only one who has come to praise and thank God. Go home. You have been healed because you believed that God could make you well.'

267 Jesus and the little children

People followed Jesus wherever he went. They wanted to be near him. One day, some people brought their babies to Jesus. They wanted him to touch them and bless them.

The disciples were not happy. They knew how busy Jesus was.

'Don't bother Jesus with babies!' they said. 'He's too busy.'

Jesus knew what his friends were saying. Instead, he said, 'Don't stop the children from coming to me, because God's kingdom belongs to them. Learn from the children. They love me. Learn to love like them, or you cannot be a part of the kingdom of God.'

268 A very rich man

A very rich man came up to Jesus. He wanted to ask him a question.

'What do I have to do to live with God for ever?' he asked.

'Keep God's laws,' replied Jesus.

'I have done so,' said the rich man, 'ever since I was a boy.'

Jesus looked at the man. He loved him very much. 'There is one more thing you can do,' said Jesus. 'Sell everything you have, give your money to the poor, and follow me.'

The rich man did not say anything. His face looked sad. He could not do as Jesus asked. He was very wealthy. He turned to go away.

Jesus looked at his friends. 'It is very hard for a rich man, who does not think he needs anything, to enter God's kingdom.'

266 Luke chapter 17, verses 11-19.

Leprosy
This disease damages the skin and nerves, and can make lumps grow all over the body. People with skin diseases were considered 'unclean' so everyone avoided them.

Samaritan
See also stories 254 and 260.

Healed
All ten were made better. But only one said thank you.

267 Luke chapter 18, verses 15-17.

Blessing
Mothers took young children to rabbis (teachers of religion) to be blessed. The rabbi would pray for the child to receive God's love and help.

Children
Jesus showed his disciples that everyone is important to God. He said that a child's simple trust in God was something adults needed to copy.

268 Mark chapter 10, verses 17-25.

God's laws
The man had kept the Ten Commandments. But Jesus saw that his wealth was more important to him than God. The Bible teaches that money is good when it is used to help others, but can be dangerous when it makes people greedy.

See Feature pages 12-13.

269 Mark chapter 10, verses 46-52.

Begging
People like Bartimaeus were very poor because their disability meant they could not work. They depended on their families to look after them, and often they had to go into the streets to beg for food or money.

Cloak
This warm, heavy, woollen garment was long and worn over the shoulders, with slits in the sides for the person's arms. Bartimaeus threw it off because it would have slowed him down – he was keen to get to Jesus!

270 Luke chapter 19, verses 1-10.

Tax collector
Someone who collected money for the Romans was thought of as a traitor. Tax collectors also charged more than they needed in order to make money for themselves (see also story 241).

📖 See Feature pages 178-79.

Sycomore
This was a fruit tree that produced wild figs. It could ç ow as high as 10m/33 feet. It had a very short trunk and many wide branches, so it was easy to climb.

Zacchaeus
To go to someone's house meant you were willing to be their friend. No one thought Jesus ought to be a friend to Zacchaeus. But the tax collector had changed his ways. He gave back all he had stolen, plus a lot more to make up for the suffering he had caused.

271 John chapter 12, verses 1-8.

269 Blind Bartimaeus

When Jesus and his friends went to Jericho, a large crowd followed them. By the side of the road sat a blind man called Bartimaeus. He was a beggar.

Suddenly he began to shout, 'Jesus! Help me!'

'Be quiet!' said someone in the crowd.

'Stop shouting!' said another.

But Bartimaeus kept on shouting, 'Jesus! Help me!'

Jesus stopped. He heard Bartimaeus' voice. 'Tell him to come to me,' he said.

'Get up!' said someone to Bartimaeus. 'You can stop shouting now. Jesus wants you!'

Bartimaeus threw off his cloak and jumped to his feet. He felt his way through the crowd, until he came to Jesus.

'What do you want me to do for you?' asked Jesus.

'I want to see,' said Bartimaeus.

'You may go,' said Jesus. 'Because you have believed, you will see.'

Immediately Bartimaeus could see! He followed Jesus.

270 The little tax collector

In Jericho there lived a rich man called Zacchaeus. He was very unpopular because he was a tax collector. When a large crowd gathered to see Jesus pass by, Zacchaeus could not see because he was very short.

Suddenly Zacchaeus had an idea. He ran on, ahead of the crowd, and climbed up a sycomore tree so that he could see Jesus coming down the road.

When Jesus reached the tree he stopped and looked up into its branches. 'Zacchaeus!' said Jesus. 'Come down! I want to stay with you at your house.'

Zacchaeus clambered down the tree in excitement. 'You are welcome to stay with me, Jesus!' he cried.

But the people in the crowd were not pleased. 'Why would Jesus want to stay with such a bad man?' they whispered.

Zacchaeus knew what the people were saying. He knew he was rich because he had not been honest.

'Jesus!' he said in a loud voice. 'I'm going to give half of all that I have to people who are poor, right now! And if I have cheated anyone, I will pay them back four times as much.'

Jesus smiled at Zacchaeus. 'Today is a wonderful day!' he said. 'Once you were lost, but today you have been saved!'

271 The jar of perfume

Jesus had been invited to a special dinner party at the home of Lazarus in Bethany. Martha was helping to serve the meal when Mary came in carrying a large jar of expensive perfume.

She went to Jesus and began to pour the perfume over his feet. Immediately the room was filled with scent. Then Mary bent down.

She wiped Jesus' feet with her hair.

Everyone watched her. Then Judas Iscariot spoke up. He looked after the money that was given to support Jesus.

'What a waste!' he said. 'That perfume could have been sold and the money given to the poor. It must have cost as much as some people are paid in a year.'

Jesus looked at Judas. He was sad and disappointed at his words. 'Leave her alone,' said Jesus. 'Remember this. There will always be poor people around you, but I will not always be here with you.'

272 Jesus goes to Jerusalem

When Jesus and his friends were on the road to Jerusalem, they stopped at the little village of Bethphage on the Mount of Olives.

'Go into the village,' said Jesus to two of his disciples, 'and you will find a donkey and her colt. Bring them to me. If anyone asks what you are doing, tell them that I need them, and they will let you take them.'

The two friends did as Jesus asked. They found the donkey and her colt, and brought them to Jesus. They put their cloaks on the backs of both animals. Jesus sat on the colt, and started to ride towards Jerusalem.

As he rode, a large crowd gathered along the sides of the road. People spread their cloaks on the ground for the colt to walk on. Some cut down branches from the trees.

Everyone was shouting. 'Hosanna!' they cried. 'King Jesus!'

Jesus rode on into Jerusalem.

273 A den of thieves

Once inside the city, Jesus went to the temple. He walked through the outer courtyard where he found the money-changers and dove-sellers busy making money for themselves.

Jesus took hold of one table after another, and overturned them. Money scattered everywhere. 'This is God's house!' he roared. 'It is a place for people to worship God, but you have made it into a den of thieves!'

Then people came to him: blind people, sick people, beggars, people who needed Jesus. They came to Jesus and he healed them.

The chief priests and the Pharisees watched Jesus. They hated what he was doing. They hated him.

But little children ran around the temple courts. They sang and they shouted, 'Hosanna! God has come to save us!'

Perfume
This would have been kept for special occasions and used in small quantities. Mary gave Jesus something which was important to her.

Judas Iscariot
Later Judas handed Jesus over to those who wished to kill him (stories 275, 280).

272 Matthew chapter 21, verses 1-9.

Mount of Olives
This was a hill just outside the walls of Jerusalem.

Donkey ride
Jesus' followers knew that the prophet Zechariah had spoken of a king coming into Jerusalem riding on a donkey. So the crowds welcomed him as a king.

Branches from trees
Date palms had branches over 3m/10ft long!

273 Matthew chapter 21, verses 12-16.

Courtyard
This was the outer courtyard, the first part of the temple area into which anyone could go. People bought animals for sacrifices here.

Moneychangers
The traders were only allowed to use a special kind of money so everyone had to change their Roman coins before they could buy anything. The money-changers made a big profit.

274 Luke chapter 21, verses 1-4.

Copper coins
These were Jewish 'leptons' and were hardly worth anything.

See Feature pages 178-79.

275 Matthew chapter 26, verses 3-5, 14-16.

High Priest
He was the senior priest at the main Jewish council meetings. Caiaphas was High Priest in AD18-36.

Silver coins
Thirty silver coins was the standard price for a slave.

Judas' betrayal
No one knows why Judas betrayed Jesus. He may have had mixed-up ideas about what Jesus came to do. Later Judas was sorry for what he had done and he killed himself.

276 Luke chapter 22, verses 7-13.

Water jar
A man carrying water was so rare that the disciples could make no mistake; women usually carried them.

Passover
This is a celebration of the day when God led the Israelites out of Egypt (stories 46 and 278).

See Feature pages 54-55.

277 John chapter 13, verses 1-17.

274 The poor widow

While he was in the temple Jesus saw the rich people putting their money into the temple treasury boxes. As he watched, a poor widow slipped two small copper coins into the box.

Jesus turned to the people around him. 'That woman has given far more than anyone else. The others could afford to give; it did not mean much to them. But that woman could not afford it. She has nothing else to live on, and yet she gave everything she had to God.'

275 Thirty silver coins

The chief priests and the elders met secretly at the palace of Caiaphas, the High Priest.

'We must find a way to destroy Jesus,' they all said.

'But we must be careful,' said some. 'Passover is only two days away. Jerusalem is full of people. If we have Jesus arrested now, there will be a riot!'

Meanwhile, Judas, one of Jesus' disciples, was also plotting. He went to find some of the chief priests. 'What will you give me if I hand Jesus over to you?' he asked.

'Thirty silver coins,' they said. This was the opportunity they had been looking for.

Judas took the money. Now all he had to do was wait.

276 Preparing for Passover

'Where shall we celebrate Passover?' asked Jesus' disciples. 'Do you want us to get anything ready?'

'Two of you can go into the city,' Jesus replied. 'You'll see a man carrying a water jar. Follow him. When he goes inside a house, find the owner and ask him where his guest room is. Tell him that I need to use it to celebrate Passover with my friends. He will take you to an upstairs room. Everything will be ready for us.'

The two men did as Jesus told them. Everything happened as Jesus had said it would.

277 Jesus washes the disciples' feet

Jesus and his disciples met in the upstairs room, ready to celebrate the Passover feast.

Jesus stood up, wrapped a towel around his waist and filled a basin with water. Then he knelt down in front of each of his friends in turn and washed their feet as a servant would.

'I won't let you wash my feet,' said Peter, when Jesus knelt before him. He did not want Jesus to do a servant's job.

'You must,' said Jesus, 'or you cannot be my friend.'

'Then wash all of me!' said Peter. 'Wash my hands and head as well.'

'There's no need,' said Jesus. 'Only your feet are dirty. The rest of you is clean.' His thoughts turned to Judas. 'Although not everyone here is clean,' he added.

Jesus said, 'I have just shown you how to serve one another. Follow my example.'

278 The Passover meal

In the upstairs room, Jesus and his friends began to eat the Passover meal. Jesus was troubled in his spirit. 'One of you is going to betray me,' he said.

The disciples looked at one another in disbelief. 'Ask him who it is,' mouthed Peter to John, who was next to Jesus.

'It is someone who is sharing this piece of bread,' said Jesus, passing it round. When he gave it to Judas, Jesus said, 'Do whatever you have to do quickly.' Judas took the bread. This was the moment. He stood up, and slipped out into the night.

At the end of the meal, Jesus held the loaf of unleavened bread. He thanked God for it. Then he broke it into pieces and passed it to his friends. 'This is my body, which is given for you,' he said. 'Remember me whenever you eat bread.'

The disciples ate the bread. Then Jesus picked up a cup of red wine. 'This wine is my blood. God will use it as a sign. It is his promise that he will save you.'

Jesus' friends drank the wine but they did not understand what Jesus was telling them until after Jesus had died.

279 Alone in the garden

Jesus and his disciples went out into the night.

'All of you will abandon me tonight,' said Jesus.

'I never will!' said Peter bravely.

'Before the cock crows in the morning, you will have denied me three times.'

He took them to a garden called Gethsemane. 'Sit here and wait for me while I pray,' he said to them. He turned to Peter, James and John. 'Come with me,' he said. The three friends followed Jesus. They could see that he was very sad. 'Keep me company,' he said.

Then Jesus walked away on his own. He fell to the ground and began to pray. 'My Father, if it is possible, please save me from all the pain and sorrow that is ahead of me. But don't do it because I have asked you. I only want to do what you want.'

Jesus walked back to where he had left Peter, James and John. They were fast asleep. 'Can't you stay awake for one hour?' he said.

Jesus went away to pray again. When he came back, his friends were asleep again. Jesus prayed for a third time, alone in the garden.

Footwashing
People wore open sandals, and the roads were very dusty. The disciples were too proud to do a job usually done by servants.

278 Matthew chapter 26, verses 20-30.

Passover meal
Several times during the meal the host would share a piece of bread and a cup of wine with the others. The bread was hard and flat, not soft and round.

'My body and blood'
Jesus gave the custom a new meaning. The bread and wine would now stand for his death through which people would be able to know God's forgiveness and new life.

279 Matthew chapter 26, verses 31-44.

Gethsemane
Jesus often went to this grove of olive trees just outside Jerusalem to pray or rest.

Peter, James and John
These were Jesus' closest friends (see also story 259).

Jesus' prayer
The Bible says Jesus was worried about the pain he was about to suffer. He could face death only because he didn't want to let his Father down.

280 Matthew chapter 26, verses 47-56.

Judas' kiss

The soldiers had torches (tar-covered sticks, set alight), but it would still be hard to see in the dark garden. The kiss (a normal greeting) showed the soldiers whom they were to arrest.

Cut ear

Jesus healed the man's ear at once. He taught his disciples never to use force or violence.

281 Matthew chapter 26, verses 57-75.

Cock crow

The cock was the only 'clock' people would have heard. Cocks would not crow until it was nearly dawn.

Peter's accent

Jesus and most of his disciples came from the north. The girl came from Jerusalem in the south.

Peter's denial

He was probably afraid that he would be arrested too.

282 Matthew chapter 27, verses 11-26.

Roman governor

Pontius Pilate was a cruel man. He was 'procurator' or governor of Judea at this time. The Jews were allowed to judge criminal trials and pass sentences on criminals, but only Pilate could order an execution.

280 Jesus is arrested

The sound of voices echoed through the garden. A large crowd, led by Judas, made their way to Jesus. They were carrying swords and clubs. Judas walked straight up to Jesus, and kissed him. 'Greetings, Rabbi!' he said.

It was the signal the crowd needed. They rushed forward and seized Jesus.

The disciples stumbled sleepily to their feet. They were afraid. One of them grabbed a sword and lashed out with it, hitting one of the High Priest's servants and slicing off his ear.

'No swords!' ordered Jesus. 'There's no need to use weapons! God could rescue me with angels. You do not need to use force to capture me.'

The crowd led Jesus away. His friends fled, leaving him alone.

281 Peter lets Jesus down

Peter ran away with the others. Only a few hours before, he had promised never to let Jesus down. He had promised to die with Jesus, if necessary. 'Peter,' Jesus had replied, 'tonight, before the cock crows, you will have disowned me three times.'

Peter watched as the crowd took Jesus to Caiaphas, the High Priest. In the darkness, Peter went and sat in the courtyard of the High Priest's house, and waited to see what would happen.

A servant girl came up to him. 'I recognize you!' she said. 'You're one of Jesus' friends!'

'No, I'm not!' said Peter getting up, making his way to the gate.

'I'm sure that man is one of Jesus' friends!' said another girl, pointing to Peter.

'Jesus?' said Peter angrily. 'I've never met him!'

'You must be one of Jesus' friends!' said someone else. 'You come from the same area. We can tell by your accent.'

Peter panicked. 'Listen!' he shrieked. 'I don't know the man! I've never had anything to do with him. I swear it!'

A cock crowed. It was morning. Suddenly, Peter remembered what Jesus had said to him.

Peter walked away and cried as if his heart would break.

282 The crowd decides

Caiaphas, the High Priest, was furious. No one could find any hard evidence against Jesus. Caiaphas and the Sanhedrin wanted Jesus dead, so they sent him to Pilate, the Roman governor.

Jesus stood in front of Pilate. He did not speak.

'You know what the chief priests and elders are accusing you of?' asked Pilate. 'Why don't you say something?'

Jesus remained silent. Pilate was worried. He did not think that Jesus had done anything which could be punished by death, but he did not want trouble. He decided to appeal to the crowd outside, waiting for a verdict. He went out to speak to them.

'It is the custom at Passover to release a prisoner,' he said. 'Shall

I release Jesus, or the murderer, Barabbas?'

The chief priests and the elders made sure their supporters were in the crowd. 'Barabbas!' they shouted.

'What shall I do with Jesus?' asked Pilate.

'Crucify him!' they screamed.

'Why?' asked Pilate. 'He's innocent!'

The crowd did not listen. 'Crucify him!' they chanted.

Pilate did not want a riot. He had Jesus flogged, and then handed him over to be crucified.

283 Carrying the cross

The Roman soldiers gathered around Jesus and made fun of him. They took off his clothes and put a robe on him. They made a crown out of thorns and stuck it on his head. They gave him a stick to hold. They dressed him up like a king.

'Your majesty!' they sneered, snatching the stick and hitting him across the head. They spat in his face. Then they gave him back his own clothes and took him away to be executed.

The soldiers saw a man called Simon in the crowd. He was from Cyrene.

'Carry this cross!' they said, grabbing Simon. And they went with Jesus to the execution place, called Golgotha, which means 'the place of the skull'.

284 Jesus is crucified

Jesus was taken to be crucified with two criminals. The soldiers nailed Jesus to a wooden cross and waited for him to die.

There were crowds of people watching. Some made fun of Jesus. 'You helped other people, but you can't help yourself!' they said. Some of the soldiers took away Jesus' clothes and played dice for them. Other soldiers made a sign. They hung it above Jesus' cross. It said, 'This is the King of the Jews'.

As Jesus hung on the cross he prayed, 'Father God, please forgive them. They don't know what they are doing.'

Even one of the criminals who hung beside Jesus mocked him. 'You're Jesus, aren't you?' he said. 'You're supposed to be God's Son. Come on then! Save us!'

'Be quiet!' said the other criminal. 'We deserve to die. But Jesus doesn't. He hasn't done anything wrong.' He turned to Jesus. 'Remember me when you are king.'

Jesus replied, 'Today you will be with me in paradise.'

Hours passed. Then the sky turned black. 'Father God!' cried Jesus. 'I am in your hands!' Then Jesus died.

A Roman centurion, who had watched Jesus die, said, 'This man really was the Son of God.'

Barabbas
As a terrorist fighting the Romans, Barabbas had killed people.

283 Matthew chapter 27, verses 27-44.

King Jesus
Jesus was charged with claiming to be 'king of the Jews'. The soldiers thought he was mad, so they mocked him.

Simon of Cyrene
Cyrene was in North Africa. Simon was probably a trader or a pilgrim in Jerusalem for the festival.

284 Matthew chapter 27, verses 45-55.

Crucifixion
A person was crucified by being nailed through the wrists and ankles to a wooden cross.

📖 See Feature pages 158-59.

Black sky
There were probably heavy storm clouds. When Jesus died, the curtain of the temple hiding the 'Holy Place' was split, a sign that Jesus had opened up a new way to know God.

Paradise
This is another name for heaven, where God is seen and known perfectly.

285 Luke chapter 23, verses 50-56.

Jesus' burial

Jewish law forbade burial on the Sabbath, which started at 6.00pm. So they didn't have time to wrap the body carefully with all the usual spices and perfumes before putting it in the tomb.

📖 *See Feature pages 22-23.*

286 John chapter 20, verses 1-18.

Linen cloths

The body had not been stolen: no thief would have unwrapped the bandages, then wound them up again. The headcloth was on one side, as if it had just been lifted off.

Jesus is raised

Jesus came back to life but his 'resurrection' body was different from before, so people didn't always recognize him (see also story 288).

287 Luke chapter 24, verses 13-35.

Cleopas

His companion may have been his wife.

The prophets

There were many things in the Old Testament that tied in with what had happened to Jesus and what he had taught. But at the time, very few people realized this. Jesus made them clear to the two people.

285 A borrowed grave

Joseph of Arimathea was a member of the Sanhedrin, the Jewish Council. Like Nicodemus, he was also a secret follower of Jesus. He had not gone along with his fellow council members who had wanted to kill Jesus.

After Jesus died, Joseph went to see Pilate, the Roman governor.

'Let me take Jesus' body and bury him, before the Sabbath begins,' he said.

When Pilate agreed, Joseph and Nicodemus took Jesus' body from the cross. They wrapped him in a linen cloth, placed his body in a newly-made tomb, and rolled the great stone across the entrance.

286 Jesus is alive!

On the third day after the Sabbath, Mary Magdalene went to Jesus' tomb. The huge stone which had covered the entrance had been moved. The tomb was empty. Jesus had gone!

Mary ran to find Peter and John. 'They've taken Jesus!' she cried. 'I don't know where he is!'

Peter and John ran to the tomb. Mary was right. Jesus was not there. All they could see were the linen cloths which Joseph had wrapped around his body.

The two men ran home, leaving Mary in the garden, crying. She went to look inside the tomb again. It was filled with light. Mary could see two angels, sitting where Jesus' body should have been. 'Why are you crying?' asked one of the angels.

'They have taken away Jesus' body,' Mary sobbed. She heard a noise behind her. Turning round, she thought she saw the gardener.

'Why are you crying?' he asked. 'Who are you looking for?'

'Sir,' she said. 'If you have taken Jesus, please tell me where he is.'

Then the gardener spoke to her. 'Mary,' he said.

Immediately Mary realized that it was not the gardener. It was Jesus.

'Master!' gasped Mary, in amazement. She went and told Jesus' friends.' I have seen Jesus! He's alive!'

287 Walking to Emmaus

On the same day Cleopas and his friend were walking along the road from Jerusalem to the village of Emmaus. They were talking about everything that had happened in Jerusalem over the past few days. They were so sad because Jesus had been put to death.

Suddenly a stranger came alongside them. 'Who are you talking about?' he asked.

Cleopas looked at the stranger. 'You must be the only person who does not know what has happened,' he replied. 'We were talking about Jesus of Nazareth. We had hoped that he was the Saviour God had promised to us. But three days ago, our chief priests and elders had him executed.'

'Think back to everything the prophets wrote about God's Saviour,' said the stranger, and he began to talk to them, explaining how it had been written long ago that the Saviour must suffer and die.

'Come to our house,' said Cleopas, as they reached Emmaus.

The stranger accepted the invitation and they sat down to eat supper. As the stranger picked up bread, gave thanks to God, and broke it, Cleopas and his friend immediately knew who the stranger was. It was Jesus!

As soon as they recognized him, Jesus vanished. They rushed back to Jerusalem to tell the others that Jesus was alive.

288 Jesus meets his friends

Jesus' friends were scared. Now that Jesus was dead, they wondered what the authorities might do to them. They stayed together in the upper room and kept the doors locked.

Suddenly Jesus appeared in front of them. 'Peace be with you,' he said. He held out his hands and showed them the deep scars where the nails had been.

'Jesus!' cried his disciples, overjoyed with happiness. 'You're alive!'

Jesus breathed on them. 'Receive the Holy Spirit,' he said, 'and remember to tell people that their sins can be forgiven.'

289 Jesus and Thomas

Thomas had not been there when Jesus appeared to his disciples in the upper room after rising from the dead.

'I don't believe it!' said Thomas. 'I won't believe that Jesus is alive, unless I see him for myself and touch his scars.'

A week later Thomas and the others met together. The doors were locked. Suddenly Jesus appeared. 'Peace be with you,' he said. Then he turned to Thomas. 'Look at my hands, Thomas. Touch them. Look at the place where the sword cut my side. Touch that too. Now stop doubting and believe!'

Thomas sank to his knees. He knew that Jesus was real and that he was alive. 'My Lord and my God,' he said.

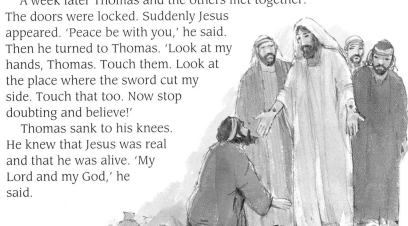

Bread
There was something familiar about the way Jesus broke the bread. Perhaps they were reminded of how he fed 5,000 people.

288 John chapter 20, verses 19-23.

Locked doors
Jesus' disciples were afraid that the leaders of the people might arrest and kill them too, to get rid of Jesus' influence for ever.

Holy Spirit
The word 'Spirit' is the same as the word for 'breath' in the original language. Jesus breathed on the disciples as a sign that God would give them his power. The Holy Spirit is God working in people's lives.

Jesus' body
It was the same, because it had the marks of the nails, but it could behave differently, such as passing through walls. The Bible says that the bodies of Jesus' followers in heaven will be different too; they won't have the same limitations as on earth.

289 John chapter 20, verses 24-29.

'My Lord'
Thomas recognized that Jesus was not just a man, but God in human form. He and the others had failed to understand this before Jesus died.

290 John chapter 21, verses 1-14.

Fishing trip
Seven disciples went fishing. They included Thomas, Nathaniel, John and James, Peter, and two others.

📖 See Feature pages 178-79.

Shoal of fish
Fishing from boats was often done in the evening or at night because the fish swam closer to the surface. During the hot daytime sun they dived to the bottom where the water was cooler.

291 John chapter 21, verses 15-19.

Peter's job
Jesus told Peter what his job would be three times, perhaps to remind Peter that he was completely forgiven for letting Jesus down. He had denied Jesus three times, too (story 281).

292 Matthew chapter 28, verses 16-20.

Holy Spirit
The disciples had been promised God's power but they had not received it yet (story 288).

Disciples' job
The task of telling people about Jesus was given to everyone who believed and followed him, not just to the eleven disciples.

290 Breakfast by the lake

For a few weeks after Jesus' death, the disciples did not know what to do. One evening Peter was back at Lake Galilee and he decided to go fishing with some of his friends. He still could not forget that he had let Jesus down so badly.

They fished all night, but caught nothing. As dawn came, they sailed back to the shore.

A man standing on the beach called, 'Have you caught anything?'

'No!' they replied.

'Try throwing your nets on the right side of the boat.'

The fishermen did as the man suggested. Immediately they felt the tug of the net as it filled with fish.

Peter looked at the man on the beach.

'It's Jesus!' he shouted. He jumped into the water and waded ashore.

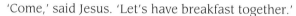

Jesus had made a small fire and had some bread there. 'Bring some of the fish you have caught,' he said. So the disciples dragged the net onto the shore and sat with Jesus on the beach.

'Come,' said Jesus. 'Let's have breakfast together.'

291 Peter's task

When breakfast was over, Jesus talked to Peter on his own.

'Peter,' he said, 'do you really love me?'

'You know I do,' said Peter.

'Then feed my lambs,' Jesus replied.

A few minutes later, Jesus spoke again. 'Peter,' he said, 'do you truly love me?'

'Yes!' said Peter. 'You know I do!'

'Then take care of my sheep,' said Jesus.

After a little while, Jesus spoke for a third time. 'Peter,' he said, 'do you love me?'

Peter was hurt. He remembered how he had disowned Jesus, how he had let him down. But he loved Jesus so much. 'You know everything,' he said to Jesus. 'You know that I love you.'

'I have a special job for you to do,' said Jesus. 'When I have gone away, I want you to look after my followers.'

292 'I will always be with you'

Jesus appeared to his disciples many times after he had risen from the dead. He carried on teaching them about God's kingdom and the good news that he wanted them to take to the whole world.

'Go to Jerusalem and wait for the Holy Spirit whom I will send,' he told them, 'and then go and tell people everywhere about me and teach them everything I have done and said. I promise you, I will always be with you.'

Not long after that Jesus left his disciples and returned to be with God his Father, in heaven.

THE EARLY CHURCH

This section tells the story of the very first followers of Jesus.
Its stories, from the book called the Acts of the Apostles, are full of great bravery
and faith. They were written down by Luke, who also wrote a Gospel
and who was an eyewitness of some of the events.

After Jesus died and rose again, he gave his followers some instructions: 'Go into the world and tell everyone about me,' he said. Until then they had only travelled around Judea, a very small country. But Jesus promised to send the Holy Spirit to give them new power to tell other people about him, and to heal those who were ill.

On the day of Pentecost, the Holy Spirit came and 3,000 people believed in Jesus when Peter first preached in Jerusalem. But some people hated the Christian message. One man, Saul of Tarsus, made it his job to have Christians killed. But one day he had a great vision of Jesus and became a Christian. Known after that as Paul, he became the greatest preacher and teacher of all.

Paul travelled around the countries on the north side of the Mediterranean Sea – modern Turkey, Greece, and finally Italy. He walked or went by sea, surviving many dangers and shipwrecks. In just a few years, groups of Christians were meeting together in many different places, in homes or hired halls, to worship Jesus and learn about him; a 'church' was the word used to describe a group of Christians meeting together in a particular place. Despite being frequently imprisoned, Paul and his friends spread the good news of Jesus far and wide.

293 Jesus returns to heaven

After Jesus rose from the dead, he appeared to his apostles at different times and in different places. He talked to them and taught them more about God. They had no doubt that he was alive.

One day they were eating a meal together.

'Stay in Jerusalem,' he told them. 'My Father God will give you the gift of the Holy Spirit in a few days' time. Do you remember when people went to be baptized by John in the River Jordan? He baptized with water, but now you will be baptized with the Holy Spirit.'

The apostles had often heard Jesus talk about the Holy Spirit, and how he would come to be with them after Jesus had gone.

About six weeks after Jesus rose from the dead, the apostles were with him on the Mount of Olives. They had been wondering about when God's kingdom would come.

'Will your kingdom come to earth when we receive the Holy Spirit?' they asked him.

'No,' said Jesus. 'Only God knows when things will happen. But when the Holy Spirit comes you will have power. The whole world will hear about me, through you.'

Suddenly Jesus began to rise through the air up into the sky, until he disappeared, covered by a cloud.

The apostles stared at the sky. Jesus had gone.

'What are you looking for?' asked two angels, dressed in white. 'Jesus has gone back to heaven, but one day he will return.'

293 Acts chapter 1, verses 1-11.

The Holy Spirit
The Holy Spirit is the 'person' of God who gives power to defeat evil and to tell others about Jesus.

Mount of Olives
This hill to the east of Jerusalem is so named because of the olive trees that used to grow there.

Jesus' ascension
This is the last appearance of Jesus on earth before he 'ascended' to heaven. It does not mean that heaven is in the sky, but it was a sign to the disciples that Jesus had returned to his Father.

294 Acts chapter 2, verses 1-11.

Pentecost
This Jewish festival marked the end of the barley harvest and was also celebrated to mark the day Moses received the Ten Commandments (story 52).

Wind and fire
God sometimes showed he was present by physical signs. Wind reminded people of his breath, which gives life; fire, of his purity and holiness. The Holy Spirit gave the disciples power to help them live and work for Jesus.

Other languages
Sometimes called 'tongues', these were a sign that the message of Jesus was for the whole world.

Be baptized
Baptism is being dipped in, or sprinkled with, water as a sign of God's forgiveness and new life given because of Jesus' death and resurrection (see story 235).

295 Acts chapter 3, verses 1-10.

Beautiful Gate
This bronze gate stood between two courtyards in the temple precincts.

294 The Holy Spirit comes

The apostles stayed in Jerusalem as Jesus had told them. It was the festival of Pentecost and the city was full of visitors from all over the world.

The apostles were together in one room. Suddenly a sound like a strong wind blew through the house, filling it with noise. Something like flames seemed to burn in the air and touch each disciple. As the Holy Spirit touched them, they all began to speak in words of other languages.

The noise from the house attracted a crowd. The apostles rushed out, still speaking. The people in the crowd were amazed.

'What's happening?' some of them said. 'I can understand what these men are saying. They are speaking in my language, talking about God. How is this possible?'

'They're drunk!' laughed others.

'No, we're not!' said Peter in a loud voice. 'It's only nine o'clock in the morning,' and he stood up to teach the crowd. First he reminded them of what the prophets had said, and about Jesus, God's chosen one, the Messiah.

When Peter described how Jesus had suffered and been put to death, the people were horrified. 'What shall we do?' they asked.

'Turn to God and be baptized, so that you can be forgiven,' Peter told them. 'Then you will receive the Holy Spirit.'

That day 3,000 people became followers of Jesus. The apostles did many miracles in the name of Jesus, and with the believers they met together to worship God, to pray and to share what they had with each other.

295 The beggar by the Beautiful Gate

One afternoon, Peter and John went to the temple to pray. As they passed the Beautiful Gate they saw a beggar. He had never been able to walk. He held out his hand. 'Give me some money,' he pleaded.

'Look at us!' said Peter. The beggar looked up hopefully.

'I don't have any silver or gold,' said Peter, 'but I do have something I can give you. In the name of Jesus, walk!'

As he spoke, Peter took hold of the man's hand. He helped him to his feet. Immediately the man could stand. He began to walk. He jumped in the air. 'Praise God!' he shouted.

As Peter and John walked on towards the temple, the beggar stayed with them. He would not let them go.

'Isn't that the man who couldn't walk?' whispered some of the people. They were amazed at what had happened to him.

296 Peter and John in prison

While Peter and John were talking to the people about Jesus, the captain of the temple guard came up with the priests and Sadducees. They arrested Peter and John and threw them into prison.

The next morning Peter and John stood before the High Priest and the other elders. 'How did you do this?' they demanded.

Peter stood up. He knew that the Holy Spirit was with him. 'I'll tell you,' he said. 'He was healed in the name of Jesus, the man you crucified, whom God brought back to life. Jesus is Saviour of the world.'

The High Priest and elders were worried. 'These men are only fishermen, but they were with Jesus for some time. There's no doubt that the beggar has been healed. Everyone is talking about it. But we must stop them speaking about Jesus again.'

'You may go,' they said to the two apostles, 'but you must not speak or teach about Jesus.'

'How can we help it?' they replied. 'We must obey God!'

The authorities let them go. There was nothing they could do.

When Peter and John returned, they began to pray with their friends, 'Help us to be bold and to keep on speaking about you. Help us to do wonderful things in the name of Jesus.'

Suddenly the whole house shook. They were filled with the Holy Spirit and they went out boldly to talk about Jesus.

297 Ananias and Sapphira

Everyone who believed in Jesus began to live in a new way, sharing their possessions and giving money to those who needed it.

Ananias was a new believer. He decided to sell some land. 'Let's give some of the money to the apostles,' he said to his wife, 'but keep some for ourselves. The apostles need never know.'

Ananias took some of the money to the apostles.

But Peter knew what Ananias had done. 'How could you do such a thing?' he said. 'You have lied to God. The land was yours, and the money was yours. You could have done with it what you liked, but you have not been honest.'

As soon as Peter finished speaking, Ananias fell down dead.

Three hours later, Sapphira, his wife, came in. She did not know her husband was dead.

'Is this the amount you and Ananias got for your land?' asked Peter, holding out the money.

'Yes,' lied Sapphira.

'Did you really think that you could trick God?' asked Peter. 'Your husband has died, and now you will die as well.'

Immediately Sapphira died. All the believers were afraid. They realized how powerful God was.

296 Acts chapter 4, verses 1-22.

Arrested
Peter and John were arrested for teaching the people that God had raised Jesus from the dead, which the religious leaders thought was untrue.

High Priest and elders
These made up the Sanhedrin, the chief Jewish Court which had power to deal with religious disputes and some crimes.

House shook
The presence of God the Holy Spirit was so powerful that it felt like an earthquake.

297 Acts chapter 5, verses 1-11.

Sharing
No one was forced to give money or possessions to the church. Ananias' sin was to pretend that he had given all the money from the sale of his land to make himself appear more generous.

Fell down dead
This dramatic and unusual sign showed the new Christians how important it was to be honest with God and with each other.

298 Acts chapter 5, verses 12-42.

Gamaliel
He was a famous Jewish teacher. Saul of Tarsus (who later became Paul, the apostle) was one of his pupils.

Flogged
They were whipped with a leather thong. Jewish law forbade any more than 40 lashes, so people were given no more than 39 lashes in case the authorities broke the law. Many people died of less than 39 lashes.

299 Acts chapter 6, verse 8 to chapter 7, verse 60.

Deacons
'Deacon' means 'one who serves'. Deacons were Christians chosen to do practical, everyday things so the apostles could focus on preaching and teaching.

Blasphemy
This means saying something considered insulting about God or an important religious truth.

Stoning
Stoning was a means of executing people who had committed bad crimes or blasphemy. They were blindfolded, put into a hole in the ground, and stones were hurled at them.

Stephen's 'spirit'
Stephen knew he was about to die. 'Receive my spirit' was another way of asking to be taken from his body to be with God.

298 More and more believers

Day by day the apostles taught and healed people in the name of Jesus and more and more people became believers. The High Priest and the elders were furious. They put all the apostles in prison.

During the night an angel came and set them free. 'Go and stand in the temple courts,' he said. 'Tell everyone about the new life God has given you.'

The next morning the High Priest and the elders sent for the prisoners. An official came back with the news. 'The doors were locked, the guards were on duty. But the cells are empty!' he exclaimed.

'The men you are looking for are in the temple, teaching the people,' said someone.

So the captain of the temple guard went and arrested the apostles again. He did not use force because he did not want a riot. The apostles stood before the Sanhedrin. 'We warned you not to teach about Jesus. You disobeyed us,' they said.

'We obeyed God,' replied Peter.

Some of the Sanhedrin were so angry that they wanted to kill them, but a wise old man spoke up. 'Leave these men alone,' said Gamaliel. 'If this is God's work, nothing will stop it.'

The Sanhedrin had the apostles flogged. Then they told them not to speak about Jesus any longer and released them.

299 The stoning of Stephen

The apostles appointed seven deacons to help organize the sharing of goods and money. Stephen was one of them. God had given him the power to do amazing things in Jesus' name.

Some Jews from Egypt were jealous of Stephen. They tried to argue with him, but they couldn't.

'Let's accuse him of blasphemy!' they said.

Stephen was brought before the Sanhedrin. He heard the lies that were spoken against him. The punishment for blasphemy was death. The Sanhedrin looked at Stephen. They saw that his face looked like an angel's face.

'Are these accusations true?' demanded the High Priest.

'Listen to me,' said Stephen bravely, and he began to tell them how, throughout the ages, God's people had refused to listen to the leaders God had given them. 'And you are just like them. God sent Jesus to lead you back to him, and you had him killed!'

Everyone was furious. They rushed at Stephen.

'I can see Jesus, standing at God's side,' he said.

'Kill him!' they cried.

They took Stephen outside the city and pelted him with stones.

'Lord Jesus,' said Stephen, 'receive my spirit and forgive these people.' At that moment he died.

A young man called Saul watched Stephen die. He was looking after the men's cloaks. He was pleased that Stephen had been killed.

300 Philip in Samaria

After Stephen's death the authorities set about destroying the Christian believers. Saul helped them. The Christians fled. Some went into hiding, others left the area. But wherever they went, they kept telling everyone about Jesus.

One of the deacons was a Greek-speaking Jew called Philip. He was a wise man, and the Holy Spirit was with him.

Philip went to a town in Samaria. He told the people about Jesus. Crowds gathered to hear him. He healed people who were ill and comforted those who were distressed. Many people, both men and women, were baptized in Jesus' name.

301 The Ethiopian treasurer

While Philip was in Samaria, an angel spoke to him. 'You must leave here,' he said, 'and travel on the desert road.'

Philip did as the angel told him. As he walked, a chariot went by. In it sat an Ethiopian official, the treasurer of Queen Candace of Ethiopia. He believed in God and had been to Jerusalem to worship him. He was reading a scroll which contained the words of the prophet Isaiah.

'Stay near the chariot,' the Holy Spirit told Philip. Philip ran up to the chariot.

The Ethiopian was looking puzzled. 'He was killed like a sheep is killed, and he was as silent as a lamb,' he read.

'Do you understand what you are reading?' asked Philip.

The Ethiopian shook his head. 'No,' he replied. 'I need someone to explain it to me.'

Philip climbed into the chariot. He explained how Isaiah had talked about a Saviour who would be killed. 'This passage is about Jesus,' Philip told the Ethiopian. 'It is good news for all who believe in him. Because Jesus died we can be forgiven!'

They passed some water by the roadside. 'Let me be baptized!' the Ethiopian said. So Philip took him down into the water and baptized him.

300 Acts chapter 8, verses 4-8.

Philip
This is not the Philip who was one of Jesus' disciples. Later in his life he settled in the sea-port of Caesarea. His four daughters had the gift of prophecy.

Samaria
The people who lived in this area, north of Jerusalem, were related to the Jews (see stories 254, 260). They expected a 'Messiah' so the message of Jesus was really good news to them.

301 Acts chapter 8, verses 26-40.

Desert road
This led to the south of Jerusalem, leading towards the coast and to Egypt.

Ethiopia
This was probably a country in north Africa, part of modern Sudan around the Nubian desert, rather than modern Ethiopia.

Isaiah
The official was reading aloud from the prophet Isaiah, chapter 53, which looks forward to Jesus suffering for people's sins as 'the lamb of God' (story 182).

Baptism
Philip had probably told the Ethiopian what Peter told the people on the day of Pentecost: to trust Jesus and to be baptized. This was a sign of God's forgiveness and of a person's membership of the Christian church. Any water nearby could be used.

THE NEW TESTAMENT WORLD

Jesus was born into a humble family in a small town in an occupied country in the furthest corner of the Roman Empire. No one could have guessed that, within a century of his birth, his name and his story would have been known in many parts of the Roman Empire by thousands and thousands of people.

Palestine

Palestine was the Roman name for a small region in the eastern part of the Roman Empire. The Jewish people resented the presence of the Roman ruling army, and did not like paying taxes to Caesar in Rome. They longed for the day when they would be free to rule their own country. Many of them were praying that God would send his Messiah to free them from Roman rule.

Jesus was born in Bethlehem, not far from Jerusalem, the capital. He spent much of his life in Galilee, but was eventually crucified in Jerusalem. His death was authorized by Pontius Pilate, the Roman governor of Judea, at the request of the ruling religious people. His followers saw him as God's Messiah.

The spread of Christianity

The Greeks had given the Mediterranean world a common language, great cities, systems of government, arts and education. By the time of Jesus, the Romans ruled a vast empire that stretched from Britain in the north, across modern-day Europe into Turkey, then into the lands of the Bible and around the Mediterranean coast of Africa.

Although the Jewish people resented Roman rule, there were no wars and the Romans had made sure there were good communications by road and sea. Although Judea was 'home' for the Jewish people, there were many Jewish communities in towns and cities throughout the empire. The first Christians spread the good news of Jesus far and wide to both Jews and Gentiles. As Greek was the common language, the gospel was passed on in Greek right across the empire. When the first Christians were persecuted and forced to leave Jerusalem, they went to many different places to spread the message.

Rome•

ITALY

GREECE

Thessalonica •

• Philippi

GALATIA

Corinth • • Athens

• Ephesus

• Colossae

SYRIA

• Antioch

MALTA

THE
MEDITERRANEAN
SEA

CRETE

CYPRUS

• Damascus

GALILEE

• Jerusalem

JUDEA

EGYPT

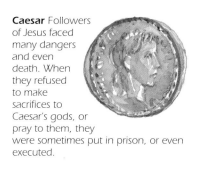

Caesar Followers of Jesus faced many dangers and even death. When they refused to make sacrifices to Caesar's gods, or pray to them, they were sometimes put in prison, or even executed.

Paul's journeys

The apostle Paul and his companions covered many hundreds of miles on foot and by sea in order to tell people about Jesus. They often followed trade routes and visited important cities. Paul took the message to present-day Turkey, to mainland Greece, Crete, Cyprus, Malta, and eventually to Rome, where he spent two years under house arrest. He was often beaten and imprisoned, and was shipwrecked, but nothing could stop him.

CRUCIFIXION

This form of execution was used by the Romans for slaves and the worst criminals, but never for Roman citizens. It was a cruel and horrible death. The criminal was nailed or tied to a cross-beam by his wrists. The cross-beam was then nailed to the upright 'tree', to which his feet were nailed. Death was from exhaustion.

Greeks and Romans They worshipped many gods and goddesses. They were also well educated and very interested in new ideas. The Romans had to worship the Emperor as a living god.

302 Acts chapter 9, verses 1-9.

Damascus
This town was in Syria, to the north of Judea.

Bright light
The people with Saul saw and heard something, but they didn't understand what it was.

303 Acts chapter 9, verses 10-19.

Ananias
This is a different man from the one in story 297. He trusted God to look after him, knowing that if he were wrong, Saul would kill him.

'Brother'
Christians think of each other as members of God's 'family'. Ananias treated Saul as a Christian from the moment he met him.

304 Acts chapter 9, verses 20-31 and Galatians chapter 1, verses 17,18.

City walls
Cities at this time had strong walls which were difficult to climb, and gates which were locked at night to protect people from bandits or invading armies. The basket would have been a strong net or wicker container normally holding wool, hay or straw.

Barnabas
He later went with Paul on his first missionary journey.

302 Saul meets Jesus

Saul hated the Christian believers. He wanted to destroy them all. He went to see the High Priest. 'Give me letters of introduction to the synagogues in Damascus. I want to find the Christians there.'

The High Priest agreed, and Saul set out. As he got near to Damascus, a bright light suddenly appeared from the sky and flashed around him. Saul fell to the ground. A voice spoke to him, 'Saul, Saul, why are you persecuting me?'

'Who are you?' asked Saul.

'I am Jesus,' said the voice, 'and you are persecuting me. Go to Damascus. You will be told what to do next.'

Saul got up. He could not see, so his companions led him by the hand into the city of Damascus.

303 A new life

In Damascus there lived a Christian believer called Ananias. In a vision God said to him, 'Ananias, go to Judas' house on Straight Street. There you will find a man called Saul who cannot see. He will be praying. He has already had a vision in which you touched him and gave him back his sight.'

Ananias was worried. 'But Saul hates Christians,' he replied. 'He has come here to destroy us!'

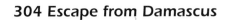

'Go!' said God. 'I have chosen Saul to tell all the people of the world, Jews and Gentiles, about me.'

Ananias found Saul. He placed his hands on him. 'Brother,' said Ananias. 'God has sent me here so that you can be filled with the Holy Spirit and see again.'

Immediately Saul could see. He was baptized.

304 Escape from Damascus

Saul stayed in Damascus for several days. He preached in the synagogue. 'Jesus is the Son of God,' he said.

The people who heard him were astonished. 'We thought that Saul had come here to destroy the Christians,' they said. 'Now he is talking like one of them.'

The Jews were confused and angry. They plotted to kill Saul, and set a guard on the city gates. But Saul had friends. At night they lowered him down through a gap in the city walls, in a basket.

Saul went to Jerusalem to join the believers there. But they were afraid of him. They knew he was a murderer. It was Barnabas who took Saul to the apostles.

'I have seen Jesus,' Saul told them, 'and Jesus has spoken to me.'

The number of believers in Jerusalem increased day by day, but when Saul's life was threatened, he left Jerusalem for Tarsus, his home town.

305 'Dorcas, get up!'

Peter visited believers in different places, teaching and encouraging them. In Lydda he healed a man called Aeneas who had been unable to move for eight years.

Not far away, in Joppa, a Christian woman called Dorcas died. Everyone was very sad because she had always worked hard, helping people who were poor. When the believers heard that Peter was in Lydda, they sent for him.

Peter went into the upstairs room where Dorcas' body lay. He sent everyone away. He prayed, and then he said, 'Dorcas, get up!'

Dorcas opened her eyes. She sat up. Many people believed in Jesus, because of what Peter had done.

306 Peter's vision

One day, while Peter was in Joppa, praying on the roof of the house, he saw a large sheet above him. It was being lowered down by its four corners. In the sheet was every kind of living creature, including reptiles and birds. Peter was hungry, but the meal was not ready.

God spoke to Peter. 'Kill what you want, and eat,' he said.

'But I can't!' said Peter. 'These animals are not clean.'

'Don't call them unclean,' said God. 'I have made them clean.'

Three times God spoke to Peter in the same way. Then the sheet disappeared. 'Three men are looking for you,' said the Holy Spirit. 'Go with them.'

Just then three men came to the house. 'Cornelius the centurion has sent us,' they said. 'He loves God. An angel told him to invite you to his house so that you could talk to him.'

307 New believers

Cornelius was both a Roman and a Gentile. He loved God, but he did not know about Jesus. He invited his close friends and relatives to come and hear what Peter had to say.

Peter told him, 'You know that it is against the Jewish law for a Jew to come into a Gentile's house. But God has shown me that no one is "unclean" in his sight. God does not have favourites.' And Peter told them everything he knew about Jesus.

While Peter was speaking, the Holy Spirit came down so that Cornelius and his family believed. The Jewish believers who were with Peter were amazed. 'Even Gentiles are filled with the Holy Spirit,' they said.

'Let these people be baptized,' said Peter, and Cornelius and his family and friends were baptized in the name of Jesus.

305 Acts chapter 9, verses 32-43.

Lydda and Joppa
Lydda was about 40km/24 miles north-west of Jerusalem. Joppa was about 20km/12 miles further west on the coast.

Raising the dead
This very unusual miracle helped people see that the message of Jesus was true. Very few people had heard of Jesus at this time.

306 Acts chapter 10, verses 9-23.

Roof
Houses had flat roofs, sometimes covered with an awning to make a shady place to sit or sleep (see also story 240).

Unclean
Jews were not allowed to eat many animals including pigs, camels, and rabbits; birds including eagles, ravens, gulls and storks; and anything in the sea which did not have both fins and scales.

307 Acts chapter 10, verses 1-8, 24-48.

Peter's vision
Strict Jews thought contact with Gentiles made them 'unclean'. Now Peter understood that God loved everyone, and Jesus had died for all people.

308 Acts chapter 12, verses 1-19.

Herod
Herod Agrippa I was the nephew of Herod Antipas who killed John the Baptist (story 255) and grandson of Herod the Great who ordered all the baby boys to be killed when Jesus was born (story 233).

James
This is the brother of John and son of Zebedee (see stories 237, 242).

Chains fell off
This is the second time Peter had a miraculous escape (see story 296).

Mary's house
This Mary is the mother of Mark and aunt of Barnabas. Mary was standing near the cross when Jesus died.

309 Acts chapter 13, verses 1-3.

Antioch
A number of years have passed. The church in Antioch (a city in the far north of Syria, about 480km/300 miles north of Jerusalem) has grown strong. Saul has made it his new base.

God's message
The prophets in Antioch agreed that God was calling Paul to go to Cyprus. They would have felt God's message come strongly to them as they prayed.

310 Acts chapter 13, verses 4-12.

308 Praying for Peter

After Peter returned to Jerusalem, King Herod had James executed. Then he put Peter in prison, guarded by sixteen soldiers. He wanted Peter to be tried in public.

While Peter was in prison, all the believers prayed.

The night before the trial Peter was asleep, chained between two soldiers. Suddenly a bright light shone in the cell, and an angel appeared. 'Get up and follow me!' said the angel. As the angel touched Peter, the chains fell off his wrists. They walked past all the guards. Then the iron gates opened by themselves, and Peter and the angel walked out into the street. The angel vanished.

Peter walked to Mary's house. A crowd of believers was there, praying for him. He knocked at the door. Rhoda, the servant girl, recognized Peter's voice but did not open the door. 'It's Peter!' she told the others.

'Don't be silly!' they replied.

Peter kept on knocking. The believers were astonished when he told them what had happened. Then he left for a secret location.

Herod was furious when the guards could not find Peter. He had them all executed.

309 Saul leaves Antioch

The Christians at Antioch were keen to serve God. Saul had spent a year with them, teaching them to be disciples of Jesus. When they heard that the Christians in Jerusalem were facing a famine, they organized a collection and sent them money.

One day, Saul and four other Christians, including his friend Barnabas, came together to worship God. They prepared themselves for God to speak. The Holy Spirit spoke to them, 'I have chosen Saul and Barnabas to do a special job for me.'

The believers placed their hands on Saul and Barnabas and prayed for them. 'God be with you wherever you go,' they said.

310 The good news in Cyprus

Saul, who was now also known as Paul, and Barnabas, with John Mark as their helper, set sail for the island of Cyprus, Barnabas' home.

When they got there, they were met by a sorcerer called Elymas, who worked for the Roman governor, Sergius Paulus. When the governor heard that Paul and Barnabas had arrived in Cyprus, he sent for them. He wanted to hear about God. But Elymas did not want them to talk to his master. 'Don't believe anything they say,' he told the governor. Elymas was an enemy of God.

Paul looked straight at Elymas. 'I know that you are full of lies and tricks,' he said. 'Because of this, you will be unable to see.'

Suddenly Elymas lost his sight. He groped around, looking for someone to help him. When Sergius Paulus saw what had happened, he believed in the power of Jesus.

311 Paul left for dead

Paul and Barnabas continued on their journey but John Mark went back to Jerusalem. From Cyprus they sailed to Galatia and visited a number of places. Eventually they went to Lystra where they saw a man who had never been able to walk. He listened as Paul spoke about Jesus.

'I believe this Jesus can make me well,' he said to himself.

Paul looked at the man. He knew what he was thinking. 'Stand up and walk!' he said. The man stood up and walked.

The crowd was amazed. 'The gods have come to visit us!' they cried. They thought Barnabas was the Greek god Zeus and Paul was Hermes. The priest of the temple of Zeus rushed out to meet them. He brought bulls to sacrifice to them and garlands.

'Stop!' shouted Paul to the crowd. 'We're not gods – we're people, just like you! We've come to tell you about the living God.'

There were some Jews in the crowd who stirred up the crowd against Paul and Barnabas. They took Paul outside the city, stoned him, and left him for dead. But Paul was still alive. Supported by the other believers, he got up and went back to the city. He left Lystra the next day.

312 The meeting in Jerusalem

Paul and Barnabas returned to Antioch, and found that false teachers were telling the Gentile Christians that they had to follow Jewish customs. To settle the argument the church sent Paul and Barnabas and the false teachers to Jerusalem to talk to the leaders there.

It was a difficult meeting, but eventually Paul and Barnabas returned with the news that Gentile Christians could please God without the Jewish laws. They also carried a letter to Antioch with some helpful advice.

Paul and Barnabas stayed for a while, and then following a disagreement, Barnabas left for Cyprus with John Mark.

Paul's journey
This visit to Cyprus, an island in the Mediterranean Sea close to the Syrian and Turkish mainland, is the first of three missionary journeys.

Sorcerer
Elymas used occult methods to see the future and cast spells. Such things are forbidden in the Bible.

311 Acts chapter 13, verse 13 and chapter 14, verses 8-20.

John Mark
Travel was hard, food was scarce, and people kept attacking the travellers. Mark may have found the experience too frightening.

Lystra
This is one of several Roman colonies which Paul visited in Galatia in modern Turkey.

Gods
Greeks and Romans thought of Zeus as the chief god, and Hermes was his spokesman. There was a legend that the two gods had once visited Lystra in disguise, and had not been recognized. The people did not want to be so unwelcoming a second time!

312 Acts chapter 15, verses 1-39.

Council of Jerusalem
Paul and Barnabas went to explain what God had done in Antioch and elsewhere. Peter also reminded the Council that God had sent the Holy Spirit to the Gentiles.

313 Acts chapter 15, verse 40 to chapter 16, verse 5.

Silas

Also known as Silvanus, he had brought the letter to Antioch after the Council of Jerusalem and seems to have stayed there. Like Paul, he was a Roman citizen which gave him certain legal rights. This is Paul's second missionary journey.

Timothy

He was the son of a Greek father and a Jewish mother. He may have become a Christian when Paul first visited Lystra.

314 Acts chapter 16, verses 6-15.

Luke joins

Luke, the author of the Acts of the Apostles, now joins the group. He may once have lived in Macedonia, in northern Greece.

Philippi

Many retired soldiers lived in this Roman colony but few Jews, so there was no synagogue there. Instead the Jews met each week by the river to pray (see also story 349).

Purple cloth

This was worn only by the very rich.

See Feature pages 178-79.

315 Acts chapter 16, verses 16-24.

Evil spirit

The girl was actually saying the right things, although it was the evil spirit, or demon, forcing her to. Many people probably thought she was mad, so Paul did not welcome her support.

313 Paul's new companions

Paul asked Silas to be his companion on his next journey. They left Antioch and went westwards, through the regions of Syria and Cilicia. They visited the different churches on the way, and encouraged all those who believed in Jesus.

Paul returned to Lystra. He met the Christians there. 'You must meet Timothy,' they said. 'He is a good man.' Paul knew that Timothy would be a good helper, so he asked Timothy to join them.

Paul, Silas and Timothy went from town to town. Everywhere they went they encouraged the believers and more and more people became followers of Jesus.

314 The friends go to Greece

Paul, Silas and Timothy carried on with their journey, guided by the Holy Spirit. A doctor called Luke joined them.

One night, Paul had a strange vision. He saw a Greek man, who was begging. 'Please come to Macedonia and help us!' he cried. Paul knew that God was speaking to him, so he and his companions set out for Philippi, the leading city in Macedonia.

Philippi was a Roman colony, and on the morning of the Sabbath, Paul and Silas went outside the city to the river where the Jews met to pray. While they were there, they noticed a group of women. They sat down and began to speak to them about Jesus.

One of the women, Lydia, was a trader in expensive purple cloth. She believed in God, and as she listened to Paul and heard what he said about Jesus, she suddenly knew in her heart that what Paul said was true: Jesus was God's Son.

'Please baptize me and my family,' she asked Paul. 'And come and stay in my home.'

315 The fortune-teller

Everywhere Paul and his friends went in Philippi they were followed by a slave-girl who had the ability to tell fortunes. She made a lot of money for her owners. She shouted out, 'These men do the work of the Most High God. They will tell you how to be saved!'

Paul was unhappy for the girl. He knew that she had an evil spirit in her. He turned to look at the girl and spoke to the spirit. 'In the name of Jesus, come out of her!' he ordered.

Immediately, the spirit left the girl. All her supernatural powers vanished. Her owners were furious. They couldn't make money from her any more. They seized Paul and Silas and took them to the authorities. 'These men are causing chaos!' they said.

The crowd agreed, and the magistrates ordered that they be beaten and put in prison. 'Guard these men carefully,' they said to the jailer. Paul and Silas were put in an inner cell and fastened in the stocks.

316 Panic in the prison

It was midnight. Paul and Silas were singing songs of praise to God and the other prisoners were listening to them.

Suddenly, the earth shook and every door in the prison burst open. The prisoners' chains came loose. Immediately the jailer woke up. He saw the doors were open. 'The prisoners have escaped!' he cried. He grabbed his sword, ready to kill himself.

'Stop!' shouted Paul. 'We're all here! No one has escaped!'

The jailer rushed in to Paul and Silas and fell on his knees. He was trembling. 'What must I do to be saved?' he asked.

'Believe in Jesus,' said Paul, and he told the jailer about Jesus.

At last the jailer got up, and took them to his house. 'Baptize me and all my family,' he said. Then he prepared a meal for Paul and Silas. He was so happy because now he knew God.

In the morning the magistrates sent a message to the jailer: 'Release those men.'

'You are free to go,' the jailer said. 'Go in peace.'

317 Trouble in Thessalonica

Paul and his friends travelled on to the city of Thessalonica. While they were there, Paul went to the synagogue for three Sabbaths and explained the scriptures.

'You know what is written,' he said. 'God promised to send a Saviour into the world, but the Saviour would suffer and die before rising from the dead. I believe that Jesus is God's Saviour.'

Jews and Greeks, men and women, heard and believed Paul's message. But some of the Jews were jealous. They went to the market place and found some tough men to start a riot.

The mob searched for Paul and Silas. They swarmed around Jason's house looking for them. But Paul and Silas were not there.

Instead, the crowd dragged out Jason and his friends. 'You have befriended dangerous troublemakers!' they shouted. 'You've broken Caesar's laws. You say that Jesus is king, as well as Caesar.'

The city authorities did not know what to do. In the end, they demanded money for bail, and let Jason and his friends go.

Stocks
This was a frame made of two pieces of wood locked over prisoners' legs so that they could not get up or walk.

316 Acts chapter 16, verses 25-40.

The jailer
If the prisoners escaped, the jailer could be executed for failing in his duty, even though on this occasion it wasn't his fault.

Magistrates
The people who ruled the city may have let the apostles go because they were also frightened or perhaps one night in prison was all they could legally impose for such a small 'crime'.

317 Acts chapter 17, verses 1-9.

Thessalonica
The capital of Macedonia, 120km/75 miles west of Philippi, was on the Egnatian Way, an important road across the top of Greece.

Sabbath
The Jewish day of rest (Saturday).

See Feature pages 82-83.

Bail
Money can be paid to a court so that someone can go free as long as they return to face trial. Jason was the owner of the house where Paul stayed.

318 Acts chapter 17, verses 16-34.

Athens and its idols
Athens was the leading city of southern Greece, full of temples and statues to Greek gods, which were mostly like human figures. The chief gods were Hermes and Athena.

See Feature pages 158-59.

Berea
Paul and his friends had fled to this town south of Thessalonica.

Areopagus
This hill was dedicated to Ares, god of war. A council met here to deal with religious and moral disputes.

319 Acts chapter 18, verses 1-22.

Corinth
This large city, 80km/50 miles west of Athens had over 500,000 people. It was a centre for the worship of Aphrodite, the Greek goddess of love (see also stories 338, 339, 340). Paul stayed here for about 18 months.

320 Acts chapter 18, verse 23 to chapter 19, verse 22.

318 The unknown god

Paul went on alone to Athens, leaving the others in Berea. The city of Athens was magnificent, full of beautiful buildings. But everywhere Paul looked there were idols, for the people liked to worship many different gods.

He went to the synagogue to talk to the Jews; and he went to the market place to talk to the Gentiles. But the people did not understand what he was saying. 'You're talking about a foreign god that has nothing to do with us!' they said.

At last they took Paul to the council of the Areopagus. 'Explain to us your message,' they said. 'We have never heard anything like it.'

Paul stood up. 'People of Athens,' he said. 'I can see that you are very religious, you have so many gods to worship. I have even seen an altar to an unknown god. Let me talk to you about this god, because I know who he is: he is the living God who made the earth.'

The people listened. Paul told them about Jesus, how he died and rose from the dead.

'What nonsense!' sneered some.

'How interesting,' said others. 'Tell us some more.'

319 Tent-makers together

Paul left Athens and went to Corinth. While he was there, he met Priscilla and Aquila. They had come from Rome, but had left there because Emperor Claudius had ordered all Jews to leave.

Priscilla and Aquila, like Paul, were tent-makers by trade. So he stayed with them and they worked together, cutting and sewing cloth made from goats' hair into tents.

Every Sabbath Paul went to the synagogue to preach. But few of the Jews would listen. 'From now on, I will speak to the Gentiles,' said Paul.

Some people heard Paul's message and believed. At last, Paul felt it was time to leave Corinth. Taking his friends Priscilla and Aquila with him, he set sail for Antioch in Syria, his home base.

320 Paul goes to Ephesus

Some time later, Paul set off on his travels again. This time he headed for the busy city of Ephesus, where he met some believers.

Paul asked them, 'Did the Holy Spirit come when you believed?'

They looked blank. 'We've never heard of the Holy Spirit,' they said.

'Were you baptized?' asked Paul.

'Yes,' they replied, 'with water, like John the Baptist did.'

Then Paul explained to them about Jesus. He put his hands on them, and immediately they were filled with the Holy Spirit.

Paul preached in the synagogue. He read the scriptures and talked about the living God. He lectured in public places, so that as many people as possible could hear about Jesus.

For two years, while he stayed in Ephesus, God enabled Paul to do extraordinary things. Even sick people were cured by touching the handkerchiefs that Paul had touched.

As for those who believed, they saw the power of God working among them, changing them and making them more like Jesus.

321 The silversmiths' riot

Demetrius, the silversmith, made money by selling models of the temple of the goddess Artemis in Ephesus. One day he called together all the other craftsmen, who, like him, made things to do with the worship of the gods.

'We earn good money,' he said. 'This man Paul could spoil it all. He is saying that there aren't any man-made gods, and lots of people, not just in Ephesus, believe him. If we're not careful we'll lose out, and the great goddess Artemis will be forgotten.'

The craftsmen took action. 'Artemis is great!' they chanted and walked through the city. Soon everyone was in uproar. The crowd seized two of Paul's friends and dragged them to the theatre.

The crowd chanted and shouted 'Artemis is great!' for two hours until a town official stood in front of them..

'Ephesians!' he shouted. 'Everybody knows that our city is the home of the great goddess Artemis. But you have dragged these men here, even though they have not said or done anything against Artemis. If Demetrius and his friends have a complaint they must go to the courts. Otherwise, we will be guilty of causing a riot. Now go home!'

The crowd gradually dispersed and the people went home.

322 Miracle in Troas

Paul left Ephesus and, after touring through Greece, went to Troas. One night he met with some other believers in an upstairs room to share bread and wine together, as Jesus and the disciples had done the night before Jesus died.

Paul started to speak. He knew that he did not have long in Troas, and so he wanted to tell them as much as possible. He was still talking at midnight.

The room was hot, and lit by oil lamps. It was so late that a young man called Eutychus, who was sitting on the window sill, went to sleep and fell out of the window, crashing onto the ground. He was killed instantly.

Paul rushed downstairs. He threw his arms round Eutychus.

'Don't worry,' he said to other believers, 'he's not dead. He's alive!'

Eutychus stood up. He went back upstairs with the others and they shared bread together, thanking God.

Paul's travels
The third missionary journey takes Paul to Ephesus, an important city on the coast of the Aegean Sea, in the Roman province of Asia (now modern Turkey). A wide road lined with columns led from the harbour to the city centre.

John the Baptist
See stories 235, 255.

321 Acts chapter 19, verses 23-41.

Artemis or Diana
This goddess was thought to be the source of fertility and love. The temple to Artemis in Ephesus was the largest building in the world of its time, and was one of the seven wonders of the world.

322 Acts chapter 20, verses 1-12.

Troas
Ships regularly crossed from Macedonia to this seaport on the Aegean coast in the north of Asia Minor (modern Turkey).

Upstairs room
This building was more like a western terraced house with several storeys. It may have been a block of apartments.

323 Acts chapter 20, verses 13-37.

Miletus
It would have taken the elders about a day to walk to this port, about 50km/30 miles south of Ephesus, crossing the Meander river.

Elders
These leaders of the church would probably have had other jobs as well.

324 Acts chapter 21, verses 1-16.

Caesarea
This port was 90km/56 miles north-west of Jerusalem on the Mediterranean coast.

Agabus
Coming from the Jerusalem area, Agabus knew how suspicious the Jewish leaders were of the Christians. He had accurately predicted a famine some years before.

Warning
Paul was not afraid to do what he believed was right, even though it might result in him being taken prisoner. He knew God could use everything for good.

325 Acts chapter 21, verses 17-32.

Roman commander
He was in charge of the soldiers who were stationed in Jerusalem. They kept law and order as well as stopping any rebellion against Roman rule.

323 Paul's long sea journey

Paul was on his way to Jerusalem. It was a long journey by sea, and on the way he stopped at the ancient port of Miletus. While he was there, Paul sent for the elders of the church in Ephesus to come to meet him.

When the ship was ready to leave, they gathered together on the quay. 'I know that I will not see you again,' said Paul. He reminded them of how he had tried to set them a good example, and warned them to obey God and remember his teaching. 'I give you to God, knowing that he will look after you,' he said.

The elders and Paul knelt together and prayed. Everyone was crying. They hugged Paul, and said goodbye as he went on board. They could not believe that they would never see Paul again.

324 Prophecy of danger

After several weeks at sea, Paul landed at Caesarea, not far from Jerusalem. He needed to rest, and stayed at Philip's house.

While he was there, a Christian called Agabus came to see Paul. God had given him the gift of prophecy. Agabus took hold of Paul's belt and began to tie up his own hands and feet with it, until he was unable to move. 'This is what the Holy Spirit says,' prophesied Agabus. 'The Jews in Jerusalem will capture the owner of this belt and give him to the Gentiles.'

'You must not go to Jerusalem!' cried the believers when they heard Agabus' message. But Paul would not listen. 'Don't cry,' he said. 'I am prepared to die in Jerusalem for Jesus, if that's what God wants.'

The believers knew that Paul would not change his mind. 'God's will be done,' they said, as they watched him go to Jerusalem.

325 Riots in Jerusalem

When Paul was in Jerusalem he went to the temple. Some Jews from Asia recognized him. 'Listen!' they shouted. 'This is the man who is telling everyone to ignore God's Law, and is saying bad things about us and our temple. We must do something about it.'

When the Jewish citizens of Jerusalem heard the accusations against Paul, they rushed into the temple, seized him, dragged him outside and tried to beat him to death.

The Roman commander heard what had happened, and ordered his troops to stop the riot. As soon as the soldiers rushed into the crowd, Paul was left alone.

326 Paul is arrested

The commander walked through the people. He looked at Paul. 'Arrest this man,' he ordered, 'and bind him in chains.' Then he asked Paul, 'What have you done to cause so much trouble?'

The crowd started to shout. Everyone was shouting something different. The commander could make no sense of it. There was so much noise, and so many different stories.

'Take him to the barracks,' he ordered.

The crowd surged forwards. 'Away with him! Kill him!' they cried.

The soldiers picked Paul up and carried him to safety.

327 Life after death

The next day the Roman commander presented Paul to the Jewish Council, the Sanhedrin, to see what would happen. Paul stood up.

'My brothers,' he said, looking at them confidently. 'My conscience is clear. I have only done what God has asked of me.'

Ananias, the High Priest, was furious when he heard Paul's words. He ordered that Paul be struck on the mouth.

Then Paul thought about how he could make them argue among themselves. He knew that some of the council members were Pharisees and others were Sadducees. 'I am a Pharisee,' he said, 'and so was my father. The only reason I have been brought here is because I believe that after I die, I will live again.'

The Pharisees also believed in life after death, so they said, 'This man has done nothing wrong.'

'Yes, he has!' shouted the Sadducees. 'There's no life after death.'

A violent argument broke out so the commander ordered his troops to take Paul back to the barracks. In the night, God spoke to Paul: 'Be brave! Now you will go to Rome, where you will tell the people about me.'

328 The plot to kill Paul

Forty Jewish men met secretly together. 'We swear not to eat or drink, until we have killed Paul!' they said.

They went to the Sanhedrin and told them of their plans. 'Ask the commander to bring Paul before the council. Pretend that you want some more information from him. We'll kill him before he gets here.'

But Paul's nephew heard of the plot. He went to visit his uncle at the barracks. 'They are planning to kill you,' he warned.

Paul told a centurion, 'Take this young man to the commander.'

The commander took Paul's nephew by the hand. 'What is it?' he asked. The young man told the commander everything.

'Go home,' said the commander. 'But don't tell anyone that you have spoken to me.'

---

326 Acts chapter 21, verse 33 to chapter 22, verse 29.

Paul the Roman
Paul's Roman citizenship gave him certain legal rights. He could not be arrested without proper charges and could not be held without a fair trial. As the commander took him in, Paul told him who he was; the soldiers had assumed he was an Egyptian bandit!

The riot
The commander allowed Paul to speak to the crowd. He told them about his faith in Jesus but they started to riot again when he said Jesus died for Gentiles as well as for Jews.

327 Acts chapter 22, verse 30 to chapter 23, verse 11.

Ananias
He was known to be a cruel man even though he was High Priest.

Pharisees and Sadducees
They were two groups within the Jewish community who believed different things about the resurrection. So Paul deliberately got them arguing amongst themselves.

328 Acts chapter 23, verses 12-22.

Forty men
These were probably extremists who wanted any excuse to use violence against people they thought were anti-Jewish.

329 Acts chapter 23, verse 23 to chapter 24, verse 27.

Soldiers
Paul was well protected: his escort was of 200 soldiers, 70 horsemen and 200 spearmen!

Caesarea
The Jewish 'king' Herod Agrippa II had built an aqueduct, theatre and harbour here.

Felix
The governor of the Roman province of Judea about AD52-59 was a former slave.

Life after death
Paul is referring to Jesus' resurrection (see also story 327). If Jesus had not risen from the dead, then there was no hope that anyone else would.

330 Acts chapter 25, verse 1 to chapter 26, verse 32.

Festus
He was governor of Judea about AD59-62 and seems to have been a good ruler. During the trial he consulted with Herod.

Appeal to Caesar
Roman citizens could have their cases heard by the emperor (Caesar) or his deputy. It was like appealing to the highest court in the empire. The emperor at this time was Nero, who later started to murder Christians.

331 Acts chapter 27, verses 1-44.

329 Paul meets Governor Felix

The commander ordered a detachment of soldiers to take Paul to Caesarea, by night. There he would see Governor Felix.

When the soldiers arrived, they handed Paul over to the governor, who kept him under guard. 'I will hear what you have to say when your accusers get here,' he said.

Five days later, Ananias, some elders, and a lawyer called Tertullus arrived.

'We do not want to waste your time,' Tertullus said. 'This man is a troublemaker.' And he told Felix what Paul had been doing.

Felix gestured to Paul to speak.

'I have witnesses who will say that what I have been accused of is untrue,' said Paul. 'However, I do admit to being a Christian, and I know that the only reason these people have wanted me brought to trial is because I have said that I believe in life after death.'

Felix adjourned the case. He ordered a centurion to guard Paul. Over the next few days, Felix and his wife Drusilla sent for Paul and asked him to tell them about Jesus, although Felix also hoped that Paul would offer him some money as a bribe.

Because Felix wanted to keep the Jews happy, he left Paul in prison. Two years later, Paul was still there, but Felix had been replaced by a new governor, Porcius Festus.

330 Paul on trial

As soon as Festus, the new governor, arrived in the province, the Jewish leaders requested a meeting with him.

'Please have Paul moved to Jerusalem,' they begged, hoping to arrange to kill Paul on his journey, 'so that he can stand trial there.'

Festus refused. Instead he arranged to go to Caesarea to see Paul with some of the elders.

The trial began. The Jews accused Paul of many things, but they could prove nothing.

'I have not broken Jewish law or Caesar's law,' insisted Paul. 'I am a Roman citizen and I have the right to appeal to Caesar.'

So Festus arranged for Paul to be moved to Rome.

331 Shipwrecked!

Paul was handed over to a centurion called Julius. They sailed from port to port, heading towards Italy. Each stage of the journey was more hazardous than the last. The winds were against them, for it was nearly the time of the autumn storms.

At last they reached Crete. Paul told Julius, 'I don't think we should sail from here. Conditions are bad. The cargo may be lost. People will die.'

Julius ignored Paul's advice. They sailed on.

Suddenly a gentle wind changed to a strong hurricane-force wind. The sky grew black. The sailors could not see the planets and the stars to guide them so the ship was driven aimlessly by the wind and waves.

Day after day the storm raged. The sailors threw the cargo into the sea. No one ate. No one thought they would survive.

Finally Paul spoke to all those on board. 'Be brave!' he shouted. 'Last night an angel told me that the ship would be wrecked but that we would not die.'

'Land!' shouted the sailors, sensing land in the darkness.

'Eat!' urged Paul. 'We need food to live.' Daylight came. The ship ran aground and broke up. Everyone struggled to shore. They had landed on the island of Malta.

332 The viper's bite

The Maltese islanders rushed to the beach to help the people from the shipwreck. It was raining and very cold, so they built a fire. Paul helped to put wood on it. He picked up a pile of brushwood, and as he threw it onto the flames, a viper slithered out of it and twisted itself around his hand, sinking its fangs into him.

The islanders saw the snake. 'That man must be a murderer,' they whispered. 'He may have escaped the storm, but now he will die from the snake bite. That's justice!'

They watched Paul, waiting for him to swell up and die.

But nothing happened. Paul carried on as if he had not been bitten.

'We were wrong,' they said to one another. 'That man can't be a murderer. He must be a god.'

333 Off to Rome

Publius, the governor of Malta, lived nearby. He welcomed the shipwrecked passengers into his home and made sure that they were well looked after.

At that time Publius' father was unwell. He lay in bed, hot and feverish and suffering from dysentery. Paul went to see the old man and prayed. Then he placed his hands on him. The fever vanished and the man was well again.

When the islanders heard what Paul had done, those who were ill came to see him and he healed them.

By the time a ship was ready to set sail, the Maltese people gave Paul food and supplies for the journey.

Paul was ready. He knew that God had already planned for him to preach the good news of Jesus, in Rome.

Sailing
This Alexandrian cargo ship tried to hug the coast rather than sail across the open sea. The weather in the Mediterranean can be bad in winter and at this time few ships would have made such a journey. Sailors found their way by using the sun and stars. They had no magnetic compasses or other navigation aids.

332 Acts chapter 28, verses 1-6.

Malta
This is an island south of Italy in the Mediterranean Sea.

Snake bite
The islanders believed that the gods always saw that justice was done. When the snake bit Paul they assumed that he was a criminal who had escaped the sea but would not escape the death he deserved.

333 Acts chapter 28, verses 7-10.

Paul in Rome
When he arrived, he was put under house arrest for two years. He could live in a rented house, and visitors would have brought him food, but he always had a guard with him.

Paul's death
It is possible that Paul was released and went on a fourth missionary journey. He was eventually executed by the emperor Nero about AD68.

LETTERS TO CHURCHES

This section is made up of a collection of letters to the first Christian churches in different places in the first century AD. Many of these letters were written by Paul the apostle, in reply to questions from new Christians about how to be followers of Jesus.

The message of Jesus had spread quickly all over the Roman Empire. Paul and other apostles started churches, and other Christians took the good news of Jesus wherever they went. At that time there was no central group of leaders who told Christians how to worship or behave, or what to believe, so leaders such as Paul wrote letters to the new believers to help them understand their faith and correct their behaviour.

Life was very hard for the first Christians. People around them worshipped many gods, and often behaved in ways which were harsh and unloving. The pressure for Christians to be like everyone else was strong. And to make matters worse, there were some people who claimed to be Christian but who were teaching churches all sorts of things which were not right. People became very confused.

Although the good roads and sea routes of the Roman Empire meant that the apostles could travel by land or sea to many different towns, it took a long time and they could not visit everyone at once. Writing letters was a good way of keeping in touch.

These letters have been preserved in the New Testament. Although modern life is very different from the life of first-century Christians, many problems are the same, and the letters contain important teachings for Christians in every century.

334 Galatians chapter 2, verse 16 and chapter 5, verses 13, 14, 22-25.

Galatia
Paul had visited some of the cities in this large Roman province in what is now Turkey, including Antioch, Lystra and Derbe. This is probably the earliest of his letters included in the Bible, and was written about AD49.

Jewish law
Some Jews who had become Christians believed they could only know God personally if they followed many ceremonies and rules. Paul said that God accepted people because they trusted Jesus, not because of the rules they followed.

334 Be like Jesus

The Christians in Galatia were confused. They thought they had to worship God in the way the Jewish people had always done in order to know God. Paul wrote them a letter to remind them of what he had already taught them:

'The only way we can please God is through faith in Jesus, not by following the Jewish law. Don't you know that Jesus came to set us free? Don't get tangled up with doing what the Law says. That will make you a slave again.

'But you mustn't use your freedom as an excuse to behave badly and do exactly as you like. Remember the commandment: "Love your neighbour as you love yourself." Let your lives be controlled by the Holy Spirit. Then you will be like Jesus. Your lives will show love, joy, peace, patience, kindness, goodness, faithfulness, gentleness and self-control.'

335 The wild tongue

James was a leader in the church based in Jerusalem. His letter was to all Christians everywhere, giving practical advice on how to live and behave.

'Everyone, and particularly those who teach, must be careful what they say,' wrote James. 'The tongue is only a small part of our body, but it makes huge claims! We control a horse by putting a bit into its mouth. A huge ship, powered by the wind, is controlled by a small rudder. A whole forest can be set on fire by a tiny spark. Our tiny tongues can cause the same damage. What we say can hurt and destroy. We must tame our tongues, so that we use them only to speak good and to praise God.'

336 When Jesus returns

The early Christians eagerly looked forward to the day when Jesus would return from heaven as he had promised. They thought it would happen very soon. But the Christians in Thessalonica were confused. Some members of their church had died, and Jesus had still not returned. 'What will happen to them when Jesus does come back?' they wondered. 'And when is it going to happen?'

Paul wrote to them: 'Do not worry about your Christian friends who have died. When Jesus returns, those who have believed in him will come back to life. Those of us who are alive when he returns will rush to meet him. Everyone who believes in Jesus will live with him for ever, but no one knows either the time or the date when this will happen. So keep on living good lives that please God.'

337 A prayer for peace

The Thessalonian Christians read Paul's letter and felt encouraged. But they were being attacked and persecuted.

'Surely Jesus must be coming back any day now,' they cried.

Paul wanted to send a second letter. He reminded them to keep on working, for no one could know when Jesus would return. Finally, he asked his secretary to stop writing. He picked up the pen, and began to write himself.

'I pray that Jesus, who is the Lord of peace, will give you peace all the time, and in every way,' he wrote. 'May the Lord Jesus be with you all.'

335 James chapter 3, verses 1-12.

James
He was probably the brother of Jesus, not the brother of John, one of Jesus' disciples. He wrote this letter about AD50.

336 1 Thessalonians chapter 4, verse 13 to chapter 5, verse 11.

Thessalonica
Paul wrote from Corinth in the south of Greece to this important city in the north. He had been there for only three weeks when he had to leave quickly after a riot (story 317).

Jesus' return
Jesus often spoke about coming back to earth at the end of the world (story 264). Paul taught that when Jesus returns all those who have died will be 'resurrected'. Those who have followed him will live with him in heaven.

337 2 Thessalonians chapter 3, verses 16-18.

Persecution
Some people treated Christians as outcasts, or mugged them, or falsely accused them of crimes to get them put in jail.

Keep working
Some of the Christians in Thessalonica had given up their jobs because they expected Jesus to return almost immediately.

338 1 Corinthians chapter 1, verses 10-12 and chapter 12, verses 12-27.

Corinth
People in this large city in southern Greece worshipped many gods and disobeyed God's laws. Paul probably wrote these letters about AD55, from Ephesus.

Jesus' 'body'
The church is called 'the body of Christ': a large group of people in which each one has an important part to play.

339 1 Corinthians chapter 13, verses 4-8.

True love
Aphrodite was the goddess of the love between men and women. Paul says real love is like Jesus' love, which means caring for someone and putting them first, with no thought of reward or thanks.

340 2 Corinthians chapter 5, verses 17-19.

Another letter
There were at least four letters from Paul to this church, but only two still exist.

Changed people
Paul explains that being a Christian isn't about simply believing and following a special code. When someone trusts Jesus, he starts to change them to become more like him. It is like starting life all over again.

338 Problems in Corinth

Things were not right within the church at Corinth. The Christians were jealous of each other. There were arguments and fighting. It was chaos.

Paul wrote to them from Ephesus, eager to show them how important it was for them to love each other and work together peacefully.

'You, the church, are like a body, made up of lots of different bits. Just imagine if a foot said, "I want to be a hand! I don't want to be part of this body any more!" Whatever the foot said, it would still be part of the body, wouldn't it? Or imagine if the whole body was made up of one massive eye! How would it hear? Or what if the eye said to the hand, "I don't need you any more!"?

'Each part of a human body is important. God made it that way. Each part is needed, or the body doesn't work properly. It's the same thing being a Christian. Each person in the church is equally important, and needed by the others to make up the "body" of Jesus here on earth.'

339 A lesson in love

Paul remembered the city of Corinth, and the many people of different races who lived there. It was a busy place, overshadowed by the huge temple to the Greek goddess of love, Aphrodite. How difficult it was for the Corinthian Christians to understand what God's love was like!

Paul wanted to explain. 'Love is patient and kind,' he wrote. 'Love does not want things that others have. It does not show off and it is not proud. Love isn't rude or selfish. It doesn't get angry easily and it doesn't bear a grudge. Love never fails.'

340 You are God's friends

A year later, Paul wrote to the Corinthians again. During that year he had visited the church, and written to them. His letter had been hard, but it had made them think, and they had begun to sort out their differences.

'Remember what happened to you when you became a Christian,' wrote Paul. 'You became a new person, a new creation. You changed inside. Your old life, and the old ways of behaving, have gone. Because of Jesus, God has made you his friends.'

341 The Christians in Rome

Paul also wrote to the Christians in Rome. He had heard about their faith and he already knew many of them. He knew that some of them were uncertain of their faith, unsure of what it meant to be a Christian.

'God is holy and perfect,' wrote Paul, 'and so are his laws. Anyone who breaks them deserves to be punished. And as everyone is guilty of breaking God's Law, everyone deserves punishment!

'But God has provided us with a way of escaping punishment!' continued Paul. 'Even though we are all guilty, we can become God's friends if we believe in Jesus.

'Remember the story of how sin and death came into the world because of one man? But now God has made sure that we can have forgiveness and life through one man, his Son, Jesus.'

342 New life in the Holy Spirit

'So,' wrote Paul, 'if we believe in Jesus there is no need to be afraid. God's Holy Spirit lives in us, helping us to do what is right, helping us to pray, showing us that we are God's children. Because the Holy Spirit is in us, we have the right to call God, "Daddy"!'

Paul knew how difficult things had been for the Christians in Rome. He wanted to encourage them.

'Now we are suffering,' said Paul, 'but one day, in the future, God's glory will be shown to the whole world. Everything in creation will be changed, and so will we! We can look forward to that time. We have something to hope for.

'God will make sure that everything will work out for good for those people who love him. If we believe that God allowed his only Son Jesus to die for us, then we can be sure that he is on our side. Jesus loves us, and nothing can separate us from his love. Death can't, and danger can't. Neither can famine or disaster. Because Jesus loves us we can expect only the best! Nothing that has ever been made can separate us from the love of God, which is ours because Jesus loves us.'

343 Living Christian lives

It was difficult living as a Christian in Rome, having a different lifestyle from all the other people around. Paul wrote with some practical guidance:

'Try to be different from the people around you. Don't be swayed by the things they say and do. Instead, keep thinking about God, and live in a way that will please him.

'Don't think of yourself as more important than anyone else. Love one another, and use the gifts that God has given you. Obey the Law, and respect those who have power over you. Remember all the good things that God has in store for you, and be happy!'

---

341 Romans chapter 3, verses 21-26 and chapter 5, verses 12-18.

Rome
Paul had not yet been to the capital city of the Roman Empire, but he had met many people from Rome. He probably wrote this long letter about AD57, from Corinth.

📖 See Feature pages 158-59.

Two men
Paul compares Adam, who brought sin into the world, with Jesus, who obeyed God even though it meant being crucified.

342 Romans chapter 8, verses 1-39.

'Daddy'
Paul wanted the Romans to think of God as caring and concerned, not stern and critical.

Paul's suffering
Paul had been several times in jail, flogged five times with leather whips and three times with canes, stoned once and left for dead, shipwrecked three times, attacked by bandits and often went without food.

All change
Paul says that when Jesus returns, all bad things will be destroyed, and nothing will die or decay again.

343 Romans chapter 12, verses 1-21.

Be different
God's character and rules show Christians what is good and bad, right and wrong.

344 Ephesians chapter 1, verses 15-23.

Ephesus
There was a temple to the goddess Diana or Artemis in this large city near the west coast of modern Turkey.

Prison cell
Paul wrote this while under house arrest in Rome, about AD60 (see stories 329-333).

Tychicus
He was a friend who took news to and from Paul and the churches he had started.

345 Ephesians chapter 6, verses 1-4.

Commandment
This is one of the Ten Commandments (story 52).

📖 See Feature pages 12-13.

346 Ephesians chapter 6, verses 10-18.

Armour
Roman soldiers wore armour when they were on duty; they worked as police as well. Paul uses each piece of armour as a picture of how a Christian can resist evil.

Righteousness
This means living God's way. Christians ask God's help to do this, to protect them against wrongdoing.

God's word
Jesus quoted the Bible at the devil (story 236) in the wilderness.

344 Thanks for the Ephesians

A few years later Paul wrote a letter to the church in Ephesus from his prison cell in Rome. He asked Tychicus to deliver it. 'Tell everyone how I am and what I am doing,' he said. He knew that his friends would be worried about him. 'Encourage them.'

Paul prayed regularly for the Christians in Ephesus and the surrounding areas. 'Ever since I heard about your faith in Jesus and the love which you share together, I have not stopped thanking God for you,' he wrote. 'I have prayed that you will be able to get to know God better, and that you will understand that the same power God used to raise Jesus from the dead is working in your lives too!'

345 Parents and children

Paul remembered all the families who were part of the churches. He wanted to give them good advice.

He thought about the children. 'Children,' he wrote. 'Do what your parents tell you. Remember the commandment which God gave Moses: "Respect your father and mother." If you do that, God promises that he will bless you.'

His thoughts turned to the parents. 'If you are a father, don't make your children angry,' he wrote. 'Instead, bring them up to respect God, and teach them about his ways.'

346 The armour of God

It was not easy to be a Christian at this time. Sometimes it felt like being in a fierce battle! Paul told his friends at Ephesus that they needed to put on the special armour God had given them.

'Be like good soldiers and stand firm,' he wrote. 'Make sure that you know what God's truth is, and wear it like a belt around your waist. Cover your hearts with the breastplate of righteousness. You are God's children – whatever happens, no one can take that away. On your feet, wear shoes to make you ready to tell other people about the good news of Jesus. In your hand, pick up the shield of faith. Whatever comes to attack you, your faith will protect you. Wear the helmet of salvation, and never doubt that Jesus died for you. In your other hand carry the sword of the Spirit, which is God's word. What God says is completely trustworthy. Depend on it.

'And keep on praying for me, so that I can keep on telling other people about Jesus.'

347 The new life

The Christians in Colossae were still not sure what to think about Jesus. Was he just a man? Or was he fully God? Paul wrote:

'Although we can't see God, we have seen Jesus, his Son. God created the whole universe through him, for he existed before the world began, and the full nature of God lives in him. When Jesus died on the cross, he made peace with God and put things right between God and the whole creation, in heaven and on earth.

'Once you were his enemies, but now you are his friends. So don't do the things you did before you believed in Jesus. Don't tell lies or get angry with one another – that belongs to your old life. You have taken off your old life and all that goes with it, and you have put on a new life which is making you more and more like Jesus.'

348 The runaway slave

Paul had a problem, and he wanted to do the right thing. While he was under house arrest in Rome, he met a runaway slave called Onesimus who had become a Christian.

Onesimus still belonged to his master, Philemon, a leader in the church at Colossae known to Paul. Paul had grown to love Onesimus, but he could not let him stay in Rome, so he wrote a letter for Onesimus to take back with him.

'To my dear friend Philemon: I always thank God for you, because I have heard about your love for God and for others. I am sending Onesimus back to you. He is like my own son. I would have liked him to stay, so that he could work with me, but I wanted your agreement first. When he comes back to you, he will be more than a slave: now he will be your Christian brother.

'So, please welcome him back as you would welcome me into your home. If he owes you anything, then I will repay you. I know that you will do what I have asked. I hope to be able to visit you soon. I know that you are praying that I will. Get the guest room ready for me!

'The grace of the Lord Jesus be with you. Paul.'

349 Copy Jesus

Paul loved the Christians at Philippi. He was sad when he heard that some of them were selfish and proud, having a high opinion of themselves and putting themselves first.

'Don't just do what you want!' wrote Paul. 'Think about other people. See what is best for them, and put them first. Just think about how Jesus behaved and how he treated other people. Try to copy him.

'Jesus was prepared to give up everything, to come to earth, and live as a man. He was even willing to die on the cross. Because he did not think about himself, but obeyed God and put others first, God has rewarded him and has given him the highest position in heaven and earth. One day, when people hear the name of Jesus, the whole world will bow down before him.'

---

347 Colossians chapter 1, verses 15-23 and chapter 3, verses 5-17.

Colossae
Paul had never been to this city, but Epaphras, a Colossian, had become a Christian when Paul was in nearby Ephesus and had taken the message back to Colossae. This letter was written from Rome about AD60.

Man or God?
Some Colossian teachers believed Jesus was either an angel or a man who became an angel after he died. Paul told them that Jesus was God in human form.

348 Philemon

Slaves
Under Roman law, a recaptured runaway slave could be put to death, so it was a brave thing for Onesimus to return.

349 Philippians chapter 2, verses 3-11.

Philippi
This rich city was in Macedonia in northern Greece (see stories 315, 316). Paul wrote this letter from prison in Rome about AD60.

Proud
Many of Philippi's new Christians were successful traders and retired soldiers, used to getting their own way.

Jesus is Lord
Paul says that Jesus, the Son of God, who has conquered sin and death, will be seen to rule all things when he returns to earth.

CRAFTS

When people lived in tents and moved from place to place, they had to make or produce everything they needed. These people were farmers who kept sheep and goats, grew crops and went out hunting. They made their own tents and clothes by weaving goats' wool and milled the grain they grew to make bread.

In later times, when people settled in towns and villages, some of them still kept animals, made clothes and grew crops, but they also started to specialize and develop different crafts and trades.

Builders

Many families built their own simple houses made of mud bricks and wood, but there were specialist carpenters who would provide timbers for house-building and also make tools, wheels, carts and other equipment for farming.

Stonemasons cut stones from the quarries to make the larger buildings and the town walls and gateways.

Farmers

By the time of Jesus, parts of Palestine were very fertile. Sheep and goats grazed on the hillsides, and many crops were grown. The two most important crops were vines and olives. Barley and wheat were the main grain crops for breadmaking. Other crops included beans and lentils, flax to provide oil and linen, and fruit and vegetables (see Feature on Food pages 54-55).

MONEY

In Old Testament times, people did not use money, but would barter their goods. This means that they would 'pay' for their goods with a sheep or a goat, for example. A rich man's wealth was counted in the number of sheep, goats and camels he had.

In New Testament Palestine, there were three currencies with coins made in gold, silver, copper and bronze. There was Roman, Greek and the local Jewish money. As the temple tax had to be paid in Greek currency, money-changers were busy. They often charged a big fee for changing money, so they had a bad reputation.

The market

In any town, the market was the place where people could sell their produce. Some traders would sell spices. There were also stalls selling cloth and clothing. Some towns were famous for their dyed cloth. In the market, specialist craftsmen like leather-workers, potters and metal-workers might sell their goods. Scribes who would write letters for a sum of money could be found in many towns. In big towns and cities, such as Jerusalem, there were also goldsmiths and silversmiths.

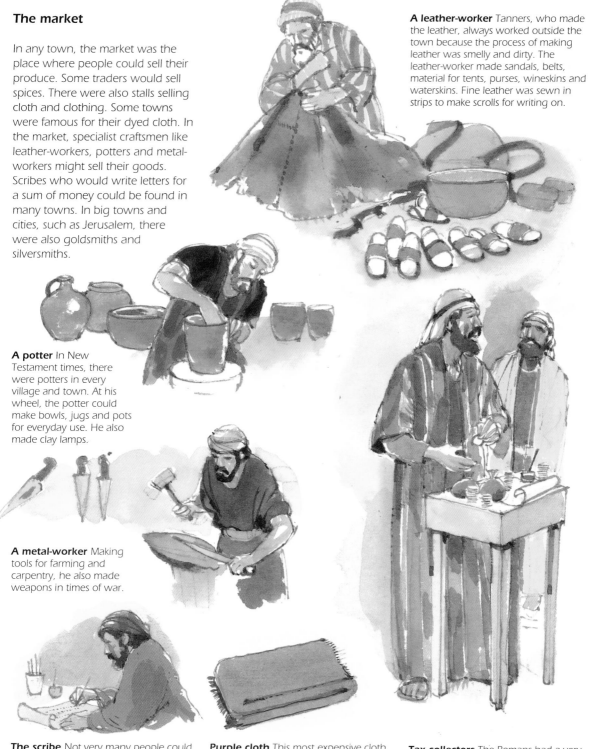

A leather-worker Tanners, who made the leather, always worked outside the town because the process of making leather was smelly and dirty. The leather-worker made sandals, belts, material for tents, purses, wineskins and waterskins. Fine leather was sewn in strips to make scrolls for writing on.

A potter In New Testament times, there were potters in every village and town. At his wheel, the potter could make bowls, jugs and pots for everyday use. He also made clay lamps.

A metal-worker Making tools for farming and carpentry, he also made weapons in times of war.

The scribe Not very many people could read or write, so the scribe would sit in the market place and write letters for other people.

Purple cloth This most expensive cloth, worn only by royalty and wealthy people, was dyed in the sea-port of Tyre. The dye came from sea-snails.

Tax collectors The Romans had a very strict taxation system. The money was collected by local tax collectors, who charged more than they gave the Romans so that they earned money themselves in the process. Tax collectors were not popular!

350 1 Peter chapter 2, verses 9-10.

Peter
This letter was written by Simon Peter, probably from Rome, about AD66. He was killed by the Roman Emperor Nero a year or two later.

Writing
People wrote on papyrus or parchment sheets or scrolls with pens made from sharpened reeds. Ink was made from soot mixed with gum from a tree. The ink was dried into a block, which was then watered down whenever it was needed.

Priesthood
Peter means that all Christians are called to serve God in the world and to help other people find Jesus.

351 1 Timothy chapter 4, verses 6-16.

Timothy
He had become a Christian through Paul's preaching at Lystra (story 311). He found it hard to stand up to people who were saying that Christians had to give up certain foods or not get married.

352 Titus chapter 1.

Titus
He was a Gentile (non-Jew) and a friend of Paul's.

Elder
This was the name given to the leader of each Christian church. Most churches were quite small and met in people's houses.

350 Chosen people

Throughout the Roman Empire, Christians were being persecuted. Peter wrote to remind them that being a Christian might lead to suffering, but to remember that God had given them new life when he brought back Jesus from the dead.

'Whatever happens, remember what God has done for you,' wrote Peter. 'He chose each one of you, so that you are now God's chosen people, and you belong to him. He has made you into a royal priesthood, so that you can come to God yourselves, and praise him for bringing you out from the darkness into the light.'

351 Instructions to Timothy

Timothy had been with Paul on some of his journeys, and Paul had left him in Ephesus to help the Christians there.

The Christians in Ephesus had been confused by false teaching. Some of them were rich, while others had nothing. Paul had heard that some families were not looking after the widows and orphans in their care but instead expected the money to come from other church members. He wrote to encourage Timothy, who had to pass on his teaching to the other leaders in the church.

'Make sure you are living as God wants you to, so you are prepared for this life and for the life we have ahead of us! And teach people to put their hope in the living God.'

Timothy was only a young man and Paul knew it would be easy for some of the older Christians in Ephesus to ignore him.

'Don't let anyone look down on you because you are young,' he wrote. 'Instead, set a good example by the way you live, and use the gift that God has given you.'

352 Titus goes to Crete

The island of Crete was one of the first places to hear the good news of Jesus. When Paul heard that the Cretan believers were fighting and disobedient to God, he sent Titus to sort things out. Later he wrote:

'Remember what I said. Appoint an elder to look after the Christians in every town. Make sure that they are known to be good people. Their children should be Christians and must not be wild and disobedient. As the elders will be doing God's work, they must not be dishonest or bad-tempered or bossy. Instead, they should be welcoming and kind, and they must remember and live by everything they have been taught.'

353 Paul's final requests

Paul was in prison again. He knew that he would die soon, so he wrote to Timothy: 'I have finished the race, and I have kept on believing. I know that Jesus will reward me and welcome me in heaven, along with everyone else who believes in him.'

Paul longed to see Timothy once more. He wrote: 'Do your best to come as quickly as you can. Demas has left me alone, and has gone to Thessalonica. Only Luke has stayed with me. Please come before winter, and bring my cloak, which I left with Carpas in Troas. I would also like my scrolls and parchments. May Jesus be with you.'

354 A letter to Jewish Christians

Some Jewish people who had become Christians were confused. They had been brought up to follow God's Law. They ate their food in a special way, they celebrated special days, and made sacrifices so that God would forgive them.

'Don't all these things matter any more?' they asked. 'What does God want us to do? Will he forgive us, even if we don't make sacrifices?'

A letter was written especially to them: 'Jesus is like the High Priest, who was chosen by God to act between God and the Jewish people. But Jesus is greater than any High Priest! He is with God and speaks to God on our behalf. And even more amazingly, he's on our side! He understands how difficult things are because he lived like us on earth. But unlike us, he never did anything wrong.

'Jesus is God's only Son, and also a perfect person. So when Jesus died, there was no need to make any more animal sacrifices. He was a sacrifice himself: he gave up his life so we could be forgiven. And because Jesus rose from the dead, his sacrifice never had to be repeated.'

355 The race

'Remember some of our great ancestors,' says the letter to Jewish Christians. 'They had faith, and believed God, even though they did not understand exactly what he was doing. Abraham believed God's promise that he would be a father, long before he and Sarah had Isaac. He believed God's promise that he would have many descendants, although he died many years before he saw the truth of that promise. Moses, Rahab, Gideon, Samuel and David, all had faith in God. They believed that his promises would come true, even though they died before they could see it. This is because God planned something better for us and them, so that everyone could be saved through Jesus, God's Saviour.

'So, let's be encouraged by the many men and women who have had faith and believed in God's promises. Living as a Christian is like running a race, with all the believers who ever lived watching us from the sidelines! We must get rid of everything that could stop us, and keep on running, fixing our eyes on Jesus, who has already run the race. If we think about him, we won't give up.'

---

353 2 Timothy chapter 4, verses 6-22.

Prison
Some friends like Demas had refused to see Paul, perhaps because they were afraid of being imprisoned too. Luke was Paul's doctor. Not long after writing this letter from Rome, Paul was executed by the Emperor Nero.

Scrolls and parchments
These were probably copies of some parts of the Old Testament, and some Christian writings as well.

📖 See Feature pages 6-7.

354 Hebrews chapter 4, verse 14 to chapter 5, verse 9.

Letter to the Hebrews
It seems the author was a Jewish Christian writing for people like himself. It was probably written about AD67.

High Priest
The chief priest entered the 'Holy of Holies' in the Temple once a year, after offering animal sacrifices for the nation's sins. Jesus' death on the cross put an end to this. Jesus had no sins of his own: he died for the sins of all the people of the world.

355 Hebrews chapter 11, verses 1-40 and chapter 12, verses 1-3.

Faith
Faith is trusting God to do what he promises. See also stories 48, 73, 91, 107, 113.

Race
The writer is thinking of a runner concentrating on the finishing line and taking no notice of anything else.

356 2 Peter chapter 3.

Peter's second letter
This was probably written shortly before he died, about AD68.

Time
God's plans go on for ever, so a long time to us is a very short time to God. We can begin to understand this when we think that what seems a long time to us is really only a very short time compared with the age of the earth.

357 Jude verses 24-25.

Jude
He was probably one of Jesus' brothers.

358 1 John chapter 1.

John
This letter was written by John, son of Zebedee, probably about AD85. He had helped lead the church in Ephesus until he was imprisoned by the Romans for his Christian beliefs.

Light
Light is often used in the Bible as a symbol for God, and darkness was used as a symbol for sin and evil. You cannot have darkness where there is light, so John is saying that God is perfect.

359 2 John.

Love one another
This was also Jesus' teaching at the 'last supper' (story 277). The way the early church cared for each other was one of things that was noticed by those who were not Christians.

356 Looking forward

Some Christian believers were very concerned to know when Jesus would return to earth. Some people laughed at them, because they did not believe he would come. Peter's second letter is about this.

'There will always be people who laugh at the idea that Jesus will come back,' it says. 'They will sneer and say "When is he going to come as he promised?"'

'Remember that to God a day is like a thousand years, and a year is like a day. It isn't that God is being slow in keeping his promise. It's that he's being very patient. He doesn't want anyone to miss out on spending eternity with him. He wants to give as many people as possible time to repent of all the things they've done wrong, and to follow him. But we can look forward to the day when Jesus comes back. It will happen!'

357 'Give glory to God!'

Jude was alarmed to hear that a few people were teaching things that were not true. They said that once you had become a Christian, you could do anything you liked. Jude wanted to warn them, because they were following their own selfish desires, and living without the Holy Spirit to guide them.

'Remember what you were told about Jesus, and stick to your faith. God can keep you from losing your way. God is our Saviour, because of what Jesus has done for us. Glory, majesty, power and authority, belong to him for ever and ever. Amen!'

358 Walking in the light

'God came into the world as a human being,' wrote John. 'I knew him. I heard him speak. I saw him with my own eyes, and I touched him with my hands. And that is what I want to tell you about!'

'God is light,' John continued. 'There is no darkness in him at all. If we claim to be God's friends, while we're still doing things that we should be ashamed of, then we are liars. But if our aim is to please God, we can be forgiven all our sins, because of what Jesus did when he died on the cross.'

John knew that God had made a promise. 'If we turn away from our sins, God has promised that he will forgive us.'

359 Love one another

John wrote another short letter:

'I have heard that you are following God's ways, and living your lives to please him. This has given me great joy. Love one another. This is not new, but something which we have been asked to do from the very beginning. How do we love one another? By obeying God and keeping his commandments.'

A VISION OF THINGS TO COME

Revelation is the last book of the New Testament and the last book in the Bible. It was written at the end of the first century AD to encourage Christians who were suffering because they followed Jesus. It is different from the other books of the New Testament, and it describes a number of visions which were 'revealed' by God to a man called John.

When this book was written, John, who had been one of Jesus' closest friends, was an old man. He had helped to lead the church in Ephesus until the city leaders, who did not like what he did, sent him away to a prison camp on the island of Patmos. At this time Christians were being persecuted because they refused to worship other gods, including the Roman Emperor.

When Christians began to suffer, some began to doubt their faith: how could Jesus let this happen? The book of Revelation gave them an answer, and a clue to what the future would hold.

The visions in it are similar to some of the prophecies in the Old Testament and use the same strange pictures people sometimes have in dreams.

These pictures show evil forces opposing God's church, trying to destroy it. But the message of the book is that evil can never succeed completely; Jesus always has the final word. Some of the pictures are of heaven; they are to remind Christians of their hope for the future. The book of Revelation helped the first Christians when life was very difficult for them, and has encouraged others ever since.

360 John sees Jesus

John was an old man when he was sent to live in exile on the island of Patmos.

One day John felt the Holy Spirit was with him in a special way. Suddenly he heard a loud, clear voice, like the sound of a trumpet, coming from behind him. 'Write down everything you see on a scroll, and send it to the churches in Ephesus, Smyrna, Pergamum, Thyatira, Sardis, Philadelphia and Laodicea.'

John swung around to see where the voice was coming from. Behind him, he saw seven golden lampstands, and among them stood someone like a human being. He was wearing a long robe with a golden sash. His face and hair were as white as snow. His eyes burned like fire, and his feet were brilliant bronze. As he spoke, his voice sounded like rushing water. In his hand he held seven stars and out of his mouth came a sharp sword. His face was shining like the sun.

John fell at Jesus' feet. He felt Jesus' hand on him. 'Do not be afraid,' he said to John. 'I am the first and the last, the Living One. I was dead, but now I am alive for ever and ever.'

360 Revelation chapter 1, verses 1-20.

Patmos
This small island in the Aegean Sea, about 80km/50 miles off the coast of modern Turkey, was not far from Ephesus, John's home.

Vision of Jesus
John's vision shows qualities of Jesus rather than his physical appearance. The robe shows him as a king; the white hair, burning eyes and shining face mean that he is pure and holy.

Seven
The lampstands represent all the churches (and seven named ones in particular). The seven stars may be the human leaders, or the general life and attitudes, of the churches.

361 Revelation chapter 4.

God's throne
The precious stones, rainbow, light and glass are all symbols that mean that God is precious, beautiful and perfect.

Twenty-four people
These seemed to John like great angels. They probably stand for all the Christians in the world who have stayed faithful to Jesus.

Four creatures
These are like spiritual guards, whose many eyes see everything. They reminded John's readers that God cannot be defeated, even if he or his church is attacked.

362 Revelation chapter 7, verses 9-17.

White robes
White stands for purity. The 'blood of the Lamb' refers to Jesus' death on the cross. The great crowd is everyone who has been forgiven by Jesus for the things they have done wrong. Their suffering came when they stood for Jesus against evil in the world.

Palm branches

These were used like flags on great festival days. People waved them when Jesus entered Jerusalem (story 272).

361 God as King

After John had finished writing, he looked up and saw a door, opening up into heaven. Then the voice spoke to him again. 'Come here! Let me show you what will happen in the future.'

Immediately, John was able to see a magnificent throne. There was someone sitting on it, whose features shone like precious stones. Around the throne circled an emerald rainbow.

God's throne was surrounded by twenty-four other thrones. On each throne sat a person dressed in white, wearing a golden crown.

God's throne flashed with light, which sparkled in a crystal-clear sea of glass, which lay before it. There was a noise like thunder.

Around the throne were four living creatures, covered with eyes. One was like a lion, another like an ox, another had the face of a man and the last one was like an eagle. Each of them had six wings and they sang continually, 'Holy, holy, holy God, who was, and is, and is to come.'

Then the twenty-four people fell down before God, and cried, 'Only you are worthy of glory and honour and power. You created everything, and everything exists because of you.'

362 The great crowd

After a while, John saw a huge crowd of people. There were so many, it was impossible to count them. As he looked, John could see men and women from all over the world, standing in front of the throne. They were dressed in white, and they held palm branches in their hands. They stood before God's throne shouting, 'Only God can save through Jesus, the Lamb!'

As they were saying this, John saw that God's throne was surrounded by angels, and the four strange creatures. They all fell down on their faces before God, and brought their worship to him.

They said, 'Praise and glory and wisdom and thanksgiving, honour and power and strength, belong to our God for ever and ever. Amen!'

One of the people who had been sitting on a throne came up to John and said, 'The crowd dressed in white are the people who have gone through great suffering. They have washed their robes, and have been made clean through the blood of the Lamb, Jesus. And now they worship God by day and night in his temple. They will never be hungry or thirsty or sad again.'

363 A new heaven and a new earth

Some time later, John saw that the earth had gone, and that there was a new heaven and a new earth.

He looked up to heaven and saw, coming from it, a wonderful new city. He heard God speak. 'Now is the time when God will live with his people, and his people will live with their God. There will be no more death or sadness or pain. No one will cry, because God will wipe every tear from their eyes. All those things will be things of the past; they will never return. I am making everything new!'

364 A river and a tree

As an angel showed John the magnificence of God's new city, he showed him a wonderful river. The water was completely clear, and it flowed down the middle of a great street. It was the river of the water of life.

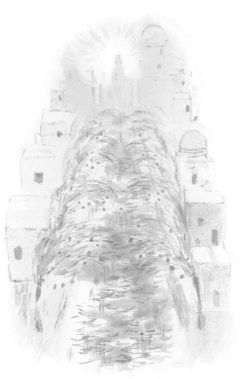

John looked to see where the river came from. He saw that it flowed straight from God's throne.

Spanning the width of the river grew the tree of life. On its branches hung fruit, and its leaves brought healing and freedom to all people of every nation.

John could see that God's throne would be in the city and that God's people would be with him all the time, for ever.

There would never be any night, nor darkness there, for their light was the light of God's presence.

365 A final promise

After John had seen and heard all these things, he fell down at the angel's feet.

'Get up!' said the angel. 'Do not worship me. Worship God!'

Then Jesus spoke. 'I am coming soon! I am the first and the last, the beginning and the end. Happy are those who have been forgiven their sins. They have the right to come into the city and enjoy the tree of life. Anyone who wants to, anyone who is thirsty, can come and drink freely from the water of life. I am coming soon!'

---

363 Revelation chapter 21.

New heaven and earth
When Jesus returns to earth the world in its present form will end. He will create a new, perfect place for the people who love him to live in for ever.

The city
This stands for the safe place where God is king and there is no suffering, pain or death any more.

364 Revelation chapter 22, verses 1-6.

River of life
This reminded John's readers of the rivers in the Garden of Eden (story 2). God's new creation restores the world to what it was until people spoiled it.

Tree of life
There was a tree like this in Eden (story 2). It stands for complete health and perfection.

No darkness
Darkness is a symbol of evil in the Bible. This reminded John's readers that heaven is full of goodness.

365 Revelation chapter 22, verses 7-21.

Coming soon
Jesus told his followers that they would never know when he would return to earth. By 'soon' he means that the sufferings of this life don't last long compared with the never-ending joy and perfect life of heaven. This was an encouragement to John's readers to stay faithful to God.

See Feature pages 120-21.

PEOPLE INDEX

Numbers refer to stories

FACTFINDER INDEX

Numbers refer to pages

Marshall Pickering is an imprint of
HarperCollins*Religious*
Part of HarperCollins*Publishers*
77-85 Fulham Palace Road, London W6 8JB

First published in Great Britain in 1999 by Marshall Pickering

1 3 5 7 9 10 8 6 4 2

Copyright © 1999 AD Publishing Services Ltd,
7 Hill Side, Cheddington, Leighton Buzzard, Beds LU7 0SP
Illustrations copyright © 1999 Tony Morris and Chris Saunderson

A catalogue record for this book is available from the British Library.

ISBN 0 551 03205 7

Printed and bound in China

THE NEW TESTAMENT WORLD

Rome •

ITALY

GREECE

MACEDONIA

Philippi •

• Thessalonica

Corinth •

• Athens

MALTA

CRET

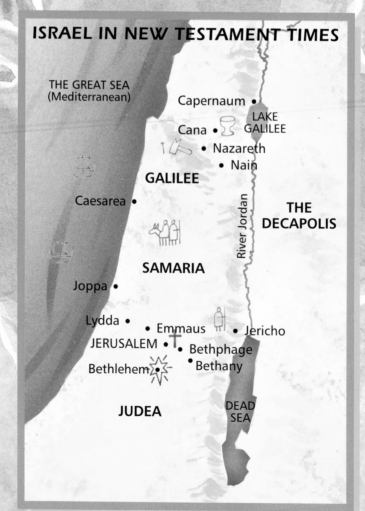

ISRAEL IN NEW TESTAMENT TIMES

THE GREAT SEA
(Mediterranean)

Capernaum •

Cana •

LAKE
GALILEE

Nazareth

Nain

GALILEE

Caesarea •

River Jordan

THE
DECAPOLIS

SAMARIA

Joppa •

Lydda •

• Emmaus

JERUSALEM •

• Jericho

Bethphage

Bethlehem •

• Bethany

JUDEA

DEAD
SEA